Lecture Notes in Computer Scie

Commenced Publication in 1973
Founding and Former Series Editors:
Gerhard Goos, Juris Hartmanis, and Jan van Leeuwen

David Naccache   Damien Sauveron (Eds.)

Information Security Theory and Practice

Securing the Internet of Things

8th IFIP WG 11.2 International Workshop, WISTP 2014
Heraklion, Crete, Greece, June 30 – July 2, 2014
Proceedings

Springer

Volume Editors

David Naccache
École Normale Supérieure
Département d'Informatique
45, rue d'Ulm, 75230 Paris, France
E-mail: david.naccache@ens.fr

Damien Sauveron
Université de Limoges
XLIM (UMR CNRS 7252)
123 avenue Albert Thomas, 87060 Limoges Cedex, France
E-mail: damien.sauveron@unilim.fr

ISSN 0302-9743   e-ISSN 1611-3349
ISBN 978-3-662-43825-1   e-ISBN 978-3-662-43826-8
DOI 10.1007/978-3-662-43826-8
Springer Heidelberg New York Dordrecht London

Library of Congress Control Number: 2014940797

LNCS Sublibrary: SL 4 – Security and Cryptology

Typesetting: Camera-ready by author, data conversion by Scientific Publishing Services, Chennai, India

Printed on acid-free paper

Springer is part of Springer Science+Business Media (www.springer.com)

Preface

Future ICT technologies, such as the concepts of ambient intelligence, cyber-physical systems and Internet of Things, provide a vision of the information society in which: people and physical systems are surrounded with intelligent interactive interfaces and objects, and environments are capable of recognising and reacting to the presence of different individuals or events in a seamless, unobtrusive and invisible manner. The success of future ICT technologies will depend on how secure these systems may be, to what extent they will protect the privacy of individuals and how individuals will come to trust them.

The 8th Workshop in Information Security Theory and Practice (WISTP 2014) addressed security and privacy issues of smart devices, networks, architectures, protocols, policies, systems, and applications related to the Internet of Things, along with evaluating their impact on business, individuals, and society. WISTP 2014 was organized by the FORTH-ICS during June 30 – July 2, 2014, in Heraklion, Greece.

The workshop received 33 submissions. Each submission was reviewed by at least three reviewers. This long and rigorous process was only possible thanks to the hard work of the Program Committee members and additional reviewers, listed on the following pages.

This volume contains the eight full papers and six short papers that were selected for presentation at WISTP 2014. Furthermore, the proceedings include the two keynotes given by Bart Preneel and Timo Kasper, to whom we are grateful.

WISTP 2014 was collocated with the 7th International Conference on Trust and Trustworthy Computing (TRUST), and keynote talks of each event were delivered to both, with the attendees having the possibility to attend sessions of both events.

We wish to thank all the people who invested time and energy to make WISTP 2014 a success: first and foremost all the authors who submitted papers to WISTP and presented them at the workshop. The members of the Program Committee together with all the external reviewers worked hard in evaluating the submissions. The WISTP Steering Committee helped us graciously in all critical decisions. Thanks also go to the 2014 General Chairs Ioannis Askoxylakis, the local organizer Nikolaos Petroulakis and their respective teams for handling the local arrangements, to the Trusted Computing Group, Intel, and Microsoft for financial cosponsoring WISTP 2014, IFIP WG 11.2 Pervasive Systems Security for scientific cosponsoring of WISTP 2014, and to Sara Foresti and Cheng-Kang Chu for their efforts as publicity chairs.

April 2014

David Naccache
Damien Sauveron

Organization

WISTP 2014 was organized by FORTH-ICS.

General Chair

Ioannis Askoxylakis   FORTH-ICS, Greece

Local Organizers

Nikolaos Petroulakis   FORTH-ICS, Greece

Workshop/Panel/Tutorial Chair

Konstantinos Markantonakis   ISG-SCC, Royal Holloway University
of London, UK

Publicity Chairs

Sara Foresti   Università degli Studi di Milano, Italy
Cheng-Kang Chu   Huawei, Singapore

Program Chairs

David Naccache   Ecole Normale Supérieure, France
Damien Sauveron   XLIM, University of Limoges, France

Program Committee

Raja Naeem Akram   University of Waikato, New Zealand
Claudio A. Ardagna   Università degli Studi di Milano, Italy
Ioannis Askoxylakis   FORTH-ICS, Greece
Gildas Avoine   INSA de Rennes, France
Lejla Batina   Radboud University Nijmegen,
The Netherlands
Lorenzo Cavallaro   Royal Holloway, University of London, UK

Hervé Chabanne   Morpho, France
Serge Chaumette   LaBRI, University Bordeaux 1, France
Mauro Conti   University of Padua, Italy
Manuel Egele   Carnegie Mellon University, USA
Flavio Garcia   University of Birmingham, UK
Dieter Gollmann   Hamburg University of Technology, Germany
Johann Groszschädl   Universität Luxemburg, Luxembourg
Yong Guan   Iowa State University, USA
Gerhard Hancke   City University of Hong Kong, Hong Kong
Süleyman Kardas   TUBITAK BILGEM UEKAE, Turkey
Issa Mohammad Khalil   Qatar Fondation, Qatar
Ioannis Krontiris   Goethe University Frankfurt, Germany
Andrea Lanzi   Università degli Studi di Milano, Italy
Corrado Leita   Lastline, UK
Albert Levi   Sabanci University, Turkey
Peng Liu   Pennsylvania State University, USA
Javier Lopez   University of Malaga, Spain
Federico Maggi   Politecnico di Milano, Italy
Vashek Matyas   Masaryk University, Czech Republic
Sjouke Mauw   University of Luxembourg, Luxembourg
Aikaterini Mitrokotsa   Chalmers University of Technology, Sweden
Flemming Nielson   Technical University of Denmark, Denmark
Vladimir A. Oleshchuk   University of Agder, Norway
Frank Piessens   Katholieke Universiteit Leuven, Belgium
Wolter Pieters   TU Delft and University of Twente,
                                   The Netherlands
David Pointcheval   Ecole Normale Supérieure, France
Axel York Poschmann   Nanyang Technological University, Singapore
Henrich C. Pöhls   Institute of IT Security and Security Law at the
                                   University of Passau, Germany
Christina Pöpper   Ruhr University Bochum, Germany
Jean-Jacques Quisquater   UCL Crypto Group, Louvain-la-Neuve,
                                   Belgium
Kui Ren   State University of New York at Buffalo, USA
Vincent Rijmen   University of Leuven, Belgium
Reihaneh Safavi-Naini   University of Calgary, Canada
Kouichi Sakurai   Kyushu University, Japan
Pierangela Samarati   Università degli Studi di Milano, Italy
Seungwon Shin   KAIST, Korea
Jose Maria Sierra   Carlos III University of Madrid, Spain
Asia Slowinska   Vrije Universiteit Amsterdam, The Netherlands
Willy Susilo   University of Wollongong, Australia
Michael Tunstall   Cryptography Research Inc, USA
Umut Uludag   TUBITAK BILGEM UEKAE, Turkey
Stefano Zanero   Politecnico di Milano, Italy
Jianying Zhou   Institute for Infocomm Research, Singapore

Additional Reviewers

Ahmadi, Ahmad
Alcaraz, Cristina
Ambrosin, Moreno
Autefage, Vincent
Barenghi, Alessandro
Ben Jaballah, Wafa
Bingol, Muhammed Ali
Cai, Shaoying
Dahan, Xavier
Dayioğlu, Ziynet Nesibe
Ege, Baris

Emura, Keita
Jafari, Mohammad
Noorman, Job
Ouoba, Jonathan
Perrin, Léo
Picek, Stjepan
Riha, Zdenek
Rios, Ruben
Riou, Sebastien
Stöttinger, Marc
Yan, Jingbo

WISTP Steering Committee

Angelos Bilas   FORTH-ICS and University of Crete, Greece
Lorenzo Cavallaro   Royal Holloway, University of London, UK
Dieter Gollmann   Hamburg University of Technology, Germany
Konstantinos Markantonakis   ISG-SCC, Royal Holloway University
                                    of London, UK
Jean-Jacques Quisquater   DICE, Catholic University of Louvain, Belgium
Damien Sauveron   XLIM, University of Limoges, France

Scientific Support

IFIP WG 11.2 Pervasive Systems Security

Main Sponsors

Since the early stages of the workshop inception the workshop organizers received positive feedback from a number of high profile organizations. With the development of a strong program and organizing committee, this was further capitalised into direct financial support. This enabled the workshop organizers to strengthen significantly their main objective for proposing a high standard academic workshop. The support helped significantly to keep the workshop registration costs as low as possible and as the same time offer a number of best paper awards. Therefore, we would like to express our gratitude and thank every single organization. We are also looking forward to work together in future WISTP events.

Abstracts of Invited Papers
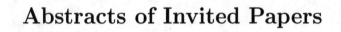

Lightweight and Secure Cryptographic Implementations for the Internet of Things (Extended Abstract)

Bart Preneel

KU Leuven and iMinds
Dept. Electrical Engineering-ESAT/COSIC,
Kasteelpark Arenberg 10 Bus 2452, B-3001 Leuven, Belgium
bart.preneel@esat.kuleuven.be

Abstract. There is a growing insight that if we build Internet functionality into every object, it will be essential for broad acceptability that security and privacy features are protected from day one. The old approach of first rolling out the system and thinking about security and privacy later will no longer work. Cryptographic algorithms form an essential element to protect the Internet of Things; moreover, this environment will impose ever higher requirements for the algorithms in terms of performance, security, and cost. For many settings algorithms tradeoffs are expected that offer an improvement of one order of magnitude compared to existing standards. This extended abstract presents a brief overview of the issues that need to be addressed for such an optimization to be successful.

The design of cryptographic algorithms corresponds to finding a tradeoff between performance, cost, and security. It is rather easy to obtain any two of these, while giving up the third one. As an example, it is easy to develop a highly secure and very fast algorithm if the implementation can be expensive.

- Performance is typically thought of as speed or throughput: how many cycles or seconds are needed to process a single byte or message. It is difficult to express performance in a single number, as the performance depends on the hardware platform (even performance numbers on two hardware platforms with the same cost can be very different) and the time to process one byte varies depending on the length of the message (there are typically setup costs). Moreover, parallelism is playing a more important role (for high end systems).
- Security can typically be expressed in number of bits of the effective key length; a more accurate but harder to estimate measure is the monetary cost for the opponent. The difficulty with estimating security is that there are a range of attacks that assume different access of the opponent to the device and that achieve difference goals. As an example, cryptographers typically consider only attackers that try to break a single instance of a cryptographic scheme, while attacking multiple instances frequently brings

economies of scales, e.g. through time-memory tradeoffs. Moreover, in the past two decades the insight has grown that implementation attacks (also known as grey box attacks), that exploit physical properties of the implementation, can be much more effective than black box attacks that only exploit the input-output behavior. Finding low-cost protections against such attacks is notoriously difficult.

– The third element is the cost: ideally, cost can be expressed in financial terms. Hardware cost depends on the gate count or chip area, but for small devices packaging costs can play a very large role. Moreover, in environments such as the Internet of Things money or hardware may not be the only constraint: devices such as passive RFID tags that receive power from the reader or devices that harvest their energy from the environment will have power constraints. Other devices are battery operated, and the challenge is to minimize energy to maximize the life time. Note that energy is the product of power and time, so an algorithm that minimizes power does not necessarily minimize energy.

The interest in lightweight cryptography has grown in the last decade. Many algorithms have been published, including block ciphers, streams ciphers, MAC algorithms, hash functions, authenticated encryption and public key algorithms. For symmetric cryptography, the focus was initially on reducing the area or gate count, but the attention has shifted to reducing energy consumption, to algorithms for low-end micro-controllers and to resistance against implementation attacks. For public-key cryptography, research has concentrated on demonstrating that it is indeed possible to implement current algorithms such as ECC (Elliptic Curve Cryptography) and NTRU on low-end platforms.

The main conclusion so far is that there is no such thing as a cryptographic algorithm suited for the Internet of Things. If one wants to push the boundaries by an order of magnitude and also resist implementation attacks, it will be essential to optimize both the algorithm and the implementation for a specific environment. At this stage it is not clear how many algorithms will be needed to satisfy the demand, but one can expect that a set of – perhaps tunable – standard algorithms will emerge. Next to the algorithm, the cryptographic protocol in which it is used plays a central role: the protocol should not use too many cryptographic algorithms and should again be optimized for a specific setting; the optimization should consider the algorithm(s), but also the communication and storage costs.

Sweet Dreams and Nightmares: Security in the Internet of Things

Timo Kasper, David Oswald, and Christof Paar

Horst Görtz Institute for IT Security, Ruhr-University Bochum, Germany
{timo.kasper,david.oswald,christof.paar}@rub.de

Abstract. Wireless embedded devices are predominant in the Internet of Things: Objects tagged with Radio Frequency IDentification and Near Field Communication technology, smartphones, and other embedded tokens interact from device to device and thereby often process information that is security or privacy relevant for humans. For protecting sensitive data and preventing attacks, many embedded devices employ cryptographic algorithms and authentication schemes. In the past years, various vulnerabilities have been found in commercial products that enable to bypass the security mechanisms. Since a large number of the devices in the field are in the hands of potential adversaries, implementation attacks (such as side-channel analysis and reverse engineering) can play a critical role for the overall security of a system. At hand of several examples of assailable commercial products we demonstrate the potential impact of the found security weaknesses and illustrate "how to not do it".

Table of Contents

Short Papers

Sweet Dreams and Nightmares:
Security in the Internet of Things

Timo Kasper, David Oswald, and Christof Paar

Horst Görtz Institute for IT Security, Ruhr-University Bochum, Germany
{timo.kasper,david.oswald,christof.paar}@rub.de

Abstract. Wireless embedded devices are predominant in the Internet of Things: Objects tagged with Radio Frequency IDentification and Near Field Communication technology, smartphones, and other embedded tokens interact from device to device and thereby often process information that is security or privacy relevant for humans. For protecting sensitive data and preventing attacks, many embedded devices employ cryptographic algorithms and authentication schemes. In the past years, various vulnerabilities have been found in commercial products that enable to bypass the security mechanisms. Since a large number of the devices in the field are in the hands of potential adversaries, implementation attacks (such as side-channel analysis and reverse engineering) can play a critical role for the overall security of a system. At hand of several examples of assailable commercial products we demonstrate the potential impact of the found security weaknesses and illustrate "how to not do it".

1 Introduction

Today's embedded devices are equipped and interconnected with various (wireless) interfaces. They often possess sensors and audiovisual peripherals, store and process private data of users and their surroundings, and can exchange information with other (embedded) devices — usually imperceptible and without a user interaction. Medical instruments, IDs, payments cards, cars, door locks, and smartphones are just a few examples for these ubiquitous devices that can directly or indirectly access the Internet. Thus, in theory all data stored and processed by the embedded devices could be collected in big data bases and analyzed, which could be harmful for the data protection of the individual. Many of the devices control critical appliances of our everyday life that in case of malfunctioning could become a threat even for the safety of the user, e.g., automotive or medical devices.

To ensure reliable, secure operation of systems, prevent fraud, and protect the data of individuals, often cryptography is employed. However, many commercial devices are not conform to the state-of-the-art in research and implement other — often proprietary and low-cost — algorithms and schemes. They seem to provide some suitable protection at first glance, but after a more thorough investigation turn out to be vulnerable to "off-the-shelf" attacks, often with a

D. Naccache and D. Sauveron (Eds.): WISTP 2014, LNCS 8501, pp. 1–9, 2014.
© IFIP International Federation for Information Processing 2014

dramatic impact. Researchers have in the past approx. 10 years started to analyze the security of cryptographic schemes implemented in commercial products, to identify and pinpoint their weaknesses, and repair them on the long term. The important process of publicly disclosing cryptographic primitives, cryptanalyzing them to separate secure from weak proposals, with the result of trusted and peer-reviewed ciphers being available for everyone today, is well known from the mathematical world. In the following, we emphasize the importance of security checks of implementations in the real world at hand of several practical examples of assailable systems in the Internet of Things (IoT).

2 Security-Analyzing NFC Applications

One widespread type of participant in the IoT are Radio Frequency IDentification (RFID) and Near Field Communication (NFC) tokens. Next, we describe cost-efficient hardware for security-analyzing them and illustrate practical attacks.

2.1 Contactless Smartcards and NFC

Many applications for ticketing, micro payments, access control, and identification rely on contactless cards that are compliant to the ISO 14443 standard [Int01], e.g., NXP's Mifare family of cards, electronic ID cards, and passports. NFC [Int04] is compatible to ISO 14443 and is widespread in embedded devices, such as smartphones, door locks, and other objects. An NFC-enabled object can function as an active reader in one moment and as a passive contactless card in the next moment.

2.2 Tools

Commercial NFC readers and cards usually contain chips that automatically execute manufacturer-specific schemes and thus provide restricted functionality. Many types of security analyses require freely programmable devices. The open-source hardware described next is handy for penetration tests, but can also serve as a flexible, low-cost alternative for realizing manufacturer-independent NFC applications.

NFC Reader. The freely programmable RFID reader presented in [KCP07] gives full control of the NFC communication and can support any contactless card or RFID tag operating at a frequency of 13.56 MHz. The customized device allows to manipulate the Radio Frequency (RF) field with a high timing accuracy of approximately 75 ns, which is a key advantage in the context of key-recovery from Mifare Classic cards.

Chameleon. The credit-card shaped Chameleon is a versatile tool for practical NFC security analyses in the field and compliance tests. On the other hand, it can also serve as a passive counterpart for an active NFC device, e.g., a smartphone in reader mode, and thus provide an energy-efficient interface for embedded systems like door locks.

Our originally published card emulator [KvMOP11] has been completely re-designed in the meantime: The new ChameleonMini can now be manufactured at a cost of less than 10 $ and is continuously maintained as an open-source project. The hardware supports Amplitude-Shift Keying (ASK) modulation (10% and 100%), can generate ASK or Binary Phase-Shift Keying (BPSK) load modulation with a subcarrier, and thus can emulate any ISO 14443, NFC, and ISO 15693 card and other types of transponders operating at 13.56 MHz. The ATXmega processor is connected to an external non-volatile memory that can store up to eight virtualized contactless cards (e.g., Mifare DESfire, Mifare Classic, Mifare Ultralight, and many others), while the processing of the relevant cryptographic schemes (e.g., Advanced Encryption Standard (AES), Triple Data Encryption Standard (3DES), or Crypto1) and the answering time is usually even faster than the original cards.

The modular firmware is programmed mostly in C, can be uploaded via a Universal Serial Bus (USB) bootloader, and is easily expandable to new cards and standards. The ChameleonMini can be controlled and configured from the USB interface with its own dedicated command set, e.g., to obtain status information, upload new card content or set a different Unique Identifier (UID). A logmode can be used to monitor and record NFC communication and a user-programmable button enables, for example, to cycle through the different virtualized cards stored inside the ChameleonMini.

We intend to make the device available at a low cost for educational purposes and aim at developing teaching material with practical know-how about both the physical layer of NFC and the higher protocol levels, including efficient implementations of cryptography for RFID. The ChameleonMini can be employed to virtualize several personal cards in one device, e.g., to open NFC-enabled door locks, operate NFC-barriers of parking lots, rent bicycles, or execute contacless payments in the system described in the next section.

2.3   Contactless Payments

The security vulnerabilities we found in the analysis of a widespread contactless payment system, as publicized in [KSP10], are overwhelming: NXP's Mifare Classic cards serve as a digital wallet, with all cards of one instantiation of the system containing an identical set of cryptographic keys. Taking into account the known weaknesses of the Crypto1 stream cipher and the flawed Random Number Generator (RNG) on these cards, this had been an extremely bad design choice: A random nonce generated by the card depends only on the time elapsed between the power-up of the card and the issuing of the authentication command by the NFC reader. Hence, the same random numbers can be reproduced in subsequent protocol runs. This and other weaknesses enable a key extraction from any Mifare Classic card with the above described customized reader, in seconds.

After extracting the secret keys of several payment cards, we examined their content and the functioning of the system with a series of practical tests. The credit balance turned out to be stored without any additional cryptographic protection — modifying it was very simple and not detected after weeks. In addition, neither the UID nor the card number stored on the card by the vendor was checked in the back-end. Note, that the content of the payment cards of other customers can be manipulated from a distance of 25 cm in milliseconds, enabling devastating attacks. After informing the system operator about the found vulnerabilities, the security of the payment system had allegedly been improved.

In March 2014, approximately five years after the initial analysis and subsequent improvement of the system, we performed a post-analysis to verify what has been changed exactly: Newly issued cards are now the much more secure (and more expensive) DESfire EV1 cards. Likewise, all NFC readers in the system were updated at a high cost, to support the new cards. However, to our surprise the system still accepts the old Mifare Classic cards, for downward compatibility reasons — with the identical key set and configuration as described above. The back-end still has no automated means to detect fraud and blacklist cards. We successfully verified that payments can still be carried out with the above described ChameleonMini in Mifare Classic emulation mode. For the tests, the user button has been programmed to increase the credit amount by 10 € on each button press, which worked very well. Upon our request, the system operator reported that some customers are known to fraudulently recharge their payment cards and use services for free, bu these crimes are tolerated as rare events.

2.4   Side-Channel Analysis of Mifare DESfire

In contrast to Mifare Classic, Mifare DESfire (MF3ICD40) cards employ a mathematically secure cipher, i.e., 3DES. They often serve for identification purposes in companies and can be found in large payment and public transport systems around the world, e.g., the Clippercard employed in San Francisco or the Opencard deployed in Prague.

In [OP11] we verify, whether an implementation attack, i.e., side-channel analysis, enables a key extraction. Side Channel Analysis (SCA) exploits information leakage in the power consumption (or timing behaviour) of a cryptographic device in order to extract its secrets. The powerful SCA attacks are especially convenient for extracting keys of implementations employing mathematically unbreakable ciphers.

In the first non-invasive Electro-Magnetic (EM) analysis of commercial cryptographic RFIDs in the literature [KOP09], the customized reader (see Sect. 2.2) again serves for the communication with the cards. Due to lack of contacts to measure the power consumption directly, the EM emanation of the RFID card is captured with near field probes and then digitized with a Picoscope 5204 1 GHz oscilloscope. The acquired measurements (and communication data) are pre-processed and then evaluated on a Personal Computer (PC). Despite the secure 3DES cipher and "RFID obstacles", we are able to extract all 112-bit keys (max. 250k measurements , i.e., approx. 7 hours, per key) and hence can gain full access to any Mifare DESfire MF3ICD40 card.

We had informed the manufacturer, NXP Semiconductors, about the described attacks several years before naming the product in a publication [OP11]. In the meantime, the MF3ICD40 DESfire cards had been discontinued and replaced by a follow-up product (DESfire EV1) incorporating side-channel resistance. Meanwhile, many NFC systems have been upgraded to the new product, e.g., newly issued Opencards in Prague are now DESfire EV1.

3 Electronic Access Control

For electronic locks and access control in buildings and cars, instead of NFC devices often active remote controls are used. The security analysis of two widespread systems is summarized in the following.

3.1 KeeLoq

The KeeLoq block cipher uses a 64-bit secret key and is widely used for Remote Keyless Entry (RKE) to cars and garages and for operating alarm systems. After the algorithm became public in 2006, various mathematical weaknesses of the cipher were found [ABDM+10]. However, mathematical attacks cannot break the most widespread "Rolling-Code" KeeLoq systems in practice: In this mode of operation, the unidirectional remote controls generate dynamic codes based on encrypting a counter with the device key of the remote control. The individual device keys are derived from the (known) serial number of the remote control by means of a (cryptographic) function involving a manufacturer key. Knowing the latter hence implies knowledge of all device keys in a KeeLoq system.

The extraction of a device key from a remote control with SCA requires at least 10 power measurements of a remote control [EKM+08]. The practical impact of this attack is tolerable, since it is comparable to duplicating a mechanical key, given physical access. The recovery of the manufacturer key (contained in all receivers of one manufacturer) is feasible with only one power measurement, without knowing neither plaintext nor ciphertext [KKMP09].

Knowing the manufacturer key, even a low-skilled intruder can spoof a KeeLoq receiver via the wireless link with technical equipment for less than 40 € and take over control of an RKE system, or deactivate an alarm system, without leaving physical traces. The case of KeeLoq illustrates that physical attacks must not be considered to be only relevant to the smartcard industry or to be a mere academic exercise. Rather, effective countermeasures need to be implemented also in electronic keys and similar wireless consumer products. The manufacturer of KeeLoq products, Microchip, agreed with the publication of our cited papers.

3.2   Simons Voss

The Simons Voss digital locking system 3060 G2 caught our attention, because it is installed in banks, universities, prisons, airports, factory sites and other locations with high demands for security and flexibility. Electronic cylinders replace their standard mechanical counterparts in the doors, while a remote control is used instead of a mechanical key. The door locks can be accessed and programmed remotely from a central PC via a wireless 868 MHz link.

After circumventing the read-out protection of the microcontrollers and reverse-engineering the contained data and program code, it became clear that in addition to a modified DES cipher a proprietary obscurity function is used as a cryptographic primitive. The first key-recovery attacks by means of SCA, or based on reading out the content of the microcontroller, evolved [OSS+14]. Since physical access to a door lock or a remote control is required, the attacks again resemble duplicating mechanical keys and may be tolerable in certain applications.

A short time after the internal functioning of the system components became clear, a devastating mathematical attack was found [SDK+13], that is clearly not tolerable: An adversary can open a door solely using the wireless link between door lock and remote control. The attack exploits (besides the bad cryptographic properties of the obscurity function) that an internal value processed by the algorithm is used as a "random number" (and thus leaked to the adversary) in the next run of the challenge-response protocol.

Eavesdropping a few (4–5) subsequent door opening attempts (and their corresponding "random numbers") allows an attacker to compute the cryptographic key of a remote control and clone it in a few seconds. For executing the attack, a valid ID of a remote control needs to be known or guessed by the adversary. In several real-world systems analyzed by us, we were able to guess a valid ID that even functions as a master key for the installation, i.e., it can open all doors of that installation. The manufacturer had been informed about the security flaws and our planned publications beforehand and meanwhile offers a firmware update, for download via the Internet, that is providing a fix for the described mathematical attack.

4   FPGAs and Bitstream Encryption

Xilinx(45–50%) and Altera(40–45%) together make up for approximiately 90% of the Field Programmable Gate Array (FPGA) market. Their products are widely used in consumer products, network routers, cars and military equipment. To protect the configuration ("bitstream") of the FPGAs that has to be loaded from an external non-volatile memory on every start-up, the market leaders offer a feature termed bitstream encryption: A designer can generate an encrypted bitstream with a secret key that is also stored in the target FPGA. A dedicated hardware on the silicon die of the FPGA then decrypts the bitstream during each start-up or reconfiguration of the FPGA. The feature enables, amongst others, to securely distribute firmware updates via insecure channels (the Internet).

After the initial successful power-analysis attacks on the 3DES implementation protecting the bitstreams of the Xilinx Virtex-2 family of FPGAs [MBKP11], similar attacks targeting the AES-256 implementation of their successors Virtex 4, Virtex 5, and the Spartan 6 evolved [MKP12]. Next, the product lines Stratix II (AES-128) Stratix III (AES-256) produced by Altera were found to have the same security vulnerabilities [MOPS13]. As in our previous publications, the manufacturers were informed about the found attacks a long time before their publication.

As a result, the vast majority of products on the market that are secured with the bitstream encryption feature can be duplicated by competitors, or secrets and IP contained in the unencrypted bitstream can be reverse-engineered. Further, scenarios like Hardware Trojans that are placed, for example, in network routers, and leak information through some covert channel, are conceivable.

5   One-Time Password Tokens

Yubikey 2 USB tokens are widely used to generate one-time passwords, e.g., for two-factor authentication instead of traditional username-password credentials. The passwords are generated by means of an AES cipher with a 128-bit secret key.

We demonstrate in [ORP13] that SCA attacks are a relevant threat for the tokens: A non-invasive side-channel analysis exploiting the EM emanations of the AES implementation requires approximately 500 EM measurements to recover the full key. Given approximately one hour of access to a Yubikey 2, an adversary can impersonate the legitimate owner and generate valid one-time passwords, even after the token has been returned. The attack leaves no physical traces on the device and can be performed using low-cost equipment.

Before publication, we notified the vendor Yubico about the found vulnerability towards SCA. Yubico acknowledged our results and has taken measures to mitigate the security issues: Tokens with an updated firmware (version 2.4) are resistant to the attacks and hence provide a significantly increased security level.

6   Conclusion

In the IoT, it is mandatory to protect privacy and security relevant information by means of cryptography. The implementation platform, i.e., the actual microcontroller, FPGA, or a similar device that stores secrets and provides the cryptographic functions, has become increasingly important for developing secure embedded systems. At the same time, the choice has become more complicated, since a large number of devices with different security features are available on the market. Besides the cryptographic strength of the employed algorithms and protocols, developers have to consider the existence and potential impact of physical attacks. The on-going research about security analyses of real-world devices provides essential know-how to the designers, e.g., for choosing respective system ingredients and parameters, as well as countermeasures. Likewise, the manufacturers obtain feedback about necessary improvements to establish the desired security strength in the next product generations.

Acknowledgement. This work was supported in part by the German Federal Ministry of Economics and Technology (Grant 01ME12025 SecMobil).

References

ABDM$^+$10. Aerts, W., Biham, E., De Moitié, D., De Mulder, E., Dunkelman, O., Indesteege, S., Keller, N., Preneel, B., Vandenbosch, G., Verbauwhede, I.: A Practical Attack on KeeLoq. Journal of Cryptology, 1–22 (2010), doi: 10.1007/s00145-010-9091-9

EKM$^+$08. Eisenbarth, T., Kasper, T., Moradi, A., Paar, C., Salmasizadeh, M., Shalmani, M.T.M.: On the Power of Power Analysis in the Real World: A Complete Break of the KeeLoq Code Hopping Scheme. In: Wagner, D. (ed.) CRYPTO 2008. LNCS, vol. 5157, pp. 203–220. Springer, Heidelberg (2008)

Int01. International Organization for Standardization (ISO). ISO/IEC 14443 Parts 1–4 (2001), http://www.iso.ch

Int04. International Organization for Standardization / International Electrotechnical Commission. ISO/IEC 18092 (Near Field Communication (NFCIP-1)) (2004)

KCP07. Kasper, T., Carluccio, D., Paar, C.: An Embedded System for Practical Security Analysis of Contactless Smartcards. In: Sauveron, D., Markantonakis, K., Bilas, A., Quisquater, J.-J. (eds.) WISTP 2007. LNCS, vol. 4462, pp. 150–160. Springer, Heidelberg (2007)

KKMP09. Kasper, M., Kasper, T., Moradi, A., Paar, C.: Breaking KeeLoq in a Flash: On Extracting Keys at Lightning Speed. In: Preneel, B. (ed.) AFRICACRYPT 2009. LNCS, vol. 5580, pp. 403–420. Springer, Heidelberg (2009)

KOP09. Kasper, T., Oswald, D., Paar, C.: EM Side-Channel Attacks on Commercial Contactless Smartcards Using Low-Cost Equipment. In: Youm, H.Y., Yung, M. (eds.) WISA 2009. LNCS, vol. 5932, pp. 79–93. Springer, Heidelberg (2009)

KSP10. Kasper, T., Silbermann, M., Paar, C.: All You Can Eat or Breaking a Real-World Contactless Payment System. In: Sion, R. (ed.) FC 2010. LNCS, vol. 6052, pp. 343–350. Springer, Heidelberg (2010)

KvMOP11. Kasper, T., von Maurich, I., Oswald, D., Paar, C.: Chameleon: A Versatile Emulator for Contactless Smartcards. In: Rhee, K.-H., Nyang, D. (eds.) ICISC 2010. LNCS, vol. 6829, pp. 189–206. Springer, Heidelberg (2011), https://github.com/emsec/ChameleonMini

MBKP11. Moradi, A., Barenghi, A., Kasper, T., Paar, C.: On the Vulnerability of FPGA Bitstream Encryption against Power Analysis Attacks: Extracting Keys from Xilinx Virtex-II FPGAs. In: Chen, Y., Danezis, G., Shmatikov, V. (eds.) ACM Conference on Computer and Communications Security, CCS 2011, pp. 111–124. ACM (2011)

MKP12.   Moradi, A., Kasper, M., Paar, C.: Black-Box Side-Channel Attacks High-
            light the Importance of Countermeasures – An Analysis of the Xilinx
            Virtex-4 and Virtex-5 Bitstream Encryption Mechanism. In: Dunkelman,
            O. (ed.) CT-RSA 2012. LNCS, vol. 7178, pp. 1–18. Springer, Heidelberg
            (2012)
MOPS13.   Moradi, A., Oswald, D., Paar, C., Swierczynski, P.: Side-Channel Attacks
            on the Bitstream Encryption Mechanism of Altera Stratix II – Facilitating
            Black-Box Analysis using Software Reverse-Engineering. In: ACM/SIGDA
            International Symposium on Field-Programmable Gate Arrays – FPGA
            2013, pp. 91–100. ACM (2013)
OP11.   Oswald, D., Paar, C.: Breaking Mifare DESFire MF3ICD40: Power Anal-
            ysis and Templates in the Real World. In: Preneel, B., Takagi, T. (eds.)
            CHES 2011. LNCS, vol. 6917, pp. 207–222. Springer, Heidelberg (2011)
ORP13.   Oswald, D., Richter, B., Paar, C.: Side-Channel Attacks on the Yubikey 2
            One-Time Password Generator. In: Stolfo, S.J., Stavrou, A., Wright, C.V.
            (eds.) RAID 2013. LNCS, vol. 8145, pp. 204–222. Springer, Heidelberg
            (2013)
OSS$^+$14. Oswald, D., Strobel, D., Schellenberg, F., Kasper, T., Paar, C.: When
            Reverse-Engineering Meets Side-Channel Analysis – Digital Lockpicking
            in Practice. In: Lange, T., Lauter, K., Lisonek, P. (eds.) Selected Areas in
            Cryptography – SAC 2013. LNCS, vol. 8282, Springer, Heidelberg (2014)
SDK$^+$13. Strobel, D., Driessen, B., Kasper, T., Leander, G., Oswald, D., Schel-
            lenberg, F., Paar, C.: Fuming Acid and Cryptanalysis: Handy Tools for
            Overcoming a Digital Locking and Access Control System. In: Canetti, R.,
            Garay, J.A. (eds.) CRYPTO 2013, Part I. LNCS, vol. 8042, pp. 147–164.
            Springer, Heidelberg (2013)

A Security Analysis of Key Expansion Functions Using Pseudorandom Permutations

Ju-Sung Kang[1], Nayoung Kim[2], Wangho Ju[2], and Ok-Yeon Yi[1]

[1] Dept. of Mathematics, Kookmin University, Korea
[2] Dept. of Financial Information Security, Graduate School, Kookmin University
77 Jeongneung-Ro, Seongbuk-Gu, Seoul, 136-702, Korea
{jskang,izerotwo,nandars2,oyyi}@kookmin.ac.kr

Abstract. Within many cryptographic systems a key expansion function is used in order to derive more keying material from the master secret. The derived additional keys may be needed for multiple entities or for different cryptographic purposes such as privacy and authenticity. In this paper we wish to examine the soundness of the key expansion functions on the view point of provable security framework. Especially we focus on the key expansion functions using PRFs(pseudorandom functions) which are recommended by NIST, and show that the variant of Double-Pipeline Iteration mode using PRPs(pseudorandom permutations) is secure, while the variants of Counter and Feedback modes using PRPs are insecure. In practice secure block ciphers such as AES can be regarded as PRPs.

Keywords: Privacy, Authenticity, Key expansion function, Keying material, Provable security, Pseudorandomness, PRF, PRP.

1 Introduction

Cryptographic keys are essential to the security of all cryptographic algorithms and protocols for some information security objectives, such as privacy or confidentiality, authenticity, digital signature, and non-repudiation in the presence of adversaries. Key management is an indispensable part of the cryptographic system and this includes dealing with the generation, exchange, storage, use, and replacement of keys. Cryptographic systems may use some kinds of keys more than one master key, so key derivation mechanism is contained in the key management part. Key derivation mechanism derives one or more secret keys from a shared secret such as a master key. Thus any key derivation mechanism has the key expansion step. For example, NIST SP 800-56C[10] specifies a key derivation mechanism that is an extraction-then-expansion procedure. This procedure consists of a randomness extraction step and a key expansion step. The randomness extraction step outputs a key derivation key from a master key. A key derivation key is then used as input to the key expansion step that derives keying material and can also be used to derive more keying material from derived keys of key expansion step. The derived additional keys from a key expansion step may be used for multiple entities or for different cryptographic objectives. Our research

D. Naccache and D. Sauveron (Eds.): WISTP 2014, LNCS 8501, pp. 10–23, 2014.
© IFIP International Federation for Information Processing 2014

interest is to examine the soundness of some key expansion functions (KEFs) for key expansion steps on the view point of provable security framework.

1.1 Related Work

Although a key derivation mechanism has the central role in applied cryptography, there has been relatively little formal work addressing the design and security analysis. Krawczyk[6] associated the notion of cryptographically strong secret keys with that of pseudorandom keys, namely, indistinguishable by feasible computation from a uniformly distributed string of the same length, and provided detailed rationale for the hash-based design of key derivation mechanisms based on the extract-then-expand approach. The extraction step generates a uniformly random or pseudorandom seed key from the master key that may be an output of an imperfect physical random number generator, and the expansion step derives several additional pseudorandom cryptographic keys from the seed key.

Gilbert[4] investigated the security of block cipher modes of operation allowing to expand an one-block input into a longer t-block output, under the Luby-Rackoff security paradigm[7,8] which is originally due to the indistinguishability in Goldreich-Goldwasser-Micali[5]. A KEF in a key derivation mechanism is a typical example of the one-block-to-many modes of operation. In [4], the author showed that, under the Luby-Rackoff security model, the key expansion function MILENAGE of 3GPP[13] is pseudorandom.

On the other hand NIST has specified three KEFs using pseudorandom functions (PRFs) in SP 800-108[11]. A PRF family $\{PRF_s(\cdot)|s \in S\}$ consists of polynomial time computable functions with an index s, a seed, such that when s is randomly selected from S and not known to adversaries, $PRF_s(\cdot)$ is computationally indistinguishable from a random function defined on the same domain and range [5]. In [11], several families of PRF-based key expansion functions are defined without describing the internal structure of the PRF, and recommended the use of either HMAC[3] or CMAC[9] as the PRF.

1.2 Our Contribution

In spite of several years after the publication of NIST SP 800-108[11], as far as we know there is no noticeable result that deals with a security analysis for three KEFs of this document. It seems that if a PRF, such as HMAC or CMAC, is used as the building block of the three KEFs in [11], we have difficulty in investigating the soundness of the given schemes. Hence we add a constraint condition that a pseudorandom permutation (PRP), such as AES, is used as the building block of the given KEFs. A PRP family is a special case of PRF families and computationally indistinguishable from a random permutation defined on the same domain. Once we regard the given KEFs of [11] as PRP-based schemes, we can investigate the security of these variant schemes in the Luby-Rackoff security model which is similar to the context of Gilbert[4].

In fact NIST SP 800-108[11] defines three families of PRF-based KEFs, so called, Counter mode, Feedback mode and Double-Pipeline Iteration mode. In this work we consider the variant schemes of three KEFs that use PRPs, and show that the variant of Double-Pipeline Iteration mode using PRPs is pseudorandom, while the variants of Counter and Feedback modes using PRPs are insecure. Moreover we provide a concrete security bound for the variant of Double-Pipeline Iteration mode where the underlying PRP is a practical block cipher. This concrete security approach is based on the security model of Bellare-Killian-Rogaway[1] and Bellare-Rogaway[2].

2   Notions of PRF and PRP

In order to examine the soundness of some KEFs, we need to introduce the rigorous notions of PRF and PRP. These are useful conceptual starting points to enable the security analysis in the design of some cryptographic functions. Cryptographic functions such as block ciphers or their modes of operation can be regarded as a pseudorandom function family indexed by a uniformly distributed key space. It is natural that we also consider a KEF as a pseudorandom function family because it is an example of block cipher modes of operation where a PRP is used as an underlying primitive in the KEF. We have to recognize that a KEF is an instance of a PRF to obtain the theoretical upper bound for the provable security. No computationally efficient adversary can distinguish with significant advantage between a randomly chosen instance of a PRF and a uniformly selected random function of the same domain and range. In this section we describe concrete security approach which is based on the Bellare-Rogaway[2] security model.

2.1   Function Families

A function family is a map $\Lambda : \mathcal{K} \times D \to R$, where $\mathcal{K}$ is the keyspace, D is the domain and R is the range of Λ. The two-input function Λ takes a key K and an input x to return a point y we denote by $\Lambda(K, x)$. For any key $K \in \mathcal{K}$ we define the map $\Lambda_K : D \to R$ by $\Lambda_K(x) = \Lambda(K, x)$. We call the function Λ_K an instance of the function family Λ. Thus Λ specifies a collection of maps indexed by the key space. Usually the probability distribution of a function family comes from some probability distributions on the keyspace $\mathcal{K}$. Unless otherwise indicated, this distribution will be the uniform distribution.

We use the following notation in this paper. For any positive integer k, n and m, we denote $\mathcal{K} = \{0,1\}^k$, $D = \{0,1\}^n$ and $R = \{0,1\}^m$, where k, n, and m are called the key-length, the input-length and the output-length, respectively. We denote by $K \xleftarrow{\$} \mathcal{K}$ the operation of selecting a random string K from $\mathcal{K}$. The notation $f \xleftarrow{\$} \Lambda$ means the operation $K \xleftarrow{\$} \mathcal{K}$ and $f = \Lambda_K$. In other words, let f be the function Λ_K where K is a randomly chosen key. We are interested in the input-output behavior of this randomly chosen instance of the family.

There are two particular function families that we need to consider in order to define PRFs and PRPs. One is $\mathcal{F}(D, R)$ the family of all functions from domain D to range R, the other is $\mathcal{P}(D)$ the family of all permutations on D. A uniformly chosen instance of $\mathcal{F}(D, R)$ is called a *random function* from D to R, and a uniformly chosen instance of $\mathcal{P}(D)$ is called a *random permutation* on D. The key describing any particular instance function is simply a description of this instance function in some canonical notation. For example, order the domain D lexicographically as $x_1, x_2, \ldots$, and let the key for a function f be the list of values $(f(x_1), f(x_2), \ldots)$. The keyspace of $\mathcal{F}(D, R)$ is simply the set of all these keys, under the uniform distribution. The key for a function in this family is a list of all the output values of the function as its input ranges over $\{0,1\}^n$. Namely, the key describing a particular instance function is exactly corresponding to the function itself. Note that the size of the key spaces of $\mathcal{F}(D, R)$ and $\mathcal{P}(D)$ are $(2^m)^{2^n}$ and $(2^n)!$, respectively.

2.2 Pseudorandom Functions and Permutations

A *pseudorandom function* is a function family with the property that the input-output behavior of a random instance of the family is computationally indistinguishable from that of a random function. Similarly, a function family is a *pseudorandom permutation* if the input-output behavior of a random instance of the family is computationally indistinguishable from that of a random permutation. In order to introduce the notions of PRF and PRP, we consider the following security model. The notion of PRP is very similar to the one of PRF. Thus we only consider the notion of PRF. Let any adversary $\mathcal{A}$ be an algorithm to distinguish a random instance of a function family from a random function. The adversary $\mathcal{A}$ has access to an oracle. The oracle will be chosen either as a random instance of a function family or as a random function by coin tossing. When the oracle selects a fuction as G we consider two different worlds. Usually in World 0, G will be chosen as a random function, while in World 1, G will be chosen as a random instance of a function family. And the adversary must determine in which world it is placed, and at the end of its computation outputs a bit.

In the formalization, we consider two different ways in which G will be chosen, giving rise to two different worlds.

World 0. The function G is drawn at random from $\mathcal{F}(D, R)$, namely, the function G is selected via $G \xleftarrow{\$} \mathcal{F}(D, R)$.

World 1. The function G is drawn at random from Λ, namely, the function G is selected via $G \xleftarrow{\$} \Lambda$.

Definition 1. *Let $\Lambda : \mathcal{K} \times D \to R$ be a function family, and $\mathcal{A}$ be an algorithm that takes an oracle for a function $G : D \to R$, and returns a bit. We consider two experiments:*

Experiment $\mathbf{Exp}_F^{prf-1}(\mathcal{A})$	Experiment $\mathbf{Exp}_F^{prf-0}(\mathcal{A})$
$K \xleftarrow{\$} \mathcal{K}$	$G \xleftarrow{\$} \mathcal{F}(D,R)$
$b \xleftarrow{\$} \mathcal{A}^{\Lambda_K}$	$b \xleftarrow{\$} \mathcal{A}^G$
Return b	Return b

The prf-advantage of $\mathcal{A}$ is defined by

$$\mathbf{Adv}_{\Lambda}^{prf}(\mathcal{A}) = Pr\left[\mathbf{Exp}_F^{prf-1}(\mathcal{A}) = 1\right] - Pr\left[\mathbf{Exp}_F^{prf-0}(\mathcal{A}) = 1\right]$$
$$= Pr\left[\mathcal{A}^G = 1 \mid G \leftarrow \Lambda\right] - Pr\left[\mathcal{A}^G = 1 \mid G \leftarrow \mathcal{F}(D,R)\right] .$$

3 PRP-Based KEFs of NIST SP 800-108

NIST has specified three KEFs using PRFs in SP 800-108[11] without describing the internal structure of the PRF, and recommended the use of either HMAC[3] or CMAC[9] as the underlying PRF. However we have difficulty in analyzing the provable security of the given KEFs where the underlying primitives are PRFs. Thus we change this PRF condition to the PRP one because a PRP family is a special case of PRF families. That is, hereafter we consider only PRP-based KEFs of the NIST recomendations. Once we regard the given KEFs of [11] as PRP-based schemes, we can investigate the provable security of these variant schemes in the Luby-Rackoff security model which is similar to the context of Gilbert[4].

3.1 PRP-Based Counter Mode

Let $\mathcal{G}$ be a PRP on $\{0,1\}^n$, then the PRP-based Counter mode is defined in Definition 2 and illustrated in Figure 1.

Definition 2. For any permutation $g \in \mathcal{G}$ and integer $t \geq 2$, $CNT[g]$ is called a PRP-based Counter mode if

$$CNT[g] : \{0,1\}^n \to \{0,1\}^{nt} ,$$
$$CNT[g](x) = (z_1, z_2, \ldots, z_t) = (g(x \oplus c_1), g(x \oplus c_2), \ldots, g(x \oplus c_t)) ,$$

where $c_1, c_2, \ldots, c_t$ are constants of $\{0,1\}^n$.

3.2 PRP-Based Feedback Mode

PRP-based Feedback mode is defined in Definition 3 and illustrated in Figure 2.

Definition 3. For any permutation $g \in \mathcal{G}$ and integer $t \geq 2$, $FB[g]$ is called a PRP-based Feedback mode if

$$FB[g] : \{0,1\}^n \to \{0,1\}^{nt} ,$$
$$FB[g](x) = (z_1, z_2, \ldots, z_t) = (g(x \oplus c_1), g(x \oplus z_1 \oplus c_2), \ldots, g(x \oplus z_{t-1} \oplus c_t)),$$

where $c_1, c_2, \ldots, c_t$ are constants of $\{0,1\}^n$.

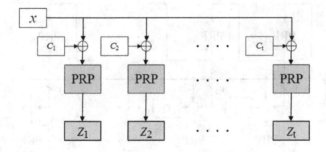

Fig. 1. PRP-based Counter mode

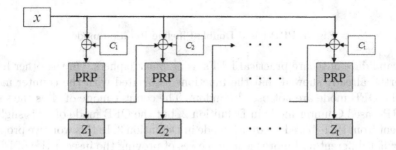

Fig. 2. PRP-based Feedback mode

3.3 PRP-Based Double-Pipeline Iteration Mode

PRP-based Double-Pipeline Iteration mode is defined in Definition 4 and illustrated in Figure 3.

Definition 4. *For any permutation $g \in \mathcal{G}$ and integer $t \geq 2$, $DP[g]$ is called PRP-based Double-Pipeline Iteration mode if*

$$DP[g] : \{0,1\}^n \to \{0,1\}^{nt},$$
$$DP[g](x) = (z_1, z_2, \ldots, z_t)$$
$$= \left(g\left(g(x) \oplus x \oplus c_1\right), g\left(g^2(x) \oplus x \oplus c_2\right), \ldots, g\left(g^t(x) \oplus x \oplus c_t\right)\right),$$

where for each $1 \leq k \leq t$, g^k denotes k times iteration of g and $c_1, c_2, \ldots, c_t$ are constants of $\{0,1\}^n$.

4 Provable Security of PRP-Based KEFs

In this section we show that the PRP-based Double-Pipeline Iteration mode is secure, while the PRP-based Counter mode and Feedback mode are insecure. Since a secure block cipher, such as AES, is regarded as the underlying PRP in practice, the PRP-based Double-Pipeline Iteration mode can be recommended

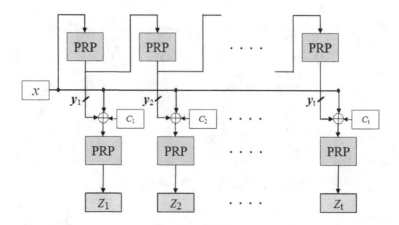

Fig. 3. PRP-based Double-Pipeline Iteration mode

as a candidate of secure practical KEFs using block ciphers. On the other hand Gilbert[4] already showed that the functions associated with the counter mode and the OFB mode are not pseudorandom. The counter mode of [4] is the same as PRP-based Counter mode in Definition 2, but the OFB mode of [4] is slightly different from PRP-based Feedback mode in Definition 3. In this work we propose somewhat different and more clear processes of proving the insecurities of PRP-based Counter and Feedback modes.

4.1   Insecurity of PRP-Based Counter Mode

Now we consider the case that $CNT[\pi]$ is derived from a random permutation $\pi \in \mathcal{P}(\{0,1\}^n)$. Then it is simple that $CNT[\pi]$ is insecure.

Theorem 1. *For any random permutation $\pi \in \mathcal{P}$, $CNT[\pi]$ is not a secure PRF.*

Proof. In order to show that $CNT[\pi]$ is not a secure PRF we specify an adversary attacking $CNT[\pi]$. Since an instance of $CNT[\pi]$ is a function from $\{0,1\}^n$ to $\{0,1\}^{nt}$, the adversary $\mathcal{A}$ will get an oracle for a function G that maps $\{0,1\}^n$ to $\{0,1\}^{nt}$. In World 0, G will be chosen as a random function from $\mathcal{F} = \mathcal{F}(\{0,1\}^n, \{0,1\}^{nt})$, while in World 1, G will be set to $CNT[\pi]$ where π is a random permutation from $\mathcal{P}(\{0,1\}^n)$. The adversary $\mathcal{A}$ must determine in which world it is placed. Let us show how the adversary $\mathcal{A}$ works.

Adversary $\mathcal{A}^G$
$\quad (z_1^{(1)}, \ldots, z_t^{(1)}) \leftarrow G\left(x^{(1)}\right)$
$\quad (z_1^{(2)}, \ldots, z_t^{(2)}) \leftarrow G\left(x^{(2)} = x^{(1)} \oplus c_1 \oplus c_2\right)$
$\quad$ **if** $z_1^{(1)} = z_2^{(2)}$ and $z_2^{(1)} = z_1^{(2)}$ **then return** 1
$\quad$ **else return** 0

If $G = CNT[\pi]$ for some π, it is certainly true that $z_1^{(1)} = z_2^{(2)}$ and $z_2^{(1)} = z_1^{(2)}$. On the other hand if G is a random function from $\mathcal{F}$, the probability of the event that $z_1^{(1)} = z_2^{(2)}$ and $z_2^{(1)} = z_1^{(2)}$ will be 2^{-2n}, the probability that $\mathcal{A}$ will return 1. Therefore the advantage of $\mathcal{A}$ is as follows:

$$\mathbf{Adv}_{CNT[\pi]}^{prf}(\mathcal{A}) = Pr\left[\mathbf{Exp}_{CNT[\pi]}^{prf-1}(\mathcal{A}) = 1\right] - Pr\left[\mathbf{Exp}_{CNT[\pi]}^{prf-0}(\mathcal{A}) = 1\right]$$
$$= Pr\left[\mathcal{A}^G = 1 \mid G \leftarrow CNT[\pi]\right] - Pr\left[\mathcal{A}^G = 1 \mid G \leftarrow \mathcal{F}\right]$$
$$= 1 - 2^{-2n}.$$

From the above formula we obtain that there exists an extremely efficient adversary whose prf-advantage against $CNT[\pi]$ is almost one. This means that $CNT[\pi]$ is not a secure PRF. $\qquad\square$

4.2   Insecurity of PRP-Based Feedback Mode

We investigate the provable security of the PRP-based Feedback mode $FB[\pi]$ derived from a random permutation π. It is also a simple argument similar to the case of PRP-based Counter mode that $FB[\pi]$ is insecure.

Theorem 2. *For any random permutation $\pi \in \mathcal{P}$, $FB[\pi]$ is not a secure PRF.*

Proof. We find an adversary with a high advantage attacking $FB[\pi]$ in order to prove that $FB[\pi]$ is not a secure PRF. Since an instance of $FB[\pi]$ is a function from $\{0,1\}^n$ to $\{0,1\}^{nt}$, the adversary $\mathcal{A}$ will get an oracle for a function G that maps $\{0,1\}^n$ to $\{0,1\}^{nt}$. In World 0, G will be chosen as a random function of $\mathcal{F} = \mathcal{F}(\{0,1\}^n, \{0,1\}^{nt})$, while in World 1, G will be set to $FB[\pi]$ where π is a random permutation from $\mathcal{P}(\{0,1\}^n)$. The adversary $\mathcal{A}$ must determine in which world it is placed. In this case $\mathcal{A}$ queries its oracle at the $x^{(1)}$ to get back $(z_1^{(1)}, \ldots, z_t^{(1)})$ and then queries its oracle at the $x^{(2)}$ to get back $(z_1^{(2)}, \ldots, z_t^{(2)})$. The adversary $\mathcal{A}$ works as follows:

Adversary $\mathcal{A}^G$
$\quad (z_1^{(1)}, \ldots, z_t^{(1)}) \leftarrow G\left(x^{(1)}\right)$
$\quad (z_1^{(2)}, \ldots, z_t^{(2)}) \leftarrow G\left(x^{(2)} = x^{(1)} \oplus c_1 \oplus c_2 \oplus z_1^{(1)}\right)$
$\quad$ **if** $z_1^{(2)} = z_2^{(1)}$ **then return** 1
$\quad$ **else return** 0

If $G = FB[\pi]$ for some π, it is obvious that

$$z_1^{(2)} = \pi((x^{(1)} \oplus c_1 \oplus c_2 \oplus z_1^{(1)}) \oplus c_1) = \pi(x^{(1)} \oplus c_2 \oplus z_1^{(1)}) = z_2^{(1)}.$$

On the other hand if G is a random function, the probability that $z_1^{(2)} = z_2^{(1)}$ will be 2^{-n}, the probability that $\mathcal{A}$ will return 1. Thus $\mathbf{Adv}_{FB[\pi]}^{prf}(\mathcal{A}) = 1 - 2^{-n}$, this shows that $FB[\pi]$ is not a secure PRF. $\qquad\square$

4.3   Provable Security of PRP-Based Double-Pipeline Iteration Mode

Now we examine the provable security of the PRP-based Double-Pipeline Iteration mode. We consider the case where $DP[\pi]$ is derived from a random permutation π and prove that $DP[\pi]$ is a secure PRF. At first we introduce a very useful fact of [12] and [4] for obtaining an upper bound on $\mathbf{Adv}^{prf}(\mathcal{A})$ based on the transition probability $Pr(\mathbf{x} \rightarrow \mathbf{y})$.

Proposition 1. *Let E be a randomly chosen instance of a function family Λ with the domain $\{0,1\}^n$ and the range $\{0,1\}^m$, F be a random function from $\mathcal{F} = \mathcal{F}(\{0,1\}^n, \{0,1\}^m)$ and q be an integer. An adversary $\mathcal{A}$ will get an oracle for a function G. In World 0, G will be chosen from $\mathcal{F}$, while in World 1, G will be set to E that is a randomly drawn from Λ. The adversary must determine in which world it is placed. Denote by X the subset of $(\{0,1\}^n)^q$ containing all pairwise distinct q-tuples $\mathbf{x} = (x^{(1)}, \cdots, x^{(q)})$. If there exist a subset Y of $(\{0,1\}^m)^q$ and two positive real numbers ε_1 and ε_2 such that*

(a) $|Y| \geq (1 - \varepsilon_1) \cdot 2^{mq}$

(b) *for each* $\mathbf{x} \in X$ *and* $\mathbf{y} \in Y$, $\quad Pr\left(\mathbf{x} \overset{E}{\rightarrow} \mathbf{y}\right) \geq (1 - \varepsilon_2) \cdot \dfrac{1}{2^{mq}}$,

then for any adversary $\mathcal{A}$ using q queries

$$\mathbf{Adv}_{\Lambda}^{prf}(\mathcal{A}) = Pr\left[\mathcal{A}^G = 1 | G \leftarrow \Lambda\right] - Pr\left[\mathcal{A}^G = 1 | G \leftarrow \mathcal{F}\right]$$
$$\leq \varepsilon_1 + \varepsilon_2 .$$

By the argument using Proposition 1, in the following Theorem 3 we obtain an upper bound on $\mathbf{Adv}_{DP[\pi]}^{prf}(\mathcal{A})$. From this we know the fact that the PRP-based Double-Pipeline Iteration mode is a secure PRF.

Theorem 3. *For any PRP-based Double-Pipeline Iteration mode*

$$DP[\pi] : \{0,1\}^n \rightarrow \{0,1\}^{nt} , \quad \forall \pi \in \mathcal{P}(\{0,1\}^n) ,$$

let $\mathcal{A}$ be an adversary with q queries such that $\frac{t^2 q^2}{2^n} \leq \frac{2}{3}$. Then we obtain that

$$\mathbf{Adv}_{DP[\pi]}^{prf}(\mathcal{A}) \leq \frac{7t^2 q^2}{2^{n+1}} .$$

Proof. Let X denote the subset of $(\{0,1\}^n)^q$ containing all pairwise distinct q-tuples $\mathbf{x} = (x^{(1)}, \ldots, x^{(q)})$ and Z be the set of q-tuples $\mathbf{z} = ((z_1^{(1)}, \ldots, z_t^{(1)}), (z_1^{(2)}, \ldots, z_t^{(2)}), \ldots, (z_1^{(q)}, \ldots, z_t^{(q)})) \in (\{0,1\}^{nt})^q$, where all tq values of $z_k^{(i)}$, $1 \leq k \leq t$ and $1 \leq i \leq q$, are distinct. By Proposition 1, it suffices to show that there exist positive real numbers ε_1 and ε_2 such that

$$|Z| \geq (1 - \varepsilon_1) \cdot 2^{ntq} \tag{1}$$

and

$$\forall \mathbf{x} \in X, \ \forall \mathbf{z} \in Z, \quad Pr\left(\mathbf{x} \stackrel{DP[\pi]}{\longrightarrow} \mathbf{z}\right) \geq (1 - \varepsilon_2) \cdot \frac{1}{2^{ntq}} \, . \qquad (2)$$

Note that

$$
\begin{aligned}
\frac{1}{2^{ntq}} \cdot |Z| &= \frac{2^n \cdot (2^n - 1) \cdots (2^n - (tq - 1))}{2^{ntq}} \\
&= 1 \cdot \left(1 - \frac{1}{2^n}\right) \cdots \left(1 - \frac{tq - 1}{2^n}\right) \\
&\geq 1 - \frac{1}{2^n}\left(1 + 2 + \cdots + (tq - 1)\right) \\
&= 1 - \frac{1}{2^n}\left(\frac{(tq - 1)(1 + tq - 1)}{2}\right) \\
&\geq 1 - \frac{t^2 q^2}{2^{n+1}} \, .
\end{aligned}
$$

Then the inequality (1) is established, if we set $\varepsilon_1 = \frac{t^2 q^2}{2^{n+1}} > 0$.

In order to estimate the transition probability of (2), we have to consider somewhat complicated cases changed by some input-output conditions associated with π's of $DP[\pi]$. For any fixed $\mathbf{x} \in X \subset (\{0,1\}^n)^q$ and $\mathbf{z} \in Z \subset (\{0,1\}^{nt})^q$, the transition probability $Pr\left(\mathbf{x} \stackrel{DP[\pi]}{\longrightarrow} \mathbf{z}\right)$ can be estimated by investigating the intermediate value $\mathbf{y} \in (\{0,1\}^{nt})^q$ of $DP[\pi]$ depicted in Figure 3. The values of the input $\mathbf{x}$ and the corresponding output $\mathbf{z}$ are known, while the exact value of the intermediate value $\mathbf{y}$ is unknown. Hence we have to collect all possible candidates about the unknown intermediate value. Let $Y \subset (\{0,1\}^{nt})^q$ be the set of all these possible candidates;

$$
Y = \Big\{ \mathbf{y} = ((y_1^{(1)}, \dots, y_t^{(1)}), \dots, (y_1^{(q)}, \dots, y_t^{(q)}))
$$

$$
\mid y_k^{(i)} \neq y_k^{(j)}, \ 1 \leq k \leq t, \ 1 \leq i \neq j \leq q \Big\},
$$

where for each $1 \leq k \leq t$ and $1 \leq i \leq q$, $y_k^{(i)} = \pi^k(x^{(i)})$. By the definition of Y,

$$|Y| = 2^{nt} \cdot (2^n - 1)^t \cdots (2^n - q + 1)^t = \left(\frac{2^n!}{(2^n - q)!}\right)^t . \qquad (3)$$

Now we introduce a subset $Y' \subset Y$ for convenience of counting distinct input values of π. Let $Y' = A \cap B \cap C$ with

$$A = \{\mathbf{y} \in Y \mid y_k^{(i)} \neq y_l^{(j)}, \ 1 \leq i,j \leq q, \ 0 \leq k,l \leq t - 1\},$$

$$B = \{\mathbf{y} \in Y \mid y_k^{(i)} \neq y_l^{(j)} \oplus x^{(j)} \oplus c_l, \ 1 \leq i,j \leq q, 0 \leq k \leq t - 1, 1 \leq l \leq t\},$$

$$\text{where } y_0^{(i)} = x^{(i)}, \text{ and}$$

$$C = \{\mathbf{y} \in Y \mid y_k^{(i)} \oplus x^{(i)} \oplus c_k \neq y_l^{(j)} \oplus x^{(j)} \oplus c_j, \ 1 \leq i,j \leq q, \ 1 \leq k,l \leq t\}.$$

For any $1 \leq i \leq q$, $1 \leq k \leq t-1$ and $1 \leq l \leq t$, we have

$$
Pr\left(\mathbf{x} \xrightarrow{DP[\pi]} \mathbf{z}\right)
$$

$$
= \sum_{\mathbf{y} \in Y} Pr\left(x^{(i)} \xrightarrow{\pi} y_1^{(i)},\ y_k^{(i)} \xrightarrow{\pi} y_{k+1}^{(i)},\ y_l^{(i)} \oplus x^{(i)} \oplus c_l \xrightarrow{\pi} z_l^{(i)}\right)
$$

$$
\geq \sum_{\mathbf{y} \in Y'} Pr\left(x^{(i)} \xrightarrow{\pi} y_1^{(i)},\ y_k^{(i)} \xrightarrow{\pi} y_{k+1}^{(i)},\ y_l^{(i)} \oplus x^{(i)} \oplus c_l \xrightarrow{\pi} z_l^{(i)}\right)
$$

$$
= |Y'| \cdot \frac{(2^n - 2tq)!}{2^n!}. \tag{4}
$$

In order to obtain a lower bound on $|Y'|$, we count $|Y - A|$, $|Y - B|$ and $|Y - C|$. At the first step we represent the set $Y - A$ with three subsets to count $|Y - A|$. For any element of $Y - A$, we consider three cases according to the condition of indexes.

Case 1. If $k = 0$ and $1 \leq l \leq t-1$, then for any $\mathbf{y} \in Y - A$ satisfies $x^{(i)} = y_0^{(i)} = y_l^{(j)}$. In this case the number of $\mathbf{y}$ such that $x^{(i)} = y_l^{(j)}$ is $\frac{|Y|}{2^n} \cdot q^2 \cdot (t-1)$, since by (3), for any fixed i, j and l, $(2^n)^{t-1} \cdot (2^n - 1)^t \cdots (2^n - q + 1)^t = \frac{|Y|}{2^n}$.

Case 2. If $1 \leq k \neq l \leq t-1$ and $1 \leq i = j \leq q$, then for any $\mathbf{y} \in Y - A$ satisfies $y_k^{(i)} = y_l^{(j)} = y_l^{(i)}$. In this case the number of $\mathbf{y}$ such that $y_k^{(i)} = y_l^{(i)}$ is $\frac{|Y|}{2^n} \cdot q \cdot \frac{(t-1)(t-2)}{2}$, since by (3), for any fixed i, k and l, $(2^n)^{t-2} \cdot (2^n - 1)^t \cdots (2^n - q + 1)^t = \frac{|Y|}{(2^n)^2}$.

Case 3. If $1 \leq k \neq l \leq t-1$ and $1 \leq i \neq j \leq q$, then for any $\mathbf{y} \in Y - A$ satisfies $y_k^{(i)} = y_l^{(j)}$. In this case the number of $\mathbf{y}$ such that $y_k^{(i)} = y_l^{(j)}$ is $\frac{|Y|}{2^n} \cdot \frac{q(q-1)}{2} \cdot \frac{(t-1)(t-2)}{2}$, since by (3), for any fixed i, j, k and l, $(2^n)^{t-2} \cdot (2^n - 1)^t \cdots (2^n - q + 1)^t = \frac{|Y|}{(2^n)^2}$.

Therefore we obtain that

$$
|Y - A| \leq \frac{|Y|}{2^n} \cdot q \cdot (t-1) \left(q + \frac{t-2}{2} + \frac{(q-1)(t-2)}{4} \right).
$$

By the similar argument, we have

$$
|Y - B| \leq \frac{|Y|}{2^n} \cdot q \left(t + (q-1)t + (t-1)^2 + (q-1)(t-1)^2 + 2(q-1)(t-1) \right)
$$

and

$$
|Y - C| \leq \frac{|Y|}{2^n} \cdot \frac{qt}{2} \left((t-1) + \frac{(q-1)(t-1)}{2} + 2(q-1) \right).
$$

Now we have a lower bound on $|Y'|$ as follows:

$$|Y'| \geq |Y| - (|Y - A| + |Y - B| + |Y - C|)$$
$$\geq |Y| - \frac{|Y|}{2^{n+1}} q \left(3qt^2 + 4qt - 3q + t^2 - 8t + 5\right)$$
$$= |Y| \left(1 - \frac{q}{2^{n+1}} \left(3qt^2 + 4qt - 3q + t^2 - 8t + 5\right)\right). \tag{5}$$

By (3), (4) and (5), we obtain that

$$Pr\left(\mathbf{x} \xrightarrow{DP[\pi]} \mathbf{z}\right)$$

$$\geq \left(1 - \frac{q}{2^{n+1}} \left(3qt^2 + 4qt - 3q + t^2 - 8t + 5\right)\right) \cdot \frac{(2^n - 2tq)!}{2^n!} \cdot \left(\frac{2^n!}{(2^n - q)!}\right)^t$$

$$\geq \left(1 - \frac{q}{2^{n+1}} \left(3qt^2 + 4qt - 3q + t^2 - 8t + 5\right)\right) \cdot \frac{1}{2^{ntq}} \left(1 + \frac{qt(3qt - 1)}{2^{n+1}}\right)$$

$$= \frac{1}{2^{ntq}}(1 - \eta)(1 + \delta),$$

where $\eta = \frac{q}{2^{n+1}} \left(3qt^2 + 4qt - 3q + t^2 - 8t + 5\right)$, $\delta = \frac{qt(3qt-1)}{2^{n+1}}$. Since $\delta \leq 1$ by assumtion $\frac{t^2 q^2}{2^n} \leq \frac{2}{3}$,

$$(1 - \eta)(1 + \delta) \geq 1 - 2\eta + \delta$$
$$= 1 - \frac{q}{2^{n+1}} \left(3qt^2 + 8qt - 6q + 2t^2 - 15t + 10\right)$$
$$\geq 1 - \frac{q}{2^{n+1}} \left(3qt^2 + 3qt^2\right) = 1 - \frac{6q^2t^2}{2^{n+1}}.$$

Thus

$$Pr\left(\mathbf{x} \xrightarrow{DP[\pi]} \mathbf{z}\right) \geq \frac{1}{2^{ntq}} \left(1 - \frac{6q^2t^2}{2^{n+1}}\right).$$

Hence we show that (2) is established with $\varepsilon_2 = \frac{6q^2t^2}{2^{n+1}}$.

Consequentially, we obtain the upper bound on advantage of adversary $\mathcal{A}$

$$\mathbf{Adv}^{prf}_{DP[\pi]}(\mathcal{A}) \leq \varepsilon_1 + \varepsilon_2 = \frac{7t^2q^2}{2^{n+1}}. \qquad \square$$

On the other hand, any random permutation $\pi \in \mathcal{P}(\{0,1\}^n)$ in Theorem 3 is implemented by a secure block cipher in the real field. Hence it is important to investigate the concrete security analysis for the PRP-based Double-Pipeline Iteration mode where the underlying PRP is a practical block cipher such as AES. Theorem 4 shows that the Double-Pipeline Iteration mode using a block cipher is also secure, if the underlying block cipher is secure on the view point of concrete security paradigm. Let E_K be a permutation family where K is randomly chosen from $\mathcal{K}$. Then a block cipher with key is regarded as a instance of the E_K.

Theorem 4. *Let $\mathcal{A}$ be any prf-adversary attacking $DP[E_K]$ with any q queries such that $\frac{t^2 q^2}{2^n} \leq \frac{2}{3}$. Then there exists an prp-adversary $\mathcal{B}$ attacking E_K with $2tq$ queries such that*

$$\mathbf{Adv}_{DP[E_K]}^{prf}(\mathcal{A}) \leq \mathbf{Adv}_{E_K}^{prp}(\mathcal{B}) + \frac{7t^2 q^2}{2^{n+1}} .$$

Proof. We specify an adversary $\mathcal{B}$ attacking E_K. Let E_K be a permutation family with induced distibution from $\mathcal{K}$, π be a random permutation from $\mathcal{P} = \mathcal{P}(\{0,1\}^n)$. The adversary $\mathcal{B}$ will get an oracle for a permutation g on $\{0,1\}^n$. In World 0, g will be chosen from $\mathcal{P}$, that is, $g = \pi$, while in World 1, g will be set to E_K where K is a randomly chosen key. The adversary $\mathcal{B}$ will run $\mathcal{A}$ as a subroutine. The $\mathcal{B}$ work like this:

Adversary $\mathcal{B}^g$
    Run adversary $\mathcal{A}$, replying to its oracle queries as follows
        For $i = 1, \cdots, q$ do
        When $\mathcal{A}$ makes an oracle query $x^{(i)}$
        $\mathbf{z}^{(i)} \xleftarrow{\$} DP[g](x^{(i)})$
        Return $\mathbf{z}^{(i)}$ to $\mathcal{A}$ as the answer
        Until $\mathcal{A}$ stops and outputs a bit, b
    Return b

Then by Definition 1, prp-adventage of $\mathcal{B}$ is

$$\begin{aligned}
\mathbf{Adv}_{E_K}^{prp}(\mathcal{B}) &= Pr\left[\mathbf{Exp}_{E_K}^{prp-1}(\mathcal{B}) = 1\right] - Pr\left[\mathbf{Exp}_{E_K}^{prp-0}(\mathcal{B}) = 1\right] \\
&= Pr\left[\mathcal{B}^g = 1 \mid g \leftarrow E_K\right] - Pr\left[\mathcal{B}^g = 1 \mid g \leftarrow \mathcal{P}\right].
\end{aligned}$$

In this case,

$$Pr\left[\mathcal{B}^g = 1 \mid g \leftarrow E_K\right] = Pr\left[\mathcal{A}^G = 1 \mid G \leftarrow DP[E_K]\right] ,$$

$$Pr\left[\mathcal{B}^g = 1 \mid g \leftarrow \mathcal{P}\right] = Pr\left[\mathcal{A}^G = 1 \mid G \leftarrow DP[\pi]\right] .$$

Therefore,

$$\begin{aligned}
\mathbf{Adv}_{E_K}^{prp}(\mathcal{B}) &= Pr\left[\mathbf{Exp}_{E_K}^{prp-1}(\mathcal{B}) = 1\right] - Pr\left[\mathbf{Exp}_{E_K}^{prp-0}(\mathcal{B}) = 1\right] \\
&= Pr\left[\mathcal{B}^g = 1 \mid g \leftarrow E_K\right] - [\mathcal{B}^g = 1 \mid g \leftarrow \mathcal{P}] \\
&= Pr\left[\mathcal{A}^G = 1 \mid G \leftarrow DP[E_K]\right] - Pr\left[\mathcal{A}^G = 1 \mid G \leftarrow DP[\pi]\right] \\
&= Pr\left[\mathcal{A}^G = 1 \mid G \leftarrow DP[E_K]\right] - Pr\left[\mathcal{A}^G = 1 \mid G \leftarrow \mathcal{F}\right] \\
&\quad + Pr\left[\mathcal{A}^G = 1 \mid G \leftarrow \mathcal{F}\right] - Pr\left[\mathcal{A}^G = 1 \mid G \leftarrow DP[\pi]\right] \\
&= \mathbf{Adv}_{DP[E_K]}^{prf}(\mathcal{A}) - \mathbf{Adv}_{DP[\pi]}^{prf}(\mathcal{A}) .
\end{aligned}$$

By Theorem 3, we obtain that

$$\mathbf{Adv}_{DP[E_K]}^{prf}(\mathcal{A}) \leq \mathbf{Adv}_{E_K}^{prp}(\mathcal{B}) + \frac{7t^2 q^2}{2^{n+1}} . \qquad \square$$

5 Conclusion

In this paper we have examined the soundness of the PRP-based KEFs, variant schemes of PRF-base schemes of NIST SP 800-108, on the view point of provable security framework, and proved that the variant of Double-Pipeline Iteration mode using PRPs is secure, while the variants of Counter and Feedback modes using PRPs are insecure. Moreover we have provided a concrete security bound for the variant of Double-Pipeline Iteration mode where the underlying PRP is a practical block cipher, since in practice a secure block cipher such as AES can be regarded as a PRP. As far as we know our results are the first work related to the security analysis for the KEFs within NIST SP 800-108.

Acknowledgements. This research was partially supported by BK21PLUS through the National Research Foundation of Korea(NRF) funded by the Ministry of Education, Science and Technology (Grant No. 31Z20130012918) and the IT R&D program of MSIP/KEIT[10041864, development on Spectrum Efficient Multiband WPAN System for Smart Home Networks].

References

1. Bellare, M., Kilian, J., Rogaway, P.: The security of the cipher block chaining message authentication code. J. Computer and System Sciences 61(3), 362–399 (2000)
2. Bellare, M., Rogaway, P.: Introduction to Mordern Cryptography, http://cseweb.ucsd.edu/~mihir/cse207/classnotes.html
3. FIPS 198-1, The Keyed-Hash Message Authentication Code, HMAC (2008)
4. Gilbert, H.: The security of one-block-to-many modes of operation. In: Johansson, T. (ed.) FSE 2003. LNCS, vol. 2887, pp. 376–395. Springer, Heidelberg (2003)
5. Goldreich, O., Goldwasser, S., Micali, S.: How to construct random functions. J. of the ACM 33(4), 210–217 (1986)
6. Krawczyk, H.: Cryptographic extraction and key derivation: The HKDF scheme. In: Rabin, T. (ed.) CRYPTO 2010. LNCS, vol. 6223, pp. 631–648. Springer, Heidelberg (2010)
7. Luby, M., Rackoff, C.: How to construct pseudorandom permutations and pseudorandom functions. SIAM J. Comput. 17, 373–386 (1988)
8. Naor, M., Reingold, O.: On the construction of pseudorandom permutations: Luby-Rackoff revisited. J. Cryptology 12, 29–66 (1999)
9. NIST Special Publication 800-108, Recommendation for Block Cipher Modes of Operation - The CMAC Mode for Authentication (May 2005)
10. NIST Special Publication 800-56C, Recommendation for Key Derivation through Extraction-then-Expansion (November 2011)
11. NIST Special Publication 800-108, Recommendation for Key Derivation Using Pseudorandom Functions (October 2009)
12. Patarin, J.: How to construct pseudorandom and super pseudorandom permutations from one single pseudorandom function. In: Rueppel, R.A. (ed.) Advances in Cryptology - EUROCRYPT 1992. LNCS, vol. 658, pp. 256–266. Springer, Heidelberg (1993)
13. 3rd Generation Partnership Project, Specification of the MILENAGE algorithm set: An example algorithm set for the 3GPP authentication and key generation functions f1, f1*, f2, f3, f4, f5 and f5*, http://www.3gpp.org

Towards More Practical Time-Driven Cache Attacks

Raphael Spreitzer[1,*] and Benoît Gérard[2]

[1] IAIK, Graz University of Technology, Austria
raphael.spreitzer@iaik.tugraz.at
[2] DGA-MI, France
benoit.gerard@irisa.fr

Abstract. Side-channel attacks are usually performed by employing the "divide-and-conquer" approach, meaning that leaking information is collected in a *divide step*, and later on exploited in the *conquer step*. The idea is to extract as much information as possible during the *divide step*, and to exploit the gathered information as efficiently as possible within the *conquer step*. Focusing on both of these steps, we discuss potential enhancements of Bernstein's cache-timing attack against the Advanced Encryption Standard (AES). Concerning the *divide part*, we analyze the impact of attacking different key-chunk sizes, aiming at the extraction of more information from the overall encryption time. Furthermore, we analyze the most recent improvement of time-driven cache attacks, presented by Aly and ElGayyar, according to its applicability on ARM Cortex-A platforms. For the *conquer part*, we employ the optimal key-enumeration algorithm as proposed by Veyrat-Charvillon *et al.* to significantly reduce the complexity of the exhaustive key-search phase compared to the currently employed threshold-based approach. This in turn leads to more practical attacks. Additionally, we provide extensive experimental results of the proposed enhancements on two Android-based smartphones, namely a *Google Nexus S* and a *Samsung Galaxy SII*.

Keywords: AES, ARM Cortex-A, key-chunk sizes, optimal key-enumeration algorithm, time-driven cache attack.

1 Introduction

Side-channel attacks have been shown to represent a powerful means of exploiting unintended information leakage on modern system architectures in order to break cryptographic implementations. One specific form of such side-channel attacks is denoted as cache attacks, which aim at the exploitation of different memory-access times within the memory hierarchy. More formally, the central-processing unit (CPU) is able to access data within the cache memory much faster than data within the main memory. These timing differences allow an attacker to break cryptographic implementations [10, 16].

Recent investigations of the timing leakage due to the cache memory, *i.e.*, cache hits and cache misses, emphasized the general applicability of these attacks [2]. However, especially on the ARM Cortex-A platform—the most commonly used architecture in

---

* This work has been supported by the Austrian Research Promotion Agency (FFG) and the Styrian Business Promotion Agency (SFG) under grant number 836628 (SeCoS).

D. Naccache and D. Sauveron (Eds.): WISTP 2014, LNCS 8501, pp. 24–39, 2014.

modern mobile devices—these investigations [18, 25] showed that timing information is leaking, but the complexity of the remaining key-search phase is usually very high. For instance, Weiß *et al.* [25] compared the vulnerability of different Advanced Encryption Standard (AES) implementations on the ARM platform. For the most vulnerable implementation, *i.e.*, Bernstein's Poly 1305-AES implementation, they presented a remaining key-search complexity of about 65 bits. Such an order of magnitude has been confirmed in [19]. While being clearly within the range of a mafia or state institution—that have far more efficient techniques to recover information anyway—such attacks may be out of reach for hackers and criminals. More precisely, such an attack would require a huge effort that could only be invested for hacking a few users.

Motivation and Contribution. The motivation of this work is to investigate potential improvements of time-driven cache attacks to determine if such attacks could be massively performed by skilled hackers. In this respect, we propose and investigate multiple enhancements to the cache-based timing attack of Bernstein [4] in order to evaluate more accurately the actual security of ARM-based devices regarding this threat.

Bernstein's timing attack is based on the so-called *divide-and-conquer* strategy. While the *divide part* aims at the gathering of the leaking information, *i.e.*, the overall encryption time, the *conquer part* focuses on the actual exploitation of the gathered information to recover the employed secret key. We study potential improvements for both steps. Thus, our contributions can be summarized as follows.

- Regarding the *divide part* we discuss the potential improvement of attacking different key-chunk sizes, *i.e.*, key chunks not corresponding to one byte. Thereby, we try to extract even more information from the observed encryption time under a secret key. Furthermore, we investigate the proposed enhancement of Aly and ElGayyar [2], *i.e.*, the exploitation of the minimum encryption time, according to its applicability on ARM Cortex-A platforms.
- Regarding the context of the *conquer part* we focus on an optimal way to iterate over potential key candidates. While Bernstein initially proposed a *threshold-based approach* to sort out potential key candidates for an exhaustive search, we apply the *optimal key-enumeration algorithm* of Veyrat-Charvillon *et al.* [23]. This allows us to iterate over potential key candidates according to their probability for being the correct one and, thus, to reduce the complexity of the remaining key-search phase.

All discussions about potential improvements are supported by tests performed on two smartphones employing an ARM Cortex-A processor, namely a *Google Nexus S* and a *Samsung Galaxy SII*. These practical experiments demonstrate that the number of key bits to be searched exhaustively can be reduced significantly, hence answering positively the motivating question: timing attacks are within the range of a skilled hacker.

Outline. The remainder of this paper is organized as follows. In Section 2, we cover the required preliminaries including AES software implementations, CPU caches, and cache attacks in general. Section 3 provides the required details of Bernstein's timing attack as well as follow-up work on Bernstein's attack. We consider potential improvements of the *divide part* in Section 4 and discuss the use of the optimal key-enumeration algorithm within the *conquer part* in Section 5. Section 6 states our practical observations of the proposed enhancements. Finally, we conclude this work in Section 7.

2 Background

This section details the basic concept of the Advanced Encryption Standard, the CPU cache memory, as well as the basic principles of cache attacks.

2.1 Advanced Encryption Standard

The Advanced Encryption Standard (AES) [12] is a block cipher operating on 128-bit states—denoted as $S = (s_0, \ldots, s_{15})$—and supports key lengths of 128, 192, and 256 bits. The initial state is computed as $S^0 = P \oplus K^0$, with $P = (p_0, \ldots, p_{15})$ being the plaintext and $K^0 = (k_0^0, \ldots, k_{15}^0)$ the initial round key. After the initial key addition, the round transformations (1) *SubBytes*, (2) *ShiftRows*, (3) *MixColumns*, and (4) *AddRoundKey* are applied multiple times, whereas the last round omits the *MixColumns* transformation. The exact number of rounds depends on the actual key length.

For the purpose of cache attacks the details of these round transformations are mostly irrelevant since software implementations usually employ so-called T-tables, denoted as T_i. These T-tables hold the precomputed round transformations and are composed of 256 4-byte elements. In every round the state bytes s_i are used to retrieve the precomputed 4-byte values which are then combined with a simple XOR operation to form the new state. The resulting state after the last round represents the ciphertext.

In this work, we consider a key length of 128 bits. However, the outlined concepts shall apply to other key lengths analogously.

2.2 CPU Caches

Since the CPU is not able to access the main memory at the desired speed, the CPU cache has been introduced. The purpose of the CPU cache—a small and fast memory between the CPU and the main memory—is to hold close frequently used data and, thus, to enhance the performance of memory accesses. The most commonly used caches are so-called *set-associative caches* where the cache is divided into equally sized cache sets, each consisting of multiple cache lines. Contiguous bytes of the main memory are then mapped to a specific cache set and can be placed in any cache line of this cache set. The actual cache line within a cache set where new data should be placed is determined by the replacement policy, which can be either random or deterministic. In case of the ARM Cortex-A platform a random-replacement policy is employed.

2.3 Cache Attacks

Combining the knowledge about T-table implementations and CPU caches leads to the concept of cache attacks. First, AES T-table implementations make use of key-dependent look-up indices to access the precomputed values of the round transformations. Second, these T-table accesses are not performed in constant time. The data might be fetched either from the CPU cache (cache hit) or from the main memory (cache miss) and, thus, leads to varying execution times. Hence, cache attacks are a specific form of side-channel attacks that aim at the exploitation of variations within the execution time.

Cache attacks are separated into three categories: (1) *time-driven attacks*, (2) *access-driven attacks*, and (3) *trace-driven attacks*. Time-driven cache attacks [4, 22] rely on the overall encryption time to recover the used secret key by means of statistical methods. Hence, these attacks represent the most general type of cache attacks. In contrast, access-driven cache attacks [9, 14, 20, 21] as well as trace-driven cache attacks [1, 6, 7] rely on more sophisticated knowledge about the implementation and the underlying hardware architecture. However, access-driven and trace-driven attacks require far less measurement samples than time-driven attacks. In short, there is a trade-off between the required knowledge and the number of required measurement samples. In this work, we focus on the investigation of the time-driven cache attack proposed by Bernstein [4].

3 Related Work

In this section, we detail the basic concept of Bernstein's timing attack [4] and outline related work based on this attack.

3.1 Seminal Work: Bernstein's Timing Attack

In 2005, Bernstein [4] proposed a timing attack against the AES T-table implementation. He suggested to gather timing information of different plaintexts under a known key $\mathbf{K}$ as well as under an unknown key $\widetilde{\mathbf{K}}$. Afterwards, correlating the timing information of these two sets of plaintexts should reveal potential key candidates. The attack consists of four different phases which are outlined within the following paragraphs.

Study Phase. Within this phase the attacker measures the encryption time of multiple plaintexts $\mathbf{P}$ under a known key $\mathbf{K}$. Without loss of generality, we assume that the zero-key is used for this phase. The information is stored in $\mathbf{t}[j][b]$ which holds the sum of all encryption times observed for plaintexts where the plaintext byte $\mathbf{p}_j = b$, and $\mathbf{n}[j][b]$ which counts the number of encrypted plaintexts where $\mathbf{p}_j = b$.

Attack Phase. In this phase the attacker collects the exact same information as in the study phase, but this time under an unknown key $\widetilde{\mathbf{K}}$ that she wants to recover. The gathered information is stored in $\widetilde{\mathbf{t}}[j][b]$ and $\widetilde{\mathbf{n}}[j][b]$, respectively.

Correlation Phase. The attacker computes the so-called plaintext-byte signature [13] of the study phase as illustrated in Equation 1. The plaintext-byte signature of the attack phase is computed analogously, except that $\mathbf{v}[j][b]$, $\mathbf{t}[j][b]$, and $\mathbf{n}[j][b]$ are replaced with $\widetilde{\mathbf{v}}[j][b]$, $\widetilde{\mathbf{t}}[j][b]$, and $\widetilde{\mathbf{n}}[j][b]$, respectively.

$$\mathbf{v}[j][b] = \frac{\mathbf{t}[j][b]}{\mathbf{n}[j][b]} - \frac{\sum_j \sum_b \mathbf{t}[j][b]}{\sum_j \sum_b \mathbf{n}[j][b]} \tag{1}$$

Afterwards, the correlations of the plaintext-byte signature within the study phase and the attack phase are computed as outlined in Equation 2.

$$\mathbf{c}[j][b] = \sum_{i=0}^{255} \mathbf{v}[j][i] \cdot \widetilde{\mathbf{v}}[j][i \oplus b] \tag{2}$$

The correlations are sorted in a decreasing order and, based on a predefined threshold, the attacker obtains a list of potential values for each key byte $\mathbf{k}_j$.

Key-Search Phase. Usually, more than one value per byte is selected in the correlation phase. Thus, the attacker performs an exhaustive search over all possible key candidates that can be formed from the selected values using a known plaintext-ciphertext pair.

3.2   Applications and Improvements of Bernstein's Attack

Bernstein's idea of exploiting the timing leakage of T-table based AES implementations has gained particular attention among the scientific community. For instance, Neve [13] and Neve *et al.* [15] performed a detailed analysis of Bernstein's timing attack. In 2012, Weiß *et al.* [25] compared the vulnerability of different AES implementations. Spreitzer and Plos [18] investigated the applicability of time-driven cache attacks, including the one of Bernstein, on mobile devices. Aly and ElGayyar [2] also investigated this timing attack and introduced an additional timing information, which is used to correlate the timing profiles obtained in the study phase with the timing profiles obtained in the attack phase. This timing information consists of the overall minimum encryption time (*global minimum*) and the minimum encryption time for a specific plaintext byte at a specific position (*local minimum*). Recently, Saraswat *et al.* [17] investigated the applicability of Bernstein's timing attack against remote servers.

4   Analysis and Improvements of the Divide Part

In this section, we detail potential improvements regarding the gathering of the required timing information. We present the corresponding experimental results in Section 6.

4.1   Attacking Different Key-Chunk Sizes

While Bernstein [4] considered the leaking timing information for exactly one key byte, we investigate a potential improvement of this attack by considering the leaking timing information of different key-chunk sizes. To this end, we briefly analyze the main concept of this idea as well as potential pitfalls.

Let n_{kc} be the number of key chunks the whole key is comprised of, and s_{kc} be the size of each key chunk, *i.e.*, the number of possible values each key chunk might take. If we attack each key byte separately ($n_{kc} = 16$, $s_{kc} = 256$), then $\mathbf{t}[j][b]$ holds the total of all encryption times where plaintext byte $\mathbf{p}_j = b$ and $\mathbf{n}[j][b]$ counts the number of plaintexts where $\mathbf{p}_j = b$, for $0 \leq j < n_{kc}$ and $0 \leq b < s_{kc}$. Hence, attacking larger parts of the key at once leads to fewer key chunks n_{kc}, but a larger number of possible values per key chunk s_{kc}. In contrast, attacking smaller parts of the key leads to a larger number of key chunks n_{kc} with fewer possible values s_{kc} for each of these key chunks.

Considering the plaintext as a 4×4 matrix, we observe that larger blocks can be formed in different ways. For instance, Figure 1 illustrates the gathering of the timing information for two consecutive plaintext bytes of one specific row. In contrast, Figure 2 illustrates the combination of two plaintext bytes within one specific column. In case of the T-table implementation provided by OpenSSL the former approach collects timing information of two bytes accessing two different T-tables and the latter collects timing information of two bytes accessing the same T-table. For the practical evaluation we

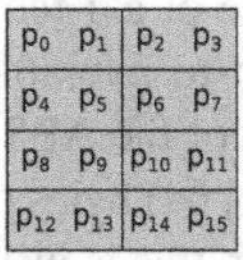

p_0	p_1	p_2	p_3
p_4	p_5	p_6	p_7
p_8	p_9	p_{10}	p_{11}
p_{12}	p_{13}	p_{14}	p_{15}

Fig. 1. Combination of bytes within a row

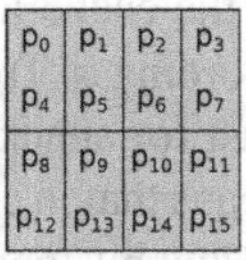

p_0	p_1	p_2	p_3
p_4	p_5	p_6	p_7
p_8	p_9	p_{10}	p_{11}
p_{12}	p_{13}	p_{14}	p_{15}

Fig. 2. Combination of bytes within a column

implemented the approach that collects timing information of two bytes accessing the same T-table. This case reduces the eventuality of corrupting key chunks with noise that might affect a specific T-table. We illustrate this within the following example. Recall that look-up indices s_i access T-table T_j, with $i \equiv j \mod 4$. Now, suppose that noise affects T-table T_0. Then in case of attacking two-byte key chunks that access the same T-table (*e.g.*, T_0), only two key chunks are affected by this noise. In contrast, if we attack two-byte key chunks that access different T-tables (*e.g.*, T_0 and T_1), four key chunks are affected by this noise.

Within the following paragraphs we investigate potential pitfalls of attacking different key-chunk sizes. Corresponding experimental results can be found in Section 6.

Memory Requirements. The memory consumption of the timing attack depends on the number of key chunks n_{kc}, the size of each key chunk s_{kc}, and the size s_d of the employed data type in bytes. Assuming the size of the data type $s_d = 8$, then for attacking each key byte separately ($n_{kc} = 16, s_{kc} = 256$) the size of one such data structure is 32 KB. Attacking two bytes at once ($n_{kc} = 8, s_{kc} = 256^2$) would result in 4 MB for each data structure and attacking even four bytes at once ($n_{kc} = 4, s_{kc} = 256^4$) would result in 128 GB for each data structure. Thus, attacking more than two bytes at once is not applicable for devices with limited resources, *e.g.*, mobile devices.

Number of Measurement Samples. The key-chunk size also has an impact on the noise reduction of the timing information. First, notice that the larger the key chunks are, the smaller should be the algorithmic noise in the gathered encryption times. This positive effect of large chunks is counterbalanced by the fact that the larger the chunks are, the smaller is the number of samples obtained for a specific chunk value[1]. Thus, there is a trade-off between the algorithmic noise and the number of samples per value. Analyzing this requires the full understanding of the noise behavior (what is the proportion of algorithmic noise compared to measurement noise and what is the noise distribution) and is out of the scope of this paper. We thus ran experiments to get an empirical evidence for the best trade-off.

Indistinguishable Key Bits. The cache-line size determines the number of contiguous T-table elements to be loaded at once in the event of a cache miss. In case of a cache-line size of 32 (resp. 64) bytes, each cache line holds 8 (resp. 16) T-table elements. This in turn means that in general one cannot distinguish between accessed elements in one specific cache line and, therefore, the number of recoverable key bits is limited. Let

---

[1] Let N be the number of encrypted plaintexts, then each possible value b of a specific block $\mathbf{p}_j$ is encrypted approximately $\frac{N}{s_{kc}}$ times.

us denote by s_c the cache-line size in bytes and by s_t the size of a T-table element in bytes. Then, according to Tromer *et al.* [21] the number of non-recoverable key bits per key byte—at least for attacks considering only the first round of the AES—is given as $\log_2 \frac{s_c}{s_t}$. This means that in case of a cache-line size of 32 (resp. 64) bytes the number of non-recoverable key bits per key byte are 3 (resp. 4). However, this is just a theoretical observation since in practice more advanced features of the architecture like *critical word first*[2] or *early restart*[3], as well as particular properties of the implementation itself, *i.e.*, disaligned T-tables, usually lead to more information leakage.

4.2   Template-Attack Approach

Template attacks [5] are optimal attacks if the attacker gets perfect knowledge of the leakage distribution on the targeted device. The idea is to make a template of the leakage, *i.e.*, computing the leakage distribution in a known-key setting, and then performing an attack by exploiting leakages and the knowledge of the computed distribution.

The templates can be made (i) by observing a twin device owned (and controlled) by the attacker or (ii) by using the target device if the attacker is able to observe encryptions performed with a known key. In both cases the attacker expects that the characterization she made during the learning phase will still be valid during the attack.

4.3   Minimum Timing Information

Recently, Aly and ElGayyar [2] suggested to compute the correlation of the minimum encryption time within the study phase and the minimum encryption time within the attack phase. Therefore, **tmin** and $\widetilde{\mathbf{tmin}}$ hold the overall minimum encryption time of all encrypted plaintexts in the study phase and the attack phase, respectively. In addition, the data structure **umin**$[j][b]$ holds the minimum encryption time of all plaintexts **p** where $\mathbf{p}_j = b$. The same holds for the attack phase, except that **umin**$[j][b]$ and **p** are replaced by $\widetilde{\mathbf{umin}}[j][b]$ and $\widetilde{\mathbf{p}}$, respectively. The computation of the correlation is based on **umin**$[j][b]-$**tmin** and $\widetilde{\mathbf{umin}}[j][b]-\widetilde{\mathbf{tmin}}$. Combining the timing information initially proposed by Bernstein and the minimum timing information, they claim to recover the whole secret key without a single exhaustive key-search computation. We assume that the attacker computes the correlation with the timing information initially proposed by Bernstein and the correlation with the minimum timing information. So for each key byte $\mathbf{k}_i$ the attacker retrieves two sets of potential key candidates. Afterwards the attacker combines the sets of potential key candidates with the lowest cardinalities.

5   Analysis and Improvements of the Conquer Part

The main challenge of the conquer part is to gather information obtained during the divide step to recover the full key.

---

[2] *Critical word first* means that in case of a cache miss the missed word is loaded first and then the CPU continues its work while the remaining words are loaded into the cache.

[3] *Early restart* means that as soon as the critical word arrives, the CPU continues its work. In practice this would impose a serious side channel.

5.1 Combining Information from the Divide Part

We briefly describe two possible approaches to recover the full key. The first one being the one currently used in timing attacks, and the second one overcoming some of the mentioned shortcomings of the first one.

Threshold Approach. Currently, timing attacks employ a threshold-based approach. This means that one fixes a threshold on the computed correlations and considers sub-key values as potential candidates only if the corresponding correlation is larger than the threshold. Notice that one may use different thresholds for the different sub-keys, either because a profiling phase has shown different behaviors for different sub-keys or because they are dynamically computed.

The threshold approach is simple to implement but has two major drawbacks. The first one is that the actual key may not be found. Indeed, if one of its sub-key values led to a small correlation, then the key will never be tested in the search-phase and, thus, the attack will provide no advantage over exhaustive search. The second drawback is a loss of information since the ordering of kept sub-key values is not exploited in the search phase. Though Neve [13, p 58] suggested that the key search "could start by the most probable key candidates", no clear indication is given how this should be accomplished. A somehow related approach has been suggested by Meier and Staffelbach [11] in 1991. However, they do not iterate over potential keys which are sorted according to their probability for being the correct one, but instead they exploit the non-uniform probability distribution of the key source. Thus, they generate the keys to be tested from the actual probability distribution.

Optimal Enumeration Approach. Veyrat-Charvillon *et al.* [23] recently proposed an optimal key-enumeration algorithm that solves the aforementioned problems at the cost of additional computations for generating the next full-key to be tested. The algorithm requires a *combination function* that computes the score of the concatenation of two key chunks based on the scores of each chunk. Using such a combination function, a global score can be computed for each full key by combining the sub-key scores. The "optimal" notion comes from the fact that the algorithm ensures that keys will be generated in a decreasing order of global scores.

5.2 Evaluating the Key-Search Complexity

Threshold Approach. The lower bound on the key-search complexity is easy to obtain. Assuming that the attacker dynamically chooses a threshold for each targeted sub-key, it will, for a given sub-key, keep at least all values with a score larger than the correct one. The cardinality of the set of keys to be tested is then equal to the product of sub-key ranks. This lower bound is very optimistic as no such magic threshold choice exists.

Concerning the upper bound, it will depend on the allowed probability of missing the correct key. For given threshold(s), upper bounds on the key-search complexity and estimates of the missing-key probability can be obtained by simulating attacks. The upper bound being the size of the key-search space and the success probability being the probability that the actual key belongs to this space.

Optimal Enumeration Approach. Following the proposition of a key-enumeration algorithm in [23], Veyrat-Charvillon *et al.* [24] proposed a key-rank estimation algorithm that bound the key-search complexity of the optimal key-enumeration algorithm for a given combination function. More precisely, their algorithm requires the combination function, the scores obtained for one attack and the correct key. When stopped, the program provides an interval $[2^x; 2^{x+\epsilon}]$ ensuring that the key rank lies in this range.

5.3   Choosing Relevant Thresholds and Combination Functions

Choosing Thresholds. Thresholds are potentially based on any kind of statistical value and provide a simple means of sorting out potential key candidates. Therefore, after performing the correlation of the timing information gathered within the study phase and the timing information gathered within the attack phase one retrieves a correlation vector $\mathbf{c}[j][b]$ (see Section 3.1). These elements are sorted in a decreasing order and byte values b with a correlation value above a predefined threshold are considered to represent potential key candidates. For instance, Bernstein suggested a threshold which is based on the *standard error of the mean*. By iterating over all possible key values b, the idea is to take a key candidate b for a key byte $\mathbf{k}_j$ only into consideration if the difference of the byte value providing the highest correlation and the correlation of b is smaller than the established threshold.

Choosing Combination Functions. From an information theoretical point of view the optimal choice for a combination function is to turn scores into sub-key probabilities and then combining these probabilities by multiplication. The so-called "Bayesian extension" in [23] uses Bayes' relation and a theoretical model of obtained scores to compute sub-key probabilities. This technique requires the attacker to model scores obtained to be able to estimate relevant probabilities. A recent work on side-channel collision attacks by Gérard and Standaert [8] has shown that even if the model does not accurately match reality, the use of a Bayesian extension may improve attacks.

In the context of timing attacks the scores obtained are similar to correlations. Actually a small modification of the scoring function as defined by Bernstein turns the scores into actual correlations without modifying the ordering of sub-key values. The modified formula for computing scores according to Pearson's correlation coefficient is outlined in Equation 3. The equation is given for an arbitrary key-chunk size s_{kc}.

$$\mathbf{c'}[j][b] = \frac{\sum_{i=0}^{s_{kc}-1} \mathbf{v}[j][i] \cdot \widetilde{\mathbf{v}}[j][i \oplus b]}{\sqrt{\sum_{i=0}^{s_{kc}-1} \mathbf{v}[j][i]^2} \cdot \sqrt{\sum_{i=0}^{s_{kc}-1} \widetilde{\mathbf{v}}[j][i \oplus b]^2}} \tag{3}$$

Then, using a Bayesian extension similar to the one in [8] (based on Fisher transform of correlation coefficients) we are able to estimate sub-key probabilities. The idea is that $\mathrm{arctanh}(\mathbf{c'}[j][b])$ follows a Gaussian distribution of variance $\frac{1}{s_{kc}-3}$ and with mean 1 if $\mathbf{k}_j = b$ and 0 otherwise. The estimated likelihood ratio between the probabilities of the j-th key chunk to be equal to b or not is then:

$$l[j][b] = \exp\left[\frac{(s_{kc}-3)(\mathrm{arctanh}(\mathbf{c}[j][b]) - 0)^2}{2} - \frac{(s_{kc}-3)(\mathrm{arctanh}(\mathbf{c'}[j][b]) - 1)^2}{2}\right],$$
$$= \exp\left[(s_{kc}-3)(\mathrm{arctanh}(\mathbf{c'}[j][b]) - 0.5)\right].$$

Table 1. Device specifications for the test devices

| Device | Processor | L1 Cache | | | | Critical Word First | OS |
		Size	Associativity	Line Size	Sets		
Google Nexus S	Cortex-A8	32 KB	4 way	64 bytes	128	yes	Android 2.3.6
Samsung Galaxy SII	Cortex-A9	32 KB	4 way	32 bytes	256	yes	Android 2.3.4

The score of a full-key candidate **k** will be given by

$$S_{\text{Bayes}} = \prod_j \mathbf{l}[j][\mathbf{k}_j]. \tag{4}$$

To investigate the relevance of such Bayesian extension, Section 6 also contains data obtained with a different combination function that does not use Fisher transform. Natural combinations of correlation coefficients are operators $+$ and $\times$. The latter one is not relevant here since two values with correlation -1 will combine to a key with correlation 1 what is not desirable. We thus propose results obtained using $+$ as a combination function to complement our study. In that case, the score of a full-key candidate **k** will be given by

$$S_{Add} = \sum_j \mathbf{c'}[j][\mathbf{k}_j]. \tag{5}$$

Remark on the Threshold Attack Lower Bound. In [24] authors perform experiments using the output of simulated template attacks. In this context the probabilities that are computed are sound (*i.e.*, not biased by a potentially wrong model) and thus the attack using key enumeration is optimal from an information theoretic point of view. A figure shows that the lower bound obtained by multiplying sub-key ranks (*i.e.*, the lower bound for threshold attacks) is far too optimistic by orders of magnitude from the actual key rank. The optimality of the attack regarding information theory implies that an attacker using threshold technique should not obtain better results and hence this experiment discards this lower bound as a relevant statistic.

6   Experimental Results

In this section, we detail the employed measurement setup and later on we analyze our observations regarding the practical evaluation. For the practical investigation of the suggested enhancements we employed two Android-based smartphones, namely a *Google Nexus S* and a *Samsung Galaxy SII*. The specifications of these two devices are summarized in Table 1. One assumption for our attack to work is that the device under attack must be rooted in order to allow for precise timing measurements via the ARM *Cycle Counter Register* [3].

Definitions. We define the gathering of the measurement samples under a known key and the gathering of the measurement samples under an unknown key as one *run*. Thus, one *run* of the attack application constitutes the gathering of the measurement samples for both of these phases. The *number of measurement samples* denotes the number of gathered samples in each of these two phases.

6.1   Attacking Different Key-Chunk Sizes

We launched the attack multiple times on both devices, targeting either four bits, one byte, or two bytes of the key. Figure 3 shows the rank evolution for a specific number of measurement samples on the *Samsung Galaxy SII*, averaged over multiple runs for one-byte chunks and two-byte chunks, respectively. More formally, these plots show the range (bounds) of key bits to be searched with the optimal key-enumeration algorithm after gathering a specific number of measurement samples. Our observations show that below 2^{21} measurement samples hardly any information leaks. Targeting four-bit chunks we observed a similar rank evolution as for one-byte chunks. Hence, we omitted this figure here.

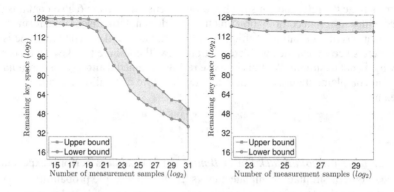

Fig. 3. Rank evolution for one-byte key chunks (left) and two-byte key chunks (right)

According to the right part of Figure 3, the noise induced by the small number of samples per chunk value is significantly larger than the noise reduction obtained by considering larger chunks, which might be due to the random-replacement policy. The problem can be illustrated as follows. Figure 4 shows the plaintext-byte signature for one specific key byte during the study phase and the attack phase, respectively. The abscissa shows the possible chunk values of a plaintext byte and the ordinate shows the average encryption time for this specific byte subtracted by the overall average encryption time, after gathering 2^{30} samples. We observe a visible pattern in both plots. Thus, the correlation yields a few possible values for this specific key byte. We also point out that most of the values lie in the range $[-0.5; 0.5]$ with peaks up to 2.5.

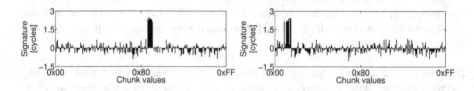

Fig. 4. One-byte chunk signatures for the study phase (left) and the attack phase (right)

In contrast, Figure 5 illustrates the chunk signatures for an attack targeting two-byte key chunks. Again, after gathering 2^{30} measurement samples. Since the pattern is not that clearly visible we marked the similar peaks appropriately. Neve [13] also performed an investigation of such signature plots for one-byte chunks. In accordance with his terminology, we note that both plots show rather *noisy* profiles with most values lying in the range $[-25; 25]$. Due to these *noisy* profiles the correlation does not reduce the key space significantly and the sub-key value for this specific key chunk cannot be determined. Though we also observed rather *noisy* profiles for attacks targeting one-byte chunks, most of the profiles established for one-byte chunks showed a clear pattern. In contrast, for two-byte key chunks we mostly observed plots where we could not find any specific pattern.

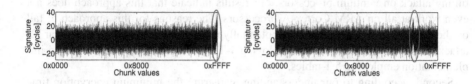

Fig. 5. Two-byte chunk signatures for the study phase (left) and the attack phase (right)

To conclude, our observations showed that attacking smaller key chunks potentially works, while attacking larger key chunks seems to leak less information for the same (realistic) number of measurement samples. Targeting even more samples is not realistic anymore, at least for mobile devices. This results from the fact that a running time of more than eight hours to gather more than 2^{30} measurement samples does not allow for a realistic scenario anymore.

6.2 Template Attack

As a first step we tried to identify the distribution of encryption times. Obviously the classical Gaussian noise model (that is quite relevant for power-based attacks) does not fit here. Moreover, the right tail of the distribution is meaningless since high encryption times are caused by interruptions. The choice of a threshold above which we consider points as outliers together with the characterization of the distribution of remaining points is not straightforward and out of the scope of the paper.

Noting the difficulty of characterizing the time distribution, we mount attacks combining the study phase and the attack phase from two different runs (that is the data sets have not been measured one after the other). We used the key-rank estimation (and the Bayesian extension as detailed in Section 5.3) to estimate the remaining workload for the key-search phase. We observe that we obtain ranks 2^{10} larger than the one obtained from attacks where the attack phase directly follows the study phase.

One reason for this observation might be the fact that ARM Cortex-A series processors employ a physically-indexed, physically-tagged (PIPT) data cache, which means that the physical address is used to map a location within the main memory to a cache set. For different runs the physical address potentially changes and, thus, the locations where memory accesses (resulting in cache evictions) occur change from run to run.

6.3 Minimum Timing Information

Aly and ElGayyar [2] argue that noise usually increases the encryption time and, thus, the exploitation of the minimum timing information should significantly improve the timing attack. Their idea is to capture only one single measurement sample without noise, which is then stored and used for the correlation later on. They successfully launched their attack against a *Pentium Dual-Core* and a *Pentium Core 2 Duo* processor. However, contrary to their conclusion that this approach significantly improves the timing attack on Pentium processors, our results indicate that this approach does not even work at all on ARM Cortex-A processors. The reasons for this approach to fail on the ARM Cortex-A processor are potentially manifold. First, Aly and ElGayyar [2] attacked an AES implementation employing 4-Tables. In contrast, we attacked an implementation employing 5 T-tables.

Second, according to our understanding, gathering the minimum encryption time misses potential useful information. As Neve *et al.* [15] put it, Bernstein's timing attack implicitly searches for cache evictions due to work done on the attacked device. Such cache evictions lead to cache misses within the encryption function and, thus, to slower encryptions. As a result, not only noise increases the encryption time, but also cache misses increase the encryption time. While noisy encryption times do not carry useful information, encryption times where a cache miss occurred definitely do so. However, gathering the minimum timing information does not capture this information because the minimum timing information seeks for encryption times where a cache hit occurred. The problem is that once we observe a cache hit, *i.e.*, a fast encryption, we store this timing information. So this approach only searches for the cache hits and in the worst case, after a certain number of measurement samples, we potentially observe a cache hit for all possible key bytes due to the random-replacement policy on ARM processors. Furthermore, in the long run, the *local minimum* as well as the *global minimum* might become equal in which case these timings do not carry any information at all. Our practical evaluation showed that after a certain number of measurement samples on the *Google Nexus S* the minimum timing information $umin[j][b] - tmin$ equals 0 for most of the key bytes. Additionally, the random-replacement policy employed in ARM Cortex-A processors strengthens this reasoning. Though Aly and ElGayyar implemented this approach on Pentium processors with a deterministic replacement policy, we consider the gathering of the minimum timing information also risky on such processors.

Concluding the investigation of the minimum timing information we point out that instead of using the minimum timing information, we stick to the exploitation of the timing information as proposed by Bernstein and only take encryption times below a specific threshold into consideration. This approach also reduces the impact of noise if the threshold is selected properly.

Table 2. Sample results on the Samsung Galaxy SII

Run	Key-Chunk Size	Samples	Bernstein				Minimum
			Optimal Threshold	Threshold	Key Enumeration		Optimal Threshold
					(4)	(5)	
1	4 bits	2^{30}	50 bits	102 bits	79.3 - 104.4	86.5 - 112.3	84 bits
2	4 bits	2^{31}	32 bits	87 bits	58.9 - 82.4	62.1 - 92.6	88 bits
3	1 byte	2^{28}	41 bits	93 bits	55.7 - 77.7	56.2 - 79.2	104 bits
4	1 byte	2^{30}	23 bits	64 bits	36.6 - 44.9	36.4 - 46.5	100 bits
5	1 byte	2^{30}	32 bits	92 bits	49.1 - 70.1	49.1 - 70.3	100 bits
6	1 byte	2^{30}	20 bits	74 bits	36.5 - 45.6	36.0 - 46.4	105 bits
7	2 bytes	2^{30}	107 bits	123 bits	118.9 - 125.3	118.9 - 125.3	104 bits
8	2 bytes	2^{30}	96 bits	128 bits	115.5 - 122.2	115.0 - 123.2	114 bits
9	2 bytes	2^{30}	90 bits	124 bits	110.5 - 119.7	110.5 - 119.9	118 bits
10	2 bytes	2^{30}	110 bits	126 bits	120.2 - 126.7	120.3 - 126.7	115 bits

Table 3. Sample results on the Google Nexus S

Run	Key-Chunk Size	Samples	Bernstein			Minimum
			Optimal Threshold	Threshold	Key Enumeration	Optimal Threshold
1	1 byte	2^{31}	64 bits	108 bits	83.5 - 109.1 bits	105 bits
2	1 byte	2^{30}	62 bits	119 bits	77.6 - 104.9 bits	95 bits
3	1 byte	2^{26}	66 bits	101 bits	79.0 - 101.3 bits	104 bits
4	1 byte	2^{30}	67 bits	96 bits	77.6 - 104.4 bits	108 bits
5	1 byte	2^{30}	58 bits	91 bits	69.6 - 90.5 bits	107 bits
6	1 byte	2^{28}	82 bits	95 bits	105.3 - 115.2 bits	110 bits
7	1 byte	2^{30}	61 bits	97 bits	84.0 - 99.0 bits	97 bits
8	2 bytes	2^{27}	121 bits	128 bits	127.8 - 128.0 bits	121 bits
9	2 bytes	2^{28}	116 bits	128 bits	125.0 - 127.8 bits	124 bits
10	2 bytes	2^{30}	118 bits	128 bits	126.1 - 127.2 bits	121 bits

6.4   Summary of Practical Results

Table 2 summarizes the results of our practical investigations on the *Samsung Galaxy SII* smartphone. For different runs, we provide the attacked key-chunk size as well as the number of samples acquired. The rest of the columns contain different $\log_2$ time complexities of the key-search phase depending on the exploited information, *e.g.*, either Bernstein's timing information or the minimum timing information from [2], and depending on the conquer-phase technique. For the threshold-based conquer phase we provide the remaining key space for: (1) an optimal threshold choice, such that for each chunk the threshold is chosen in a way that only values with better scores than the correct one are selected (cf. Section 5.2), and (2) a threshold based on the *standard error of the mean* as suggested by Bernstein [4]. The key-enumeration column contains bounds of the obtained key rank if the optimal key-enumeration algorithm from [23] is used. In Table 2 this column is separated into two, the first one being the result of the use of the Bayesian extension (see Equation 4) the second being obtained by addition of correlations (see Equation 5). We clearly observe that using the optimal key-enumeration algorithm instead of the threshold-based approach has a strong positive impact on the key-search complexity. For instance, in case of run 4 and run 6—that require far more than 2^{60} keys to be tested in case of the threshold-based approach—the optimal key-enumeration algorithm recovers the key in less than 2^{46} tests. Concerning the gained improvement of using the Bayesian extension, we observe that it is very small when attacking one-byte chunks but becomes more significant when attacking four-bit chunks.

Furthermore, for ARM Cortex-A processors we cannot confirm that the minimum timing information improves the timing attack. The last column in Table 2 shows that this information hardly leaks any information. Table 3 summarizes the exact same information for the *Google Nexus S* smartphone. Since we observed only minor differences between the usage of the Bayesian extension (Equation 4) and the usage of addition as a correlation function, we only provide the bounds based on the former approach.

7 Conclusion

In this work, we analyzed multiple improvements of Bernstein's timing attack. Considering these improvements we also provided practical insights on two devices employing an ARM Cortex-A processor. We performed theoretical investigations of attacking different key-chunk sizes and presented potential pitfalls. Our practical investigations on ARM-based devices showed that attacking one-byte chunks seems to be the best choice for resource-constrained devices. Furthermore, these investigations showed that the minimum timing information [2] does not improve the cache timing attack on the ARM Cortex-A devices at all. We also showed that due to the PIPT data cache of ARM Cortex-A processors, template attacks seem to be useless here. Nevertheless, a thorough analysis of the noise behavior might lead to more positive results. We let this point as an open question.

The most important contribution of this work is the shift from the threshold-based approach for the selection of potential key candidates towards the application of the optimal key-enumeration algorithm. Instead of selecting potential key candidates on a threshold basis, we iterate over potential keys according to their probability for being the correct key. As our observations showed, this approach significantly reduces the complexity of the remaining key-search phase, which brings this attack to a complexity that can be considered as practically relevant.

References

[1] Acıiçmez, O., Koç, Ç.K.: Trace-Driven Cache Attacks on AES (Short Paper). In: Ning, P., Qing, S., Li, N. (eds.) ICICS 2006. LNCS, vol. 4307, pp. 112–121. Springer, Heidelberg (2006)

[2] Aly, H., ElGayyar, M.: Attacking AES Using Bernstein's Attack on Modern Processors. In: Youssef, A., Nitaj, A., Hassanien, A.E. (eds.) AFRICACRYPT 2013. LNCS, vol. 7918, pp. 127–139. Springer, Heidelberg (2013)

[3] ARM Ltd. ARM Technical Reference Manual, Cortex-A8, Revision: r3p2 (May 2010)

[4] Bernstein, D.J.: Cache-timing attacks on AES (2005),
    http://cr.yp.to/antiforgery/cachetiming-20050414.pdf

[5] Chari, S., Rao, J.R., Rohatgi, P.: Template attacks. In: Kaliski Jr., B.S., Koç, Ç.K., Paar, C. (eds.) CHES 2002. LNCS, vol. 2523, pp. 13–28. Springer, Heidelberg (2003)

[6] Gallais, J.-F., Kizhvatov, I.: Error-Tolerance in Trace-Driven Cache Collision Attacks. In: COSADE, Darmstadt, pp. 222–232 (2011)

[7] Gallais, J.-F., Kizhvatov, I., Tunstall, M.: Improved Trace-Driven Cache-Collision Attacks against Embedded AES Implementations. In: Chung, Y., Yung, M. (eds.) WISA 2010. LNCS, vol. 6513, pp. 243–257. Springer, Heidelberg (2011)

[8] Gérard, B., Standaert, F.-X.: Unified and Optimized Linear Collision Attacks and their Application in a Non-Profiled Setting: Extended Version. J. Cryptographic Engineering 3(1), 45–58 (2013)

[9] Gullasch, D., Bangerter, E., Krenn, S.: Cache Games - Bringing Access-Based Cache Attacks on AES to Practice. In: IEEE Symposium on Security and Privacy, pp. 490–505. IEEE Computer Society (2011)

[10] Kelsey, J., Schneier, B., Wagner, D., Hall, C.: Side Channel Cryptanalysis of Product Ciphers. In: Quisquater, J.-J., Deswarte, Y., Meadows, C., Gollmann, D. (eds.) ESORICS 1998. LNCS, vol. 1485, pp. 97–110. Springer, Heidelberg (1998)

[11] Meier, W., Staffelbach, O.: Analysis of Pseudo Random Sequence Generated by Cellular Automata. In: Davies, D.W. (ed.) Advances in Cryptology - EUROCRYPT 1991. LNCS, vol. 547, pp. 186–199. Springer, Heidelberg (1991)

[12] National Institute of Standards and Technology (NIST). FIPS-197: Advanced Encryption Standard (November 2001)

[13] Neve, M.: Cache-based Vulnerabilities and SPAM Analysis. PhD thesis, UCL (2006)

[14] Neve, M., Seifert, J.-P.: Advances on Access-Driven Cache Attacks on AES. In: Biham, E., Youssef, A.M. (eds.) SAC 2006. LNCS, vol. 4356, pp. 147–162. Springer, Heidelberg (2007)

[15] Neve, M., Seifert, J.-P., Wang, Z.: A refined look at Bernstein's AES side-channel analysis. In: Lin, F.-C., Lee, D.-T., Lin, B.-S.P., Shieh, S., Jajodia, S. (eds.) ASIACCS, p. 369. ACM (2006)

[16] Page, D.: Theoretical Use of Cache Memory as a Cryptanalytic Side-Channel. IACR Cryptology ePrint Archive, 2002:169 (2002)

[17] Saraswat, V., Feldman, D., Kune, D.F., Das, S.: Remote Cache-timing Attacks Against AES. In: Proceedings of the First Workshop on Cryptography and Security in Computing Systems, CS2 2014, pp. 45–48. ACM, New York (2014)

[18] Spreitzer, R., Plos, T.: On the Applicability of Time-Driven Cache Attacks on Mobile Devices. In: Lopez, J., Huang, X., Sandhu, R. (eds.) NSS 2013. LNCS, vol. 7873, pp. 656–662. Springer, Heidelberg (2013)

[19] Spreitzer, R., Plos, T.: On the Applicability of Time-Driven Cache Attacks on Mobile Devices (Extended Version). IACR Cryptology ePrint Archive, 2013:172 (2013)

[20] Takahashi, J., Fukunaga, T., Aoki, K., Fuji, H.: Highly Accurate Key Extraction Method for Access-Driven Cache Attacks Using Correlation Coefficient. In: Boyd, C., Simpson, L. (eds.) ACISP. LNCS, vol. 7959, pp. 286–301. Springer, Heidelberg (2013)

[21] Tromer, E., Osvik, D.A., Shamir, A.: Efficient Cache Attacks on AES, and Countermeasures. J. Cryptology 23(1), 37–71 (2010)

[22] Tsunoo, Y., Saito, T., Suzaki, T., Shigeri, M., Miyauchi, H.: Cryptanalysis of DES Implemented on Computers with Cache. In: Walter, C.D., Koç, Ç.K., Paar, C. (eds.) CHES 2003. LNCS, vol. 2779, pp. 62–76. Springer, Heidelberg (2003)

[23] Veyrat-Charvillon, N., Gérard, B., Renauld, M., Standaert, F.-X.: An Optimal Key Enumeration Algorithm and Its Application to Side-Channel Attacks. In: Knudsen, L.R., Wu, H. (eds.) SAC 2012. LNCS, vol. 7707, pp. 390–406. Springer, Heidelberg (2013)

[24] Veyrat-Charvillon, N., Gérard, B., Standaert, F.-X.: Security Evaluations beyond Computing Power. In: Johansson, T., Nguyen, P.Q. (eds.) EUROCRYPT 2013. LNCS, vol. 7881, pp. 126–141. Springer, Heidelberg (2013)

[25] Weiß, M., Heinz, B., Stumpf, F.: A Cache Timing Attack on AES in Virtualization Environments. In: Keromytis, A.D. (ed.) FC 2012. LNCS, vol. 7397, pp. 314–328. Springer, Heidelberg (2012)

Orthogonal Direct Sum Masking

A Smartcard Friendly Computation Paradigm in a Code, with Builtin Protection against Side-Channel and Fault Attacks

Julien Bringer[1], Claude Carlet[2], Hervé Chabanne[1,3],
Sylvain Guilley[3,4], and Houssem Maghrebi[1]

[1] Morpho, 18 Chaussée Jules César, 95520 Osny, France
[2] LAGA, UMR 7539, CNRS, Department of Mathematics,
University of Paris XIII and University of Paris VIII,
2 rue de la liberté, 93 526 Saint-Denis Cedex, France
[3] Institut Mines Télécom, Crypto Group,
37/39 rue Dareau, 75 634 Paris Cedex 13, France
[4] Secure-IC S.A.S., 80 avenue des Buttes de Coësmes,
35 700 Rennes, France

Abstract. Secure elements, such as smartcards or trusted platform modules (TPMs), must be protected against implementation-level attacks. Those include side-channel and fault injection attacks. We introduce ODSM, Orthogonal Direct Sum Masking, a new computation paradigm that achieves protection against those two kinds of attacks. A large vector space is structured as two supplementary orthogonal subspaces. One subspace (called a code $\mathcal{C}$) is used for the functional computation, while the second subspace carries random numbers. As the random numbers are entangled with the sensitive data, ODSM ensures a protection against (monovariate) side-channel attacks. The random numbers can be checked either occasionally, or globally, thereby ensuring a detection capability. The security level can be formally detailed: it is proved that monovariate side-channel attacks of order up to $d_{\mathcal{C}} - 1$, where $d_{\mathcal{C}}$ is the minimal distance of $\mathcal{C}$, are impossible, and that any fault of Hamming weight strictly less than $d_{\mathcal{C}}$ is detected. A complete instantiation of ODSM is given for AES. In this case, all monovariate side-channel attacks of order strictly less than 5 are impossible, and all fault injections perturbing strictly less than 5 bits are detected.

Keywords: Masking countermeasure, trans-masking, fault detection, orthogonal supplementary spaces, linear codes, minimal and dual distances, AES.

1 Introduction

Side-channel analysis (SCA) and fault analysis (FA) are nowadays well known and most designers of secure embedded systems are aware of them. Since the first public reporting of these threats in 1996, a lot of effort has been devoted

D. Naccache and D. Sauveron (Eds.): WISTP 2014, LNCS 8501, pp. 40–56, 2014.

towards the research about these attacks and the development of corresponding protections. Several countermeasures have been proposed, but usually tackling only side-channel analysis [16] or (exclusively) fault analysis [15].

Masking is one of the most efficient countermeasures to thwart SCA. The most critical part when applying masking to secure cryptographic implementations, is to protect their non-linear operations (e.g., the *substitution boxes*, S-boxes). Commonly, there are three strategies [20]: the *global look-up table* (GLUT), the *table re-computation method*, and the *S-box secure calculation*. The GLUT method seems to be the most appropriate method: its timing performances are ideal since it requires only one memory transfer. However, the GLUT method has an exponential increase of the table size with the amount of entropy (e.g., the number of masks used).

A recent line of works known as Low-Entropy Masking Schemes (LEMS) has investigated possibilities to preserve the security level of masked implementations with reduced randomness requirements [3]. In fact, the mask is generated within a subset of all possible values. For instance, the set of masks could be a set of codewords, to reduce the overhead in terms of computational resources and entropy. Therefore, the LEMS scheme is still compatible with a table re-computation method, and a representative computation is sketched below:

- One random number d is drawn.
- (Optionally: tables are recomputed with d as a mask).
- User data (e.g., plaintext) is masked.
- Computations are done within such masked representation.
- The result (e.g., ciphertext) is demasked.

This is obviously only a first-order masking scheme, because it is still possible to combine two leaks resulting from a reuse of the mask, for instance the information leaked during the table recomputation and then during the computation. But, it can also be made more complicated by using shuffling [27] (especially during the table recomputation).

Related Works. The GLUT and table recomputation masking schemes have been described several times in the case of AES [17,12,5]. However, those countermeasures stick to the word size k (e.g., $k = 8$ for AES), possibly with multiple shares of size k. In this paper, we propose a new LEMS scheme, called *Orthogonal Direct Sum Masking* (ODSM). Like the wire-tap masking [7], it can work with any amount of added entropy (not necessarily by increments of k bits). Compared to wire-tap masking, ODSM takes advantage of an orthogonal projection to ease operations in a linear code of length $n > k$ and dimension k.

Contrasted to the state-of-the-art masking and fault protection, our masking scheme presents many innovative features. In fact, using one share, ODSM ensures a practical security against monovariate SCA (but still high-order) and provides the possibility of removing the mask without the knowledge of it. Moreover, an overwhelming advantage of this new scheme over any other masking technique, is the capability to detect some injected faults while the main goal is to ensure security against SCA. Indeed, such synergy between SCA and FA protections does not exist for other masking schemes [6]. Nonetheless, we note that *dual-rail logic* too enjoys the simultaneous protection against SCA and FA [2].

Eventually, for algorithms with large S-boxes, like AES ($k = 8$, to be compared with $k = 4$ for PRESENT), we show how to switch from ODSM to the classical first-order perfect masking using table recomputations.

Contributions. We introduce a masking scheme provably secure against monovariate attacks that uses a customizable entropy (namely $n - k$ bits, choice of the designer). With respect to the state-of-the-art, an encoding function mixes optimally the randomness with the sensitive data, in order to achieve the best protection against side-channel attacks. Additionally, the $n - k$ redundant bits injected in the computation can be leveraged to check for the injection of errors. We show that the minimal distance d_C of the $[n, k, d_C]$ code determines the minimal weight of errors to be injected for (possibly) bypassing the error sanity checks of the ODSM scheme. We also apply the ODSM to the AES, with full details on the way the computations in the linear codes are performed.

Outline. The rest of the article is organized as follows. The theory about the linear algebra and codes, and how it is applied in the ODSM countermeasure, are the topic of Sec. 2. The practical implementation of the ODSM scheme for the AES cipher and possible improvements are given in Sec. 3. Section 4 provides some discussions about the advance on the field of implementation security conveyed by ODSM, and especially a comparative analysis with other schemes, plus a presentation of ODSM distinguishing features. Conclusions and perspectives are in Sec. 5. Technical results and examples are relegated in the appendices A and B.

2   Theoretical Foundations

In this section, we first recall in Sec. 2.1 the basic notions of linear algebra and linear codes needed to describe our masking scheme. We intentionally skip the proofs of well-known propositions, but provide proofs for non classical results. Then, Sec. 2.2 contains the generic description of the ODSM; the construction is fully defined by a linear code C (with specific properties). The ODSM scheme is briefed in Sec. 2.3. The security attributes of this masking scheme are given in Sec. 2.4, thanks to properties of the code C.

2.1   Basic Notions of Linear Algebra and Linear Codes

Let k and n be two integers, such that $k \leq n$. The set of n-bit vectors, noted $\mathbb{F}_2^n$, is endowed with a structure of space vector. Let C be a subspace of $\mathbb{F}_2^n$ of dimension k. Then, C is a linear code of length n and dimension k.

Definition 1 (supplement of a space vector). *C can be completed with some vectors in order to spawn $\mathbb{F}_2^n$. Those vectors define the supplement D of C in $\mathbb{F}_2^n$. We write $\mathbb{F}_2^n = C \oplus D$ to say that $\mathbb{F}_2^n$ is the direct sum of C and D.*

Remark 1. We note that the same symbol "$\oplus$" is used for the direct sum and for the addition of vectors, which is uncommon but which does not create any ambiguity.

A linear code is spawned by a basis: the matrix whose rows consist in the basis vectors is called a *generating matrix*. We denote by G (resp. H) the generating matrix of $\mathcal{C}$ (resp. $\mathcal{D}$, the supplement of $\mathcal{C}$). Then, we have that every element $z \in \mathbb{F}_2^n$ can be written uniquely as:

$$z = c \oplus d , \tag{1}$$

where $c \in \mathcal{C}$ and $d \in \mathcal{D}$. Now, as all $c \in \mathcal{C}$ (resp. $d \in \mathcal{D}$) can also be written uniquely as xG (resp. yH), for a given $x \in \mathbb{F}_2^k$ (resp. $y \in \mathbb{F}_2^{n-k}$), we have the following equation:

$$z = xG \oplus yH . \tag{2}$$

In the following definitions, we formalize the notions of minimal and dual distance of a linear code.

Definition 2 (minimal distance). *The minimal distance $d_{\mathcal{C}}$ of a linear code $\mathcal{C}$ of length n and dimension k is the minimal Hamming distance of any two different elements of $\mathcal{C}$. We say that $\mathcal{C}$ has parameters $[n, k, d_{\mathcal{C}}]$.*

Definition 3 (dual distance). *The dual distance $d_{\mathcal{C}}^{\perp}$ of a code $\mathcal{C}$ is the minimal Hamming weight $w_H(z)$ of a nonzero vector $z \in \mathbb{F}_2^n$ such as $\sum_{c \in \mathcal{C}} (-1)^{z \cdot c} \neq 0$, where $z \cdot c$ is the scalar product between z and c ($z \cdot c = \sum_{i=1}^n z_i c_i$, or equivalently $z \cdot c = z c^{\mathsf{T}} \in \mathbb{F}_2$ using matrix notations). We recall that the Hamming weight $w_H(z)$ of a vector z is $w_H(z) = \sum_{i=1}^n z_i$.*

Definition 4 (orthogonal). *The orthogonal of a set $\mathcal{C} \subseteq \mathbb{F}_2^n$ is the space vector $\mathcal{C}^{\perp}$ defined as $\{d \in \mathbb{F}_2^n | \forall c \in \mathcal{C}, d \cdot c = 0\}$. When $\mathcal{C}$ is a linear code, $\mathcal{C}^{\perp}$ is called the dual code of $\mathcal{C}$. The generating matrix of $\mathcal{C}^{\perp}$ is called the parity matrix of $\mathcal{C}$.*

Proposition 1. *For a linear code $\mathcal{C}$, $d_{\mathcal{C}}^{\perp} = d_{\mathcal{C}^{\perp}}$.*

Indeed, in linear algebra, the dual code $\mathcal{C}^{\perp}$ can be seen as the *kernel* (or *null space*) of the code $\mathcal{C}$. We have the following Theorem.

Theorem 1 (rank-nullity). $\dim(\mathcal{C}) + \dim(\mathcal{C}^{\perp}) = \dim(\mathbb{F}_2^n) = n$, *where* $\dim(\cdot)$ *is the dimension of the vector space.*

As a direct consequence of Theorem 1, we have $\dim(\mathcal{C}^{\perp}) = n - k$. However, $\mathcal{C}$ and $\mathcal{C}^{\perp}$ are not necessarily supplementary, i.e., we do not have $\mathcal{C} \cap \mathcal{C}^{\perp} = \{0\}$. For instance, if $\mathcal{C}$ is autodual, then $\mathcal{C} = \mathcal{C}^{\perp}$.

In the following Proposition 2, we exhibit a necessary and sufficient condition to have $\mathcal{C}$ and $\mathcal{C}^{\perp}$ supplementary in $\mathbb{F}_2^n$.

Proposition 2 (Condition for $\mathbb{F}_2^n = \mathcal{C} \oplus \mathcal{C}^{\perp}$). *Without loss of generality (a permutation of coordinates might be necessary), we can assume that the generating matrix of $\mathcal{C}$ is systematic, and thus takes the form $[I_k \| M]$, where I_k is the $k \times k$ identity matrix. The supplement $\mathcal{D}$ of $\mathcal{C}$ is equal to $\mathcal{C}^{\perp}$ if and only if (iff) the matrix $I_k \oplus MM^{\mathsf{T}}$ is invertible.*

Proof. Because of the dimensions, the supplement of $\mathcal{C}$ (named $\mathcal{D}$) is equal to $\mathcal{C}^{\perp}$ if and only if $\mathcal{C} \cap \mathcal{C}^{\perp} = \{0\}$. In the systematic form, $\mathcal{C}$ has the generating matrix $[I_k \| M]$ and parity matrix $[M^{\mathsf{T}} \| I_{n-k}]$. So, the condition is that: $\forall (x, y) \in \mathbb{F}_2^k \times \mathbb{F}_2^{n-k}$, the system of two equations $x = y M^{\mathsf{T}}$ and $x M = y$ has only $(0, 0)$ as solution. This is equivalent to saying that the equation $x = x M M^{\mathsf{T}}$ has only the trivial solution, and thus that the matrix $I_k \oplus M M^{\mathsf{T}}$ is invertible.   □

When $\mathcal{D} = \mathcal{C}^{\perp}$, there is an orthogonal projection. Indeed, we thus have $G H^{\mathsf{T}} = 0$ (the all-zero $k \times (n - k)$ matrix). In this case, H is the *parity matrix* of code $\mathcal{C}$. So, in Eq. (2), x and y can be recovered from z, as follows:

$$x = z G^{\mathsf{T}} (G G^{\mathsf{T}})^{-1} , \tag{3}$$

$$y = z H^{\mathsf{T}} (H H^{\mathsf{T}})^{-1} . \tag{4}$$

Notice that given that G is a basis for $\mathcal{C}$, it is composed of linearly independent vectors of $\mathbb{F}_2^n$. Hence $G G^{\mathsf{T}}$ is a $k \times k$ invertible matrix. Similarly, provided H is a basis for $\mathcal{D}$, $H H^{\mathsf{T}}$ is a $(n - k) \times (n - k)$ invertible matrix.

It follows from Eq. (1) that the projection $P_{\mathcal{C}}$ (resp. $P_{\mathcal{D}}$) of $z \in \mathbb{F}_2^n$ on $\mathcal{C}$ (resp. $\mathcal{D}$) is given by:

$$P_{\mathcal{C}} : \mathbb{F}_2^n \to \mathcal{C}, \quad z \mapsto c = z G^{\mathsf{T}} (G G^{\mathsf{T}})^{-1} G , \tag{5}$$

$$P_{\mathcal{D}} : \mathbb{F}_2^n \to \mathcal{D}, \quad z \mapsto d = z H^{\mathsf{T}} (H H^{\mathsf{T}})^{-1} H . \tag{6}$$

2.2   Definition of the Masking Scheme

Data Representation. For the masking scheme, we choose $\mathcal{C}$ and $\mathcal{D}$ such as $\mathcal{D} = \mathcal{C}^{\perp}$. Using the property of Eq. (1), we suggest to represent any vector z of $\mathbb{F}_2^n$ as the sum of two codewords $z = c \oplus d$. The coded sensitive data is $c \in \mathcal{C}$, while the mask is $d \in \mathcal{D}$.

So, to protect a k bit sensitive data x, $(n - k)$ random bits are required. Those are denoted by y; the mask is equal to $d = y H$. The idea is that the information are codewords, and that the masks act as intentionally added noise. But, as the information and the noise live in two supplementary subspaces, it is always possible to recover both, using Eq. (3) and Eq. (4).

Computation. The goal is to carry out the computation within the orthogonal direct sum representation of Eq. (2). We assume that all the steps in computations can be represented as $\mathbb{F}_2^k \to \mathbb{F}_2^k$ functions. For instance, this is indeed the case for AES [19]. This block cipher manipulates bytes ($k = 8$). Even operations that operate on larger structures, such as MixColumns ($\mathbb{F}_2^{32} \to \mathbb{F}_2^{32}$), can be decomposed as operations on bytes, by using `xtime` [19, Sec. 4.2.1], for instance. In the sequel, we simply denote by *word* a k-bit word (and precise "n-bit" otherwise).

In this section, we give mathematical definitions of the ODSM scheme; examples are provided in Sec. 3.

We make the difference between three different operations:

(*i*) two-operand operations, that are usually exclusive-or operations, between two words;

(*ii*) linear transformations of one word, referred to as $\mathcal{L}$ (of matrix L);

(*iii*) non-linear transformations of one word, referred to as S (like the "S" of an S-box).

Computation of Type (i). The exclusive-or in $\mathbb{F}^k$ is a straightforward operation to port after encoding in $\mathbb{F}_2^n$, because it remains *the same* in $\mathbb{F}_2^n$ (it is the *additive law* in both space vectors). For instance, the key addition step is as follows: let $z_1 = x_1 G \oplus y_1 H$ be the coded and masked element of $\mathbb{F}_2^n$ used in ODSM to represent the plaintext byte x_1, and k the key. Then, the secure key addition is:

$$z_2 = z_1 \oplus kG = (x_1 \oplus k)G \oplus y_1 H \ . \tag{7}$$

Computation of Type (ii). Any linear operation $\mathcal{L} : \mathbb{F}_2^k \to \mathbb{F}_2^k$ can be turned into a masked operation, where the mask is unchanged by choice. This masked linear operation is denoted by $\mathcal{L}' : \mathbb{F}_2^n \to \mathbb{F}_2^n$. We call L and L' the matrices of the linear operations (i.e., $\mathcal{L}(x) = xL$ and $\mathcal{L}'(z) = zL'$). The matrix L' is defined from L by:

$$L' = G^{\mathsf{T}} \left(G \cdot G^{\mathsf{T}} \right)^{-1} LG \oplus H^{\mathsf{T}} \left(H \cdot H^{\mathsf{T}} \right)^{-1} H \ . \tag{8}$$

Indeed, let $z = xG \oplus yH$, one has:

$$zL' = \underbrace{\left(zG^{\mathsf{T}} \left(G \cdot G^{\mathsf{T}} \right)^{-1} \right)}_{x} LG \oplus \underbrace{\left(zH^{\mathsf{T}} \left(H \cdot H^{\mathsf{T}} \right)^{-1} \right)}_{y} H$$

$$= (xL)G \oplus yH \ . \tag{9}$$

Thus, the linear operation consists in a product of the n-bit word by an $n \times n$ matrix. Even if this matrix is stored "uncompressed" in memory, it consists only in n words of n bits (whereas an S-box would require 2^n words of n bits).

Computation of Type (iii). Non-linear operations $S : \mathbb{F}_2^k \to \mathbb{F}_2^k$ are simply recomputed. As for the case of linear functions, we denote by $S' : \mathbb{F}_2^n \to \mathbb{F}_2^n$ the masked non-linear operation. It is computed (off-line, once for all) as:

$$\forall z \in \mathbb{F}_2^n, \quad S'(z) = S(zG^{\mathsf{T}}(GG^{\mathsf{T}})^{-1})G \oplus zH^{\mathsf{T}}(HH^{\mathsf{T}})^{-1}H \ , \tag{10}$$

where we also make the assumption that the mask value is unchanged when traversing S'. Indeed, let us write $z = xG \oplus yH$. Thus $S'(z) = S(x)G \oplus yH$.

2.3 Orthogonal Direct Sum Masking (ODSM)

The purpose of this short subsection is to recapitulate the principle of ODSM.

From a side-channel analysis perspective, it is a masking scheme that belongs to the class of:

- *Boolean additive* masking schemes (i.e., the mask is inserted with $+$ in $\mathbb{F}_2^n$)
- Global Look-Up Table (GLUT), compatible with the table recomputation scheme [20] (see how to practically switch between schemes at Sec. 3.3)
- Low-entropy masking schemes [29] (the injected entropy is an integer $n - k$ that can be equal to 1, 2, etc.)

Every new encryption unfolds as presented in Alg. 1, where the state is denoted by z. The steps in gray represent optimizations in memory size (they are optional, because fault detection is disabled when they are implemented).

Algorithm 1. Big picture for the secure computation of a block cipher using ODSM

1: Draw a random variable y uniformly distributed in $\mathbb{F}_2^{n-k}$
2: (Optionally: precompute the masked non-linear tables $S'_{\text{recomp}} : \mathbb{F}_2^k \to \mathbb{F}_2^k$ from the genuine S-box $S : \mathbb{F}_2^k \to \mathbb{F}_2^k$ as per Eq. (13) — this aspect will be detailed in Sec. 3.3, since it is an optimization)
3: Encode and mask the plaintext x, as $z = xG \oplus yH$ (refer to Eq. (2))
4: Schedule the key (its protection is out of the scope of this paper; Indeed, the key is considered as non-sensitive, from a SCA standpoint — see discussion in [22, §4])
5: Iterate, for each operation of the block cipher:
   (i) if it is a key addition, multiply the key word by G and add it to z, as per Eq. (7)
   (ii) if it is a *linear* operation, apply L' to z as per Eq. (8)
   (iii) if it is a *non-linear* operation, apply S' to z as per Eq. (10)
   (or apply S'_{recomp} through procedure depicted in Alg. 4 if this option is selected)
6: Whenever required, use the relation Eq. (6) to verify that the mask has not been altered (in case of a fault attack)
7: At the end of the computation, use the relation Eq. (3) to obtain the unmasked ciphertext

---

2.4 Security Properties

Security against SCA. We recall that a *sensitive variable* depends on the plaintext __and__ on the key. Thus, neither the plaintext (nor the ciphertext) nor the key (master or round keys) are sensitive (see e.g., [22, §4]). This means that we consider only vertical attacks, where the attacker needs to collect a sufficient amount of traces to recover the secret.

It can be seen from subsection 2.3 that ODSM has been designed such that all sensitive variables are masked (by $d = yH$), as in Eq. (2). The verification against fault attacks (line 6 of Alg. 1) is non-sensitive, because it leaks the mask, which is not sensitive *alone* (we also assume that it cannot be recovered in one trace, i.e., horizontal attacks [24] do not apply). Such masking scheme has been proved perfectly masked (against monovariate attacks) by Blömer et al. in [5].

Now, if the device is leaking at order one (i.e., there is no "glitch" nor "cross-coupling"), then, the order of resistance of the ODSM scheme is quantified by Theorem 2, whose extensive proof is given in Appendix A.

Theorem 2 (Order of resistance). *ODSM can be attacked by monovariate high-order SCA only at order $j \geq d_C$.*

Remark 2. ODSM enjoys only a security against monovariate attacks (i.e., combining two leakage samples exhibits a dependency with the sensitive variable). However, let us mention this is the state-of-the-art of practically implementable masking schemes. Provably secure second-order masking schemes (e.g., [21,22,11]) are admittedly complex to be implemented in practice, owing to their long execution time. Besides, bi-variate attacks can be made very challenging by coupling the masking scheme with *shuffling*. Indeed, in block ciphers such as the AES,

- byte-oriented operations (AddRoundKey, SubBytes, ShiftRows) can be conducted in whatever order (16 possibilities per byte),
- column-oriented operations (MixColumns – unless the implementation with `xtime` is used, in which case this is also a byte-oriented operation) can be conducted in whatever order (amongst the 4! possible orders).

Security against Fault Injection Attacks. In Alg. 1, the state z, throughout the computation, is masked by the same quantity yH, for a $y \in \mathbb{F}_2^{n-k}$ chosen randomly at the beginning of the computation. So, the value of the mask can be checked from times to times (as indicated in line 6 of Alg. 1). The verification takes the following form:

$$P_D(z) \overset{?}{=} yH \ . \tag{11}$$

This operation is sibling to the computation of a *syndrome*.

Let us analyse the exact conditions for the detection to work. We consider a perturbation as the addition to the state z of a random error ε ($z \leftarrow z \oplus \varepsilon$). Like z (recall $z = xG \oplus yH$, see Eq. (2)), the fault can be uniquely written as:

$$\varepsilon = eG \oplus fH \ , \text{ where } e \in \mathbb{F}_2^k \text{ and } f \in \mathbb{F}_2^{n-k} \ . \tag{12}$$

The fault is undetected if $P_D(z \oplus \varepsilon) = (y \oplus f)H = yH$, which is equivalent to have $f = 0$.

If the faults ε are uniformly distributed over $\mathbb{F}_2^n$, then the probability of non-detection is $2^{-(n-k)}$. This probability can be regarded as high. Indeed, it is known that very few faults (sometimes only one or two [23]) can expose the complete key of an AES. However, there are two reasons for the fault injections on ODSM to be more difficult to carry out in practice.

First of all, multiple checks can be done during the algorithm, without any overhead (apart the test of Eq. (11)), because the mask yH is, by design, an invariant throughout the computation.

Second, the undetected faults are indeed very special and most probably difficult to produce in practice. Indeed, $f = 0$ means that $\varepsilon \in \mathcal{C}$ (recall Eq. (12)). Now, we assumed *conservatively* that faults were *uniformly* distributed. Experimentally, it is rather easier to produce faults that have a low Hamming weight. Indeed, when setting up the perturbation source, the stress is first applied gently, and then increased until some effect becomes observable. This approach allows to avoid the activation of sensors due to too heavy a stress, and also to avoid the circuit simply from crashing due to excessive malfunctions. So, for instance considering *overclocking*, the clock frequency is gradually increased, until the first error appears [1]. As a matter of fact, there will be initially only one fault on the *critical path*, thereby causing only 1 bit-flip. This means that easy to inject faults have low Hamming weight. But as ε must be in $\mathcal{C}$ (and nonzero) to have an effect while being undetected, it must have a Hamming weight of at least $d_{\mathcal{C}}$. The likelihood of such faults is probably setup-dependent, but is "informally speaking" much smaller than the announced probability of $2^{-(n-k)}$.

3 Implementation of AES Following the ODSM Scheme

3.1 Example with a Binary Linear Code $\mathcal{C}$ of Parameters $[16, 8, 5]$

Most smartcards and TPMs are still byte-oriented. In this section, we present the case $k = 8$ and $n = 16$, suitable for the AES. Indeed, choosing $n < 16$ would result in ignoring some bits in the processor registers and memory words. At the opposite, if a hardware target (ASIC or FPGA) had been chosen, any value of n would have been eligible, thereby allowing for finer security / overhead tradeoffs.

The problem is to find a code of length n ($n \leq 16$) and of dimension $k = 8$, with minimal distance as large as possible, such as its dual is its supplementary. It happens that there exists a linear code with the expected properties and good parameters: the code of parameters $[16, 8, 5]$ (see generator matrix G in Appendix B) has a supplementary dual, and minimal distance $d_{\mathcal{C}} = 5$ (which is maximal for a linear code). Any linear code of length $n < 16$ and dimension $k = 8$ has a minimal distance strictly smaller than 5. As the $[16, 8, 5]$ code is very attractive, we use it as an example in this paper.

Remark 3. By Theorem 2, using this linear code, we protect the AES against all monovariate high-order attacks of order $j \leq 4$. Moreover, all fault injections perturbing 4 bits or less are detected.

3.2 Efficient Implementation of Linear Functions

First of all, we notice that matrices described in Sec. 2 are precomputed. As for AES, the matrices for G and H (See Eq. (16)), and for $G^{\mathsf{T}} \cdot (G \cdot G^{\mathsf{T}})^{-1}$ and $H^{\mathsf{T}} \cdot (H \cdot H^{\mathsf{T}})^{-1}$ (Eq. (17)) are precomputed. Also, the one non-trivial linear operation, namely $\texttt{xtime}$ (Eq. (18)) is also stored masked, as L' (Eq. (19)).

Besides, the computation of vector–matrix products, a priori of $n \times n$ complexity, can be enhanced by using the natural parallel feature of processors.

For instance, one can compute a vector–matrix product in a *bitslice* manner [4]. The algorithm for the computation of vector–matrices products is given in Alg. 2. Moreover, a version in C language is in Alg. 3.

Algorithm 2. Vector–matrix product (bitslice approach on $k = 8$ bits)

Input: $v \in \mathbb{F}_2^8$ and $M \in (\mathbb{F}_2^8)^8$, whose rows are denoted by $r[i] \in \mathbb{F}_2^8$ (for $1 \leq i \leq 8$)
Output: $w = vM \in \mathbb{F}_2^8$
  1: $w \leftarrow 0$ (a vector of 8 bits [i.e., a *line*, as opposed to a *column*])
  2: **for** $i \in [\![1,8]\!]$ **do**
  3:     $w \leftarrow w \oplus v \wedge r[i]$ ▷ The AND ($\wedge$) is done bitwise
  4: **end for**
  5: **return** w

Algorithm 3. C code, corresponding to Alg. 2

```
#include <stdint.h>
uint8_t w=0;
for( unsigned i=0; i<8; ++i )
        w ^= v & r[i];
return w;
```

The vector–matrix products are processed by blocks of 8×8. We notice that G and H can be written in systematic form, as in Eq. (16). Thus, as the first (resp. last) block of G (resp. H) is I_8, no computation is involved. Moreover, G and H take only 64 bits of ROM each.

3.3   Efficient Implementation of Non-linear Functions

The GLUT approach presented in Sec. 2 has the advantage of being efficient, but even for small n, it is costly in memory size. For instance, for AES, the GLUT size in memory is $n2^n$ bits (see Eq. (10)). Therefore, the table recomputation approach would be welcome. It happens that ODSM has the nice property to support both approaches.

A mask, or a pair of masks $(x', x'') \in \mathbb{F}_2^k \times \mathbb{F}_2^k$, for the S-box recomputation is chosen randomly. It can very well be that $x' = x''$ without jeopardizing the monovariate security against side-channel attacks. Then, we compute for all $x \in \mathbb{F}_2^k$:

$$S'_{\text{recomp}}(x) = S(x \oplus x') \oplus x'' \ . \tag{13}$$

The "trans-masking" operation (for switching between ODSM and precomputed tables) is described in Alg. 4. It is a rare example of *straightforward* switch between two masking schemes (see [13,26] for other examples).

Algorithm 4. Masked application of an S-box on z with a switching between ODSM and a precomputed table. Input: $z = xG \oplus yH$ / Output: $z' = S(x)G \oplus yH$

1: $z \leftarrow z \oplus x'G$,	[Masked with x' in $\mathcal{C}$ and d in $\mathcal{D}$]
2: $x \leftarrow zG^{\mathsf{T}}(GG^{\mathsf{T}})^{-1}$,	[Perfect masking with x' in $\mathbb{F}_2^k$]
3: $x \leftarrow S'_{\text{recomp}}(x)$,	[Secure masked look-up]
4: $z' \leftarrow xG \oplus yH$,	[Remasking with $d = yH$ in $\mathcal{D}$]
5: $z' \leftarrow z' \oplus x''G$.	[Demasking x'' in $\mathcal{C}$]

Nonetheless, we stress two drawbacks of the table recomputation approach:

1. It incurs a time penalty for the recomputation preliminary stage (Eq. (13)).
2. Fault detection is not possible during the evaluation of the precomputed table, because the $(n-k)$ redundant bits are no longer used (the computation falls back on k bits). Still, the security against monovariate side-channel analysis is granted, since the sensitive variable is manipulated *perfectly masked* with (x', x''). So, for AES, we recommend to do the check $P_{\mathcal{D}}(z) \overset{?}{=} yH$ before all look-ups in a precomputed table.

4 Discussion

Remark 4. We highlight in this remark the difference with coding xG in an *Additive White Gaussian Noise* (AWGN) channel, in the context of *digital coding theory*. Our ODSM scheme shares with error detection coding that the errors of low weight can be detected (see analysis in subsection 2.4). But in addition, it manages to handle data in the presence of intentional "noise" of large Hamming weight, namely all the nonzero vectors of H. The wire-tap coding [7] shares the same features.

Remark 5. In the masking with several shares (e.g., Goubin and Patarin [14]), the mask changes throughout the implementation. Indeed, for instance, with two shares Z_1 and Z_2, a linear function $\mathcal{L}$ is applied by calling $\mathcal{L}$ on each share. As a matter of fact, if initially the sensitive variable is $Z = Z_1 \oplus Z_2$, the value of $\mathcal{L}(Z)$ is indeed shared as $\mathcal{L}(Z_1)$ on the one hand, and $\mathcal{L}(Z_2)$ on the one hand. Therefore, after demasking, the exclusive-or of $\mathcal{L}(Z_1)$ and $\mathcal{L}(Z_2)$ yields $\mathcal{L}(X)$. But if Z_2 is a random mask, then it takes value $\mathcal{L}(Z_2)$ after the function $\mathcal{L}$. In contrast, in ODSM, the mask is constrained to be untouched during the whole computation. This makes verifications much more convenient since the same verification can be done irrespective to the place in the cryptographic algorithm (said differently, the verification is not contextual).

Remark 6. When $n = k+1$, the ODSM countermeasure is equivalent to the low-entropy masking scheme proposed in [3]. It consists in having only two vectors in $\mathcal{D}$, namely $(0000)_2$ and $(1111)_2$ (the scheme is applied to the nibble-oriented PRESENT, i.e., $k = 4$). It is shown in [3] to resist first-order SCA (theoretically and by laboratory experiments).

5   Conclusions and Perspectives

The ODSM masking scheme has two *security distinctive features* over other countermeasures against SCA and FA:

1. It resists monovariate attacks of degree $d_{\mathcal{C}} - 1$ ($d_{\mathcal{C}} \geq 1$ if $\mathcal{C}$ is simple and non-empty, but in practice $d_{\mathcal{C}} \gg 1$, e.g. $d_{\mathcal{C}} = 5$ when $\mathcal{C}$ is a $[16, 8, 5]$ code).
2. It can detect faults with probability $1 - 2^{-(n-k)}$ assuming the attacker is able to inject faults uniformly in $\mathbb{F}_2^n$; However, in practice, undetected faults ε must meet a strong criteria, namely $\varepsilon \in \mathcal{C}$, which implies in particular that $w_H(\varepsilon) \geq d_{\mathcal{C}}$, which is for instance 5 for the $[16, 8, 5]$ code $\mathcal{C}$.

Both properties result from the fact the computation in ODSM is carried out, from end to end, in a coset $\mathcal{C} \oplus d$ of the linear code $\mathcal{C}$, where $d \in \mathcal{D} = \mathcal{C}^{\perp}$ is a random mask chosen before every new encryption. The initial randomness of d allows for the protection against monovariate and vertical SCA, whereas the constantness of d throughout the encryption allows for episodic checks against FA. The adaptation of the $[16, 8, 5]$ solution to other *form factors* (i.e., different values of k & n) raises the interesting problem of finding codes with orthogonal supplementary and large minimal distance. In case such codes do not exist, the *orthogonal* protection could be advantageously be replaced by an *oblique* projection.

Acknowledgments. This work has been partially funded by the ANR project E-MATA HARI. The authors would like to thank Shivam Bhasin, Nicolas Bruneau and Zakaria Najm for insights in the demonstration of Theorem 2 provided in Appendix A. Morpho and Télécom-ParisTech are funders of the "Identity & Security Alliance".

References

1. Agoyan, M., Dutertre, J.-M., Naccache, D., Robisson, B., Tria, A.: When Clocks Fail: On Critical Paths and Clock Faults. In: Gollmann, D., Lanet, J.-L., Iguchi-Cartigny, J. (eds.) CARDIS 2010. LNCS, vol. 6035, pp. 182–193. Springer, Heidelberg (2010)
2. Bhasin, S., Danger, J.-L., Flament, F., Graba, T., Guilley, S., Mathieu, Y., Nassar, M., Sauvage, L., Selmane, N.: Combined SCA and DFA Countermeasures Integrable in a FPGA Design Flow. In: ReConFig, Cancún, Quintana Roo, México, December 9-11, pp. 213–218. IEEE Computer Society (2009), http://hal.archives-ouvertes.fr/hal-00411843/en/, doi:10.1109/ReConFig.2009.50
3. Bhasin, S., Danger, J.-L., Guilley, S., Najm, Z.: A Low-Entropy First-Degree Secure Provable Masking Scheme for Resource-Constrained Devices. In: Proceedings of the Workshop on Embedded Systems Security, WESS 2013, Montreal, Quebec, Canada, pp. 7:1–7:10, September 29. ACM, New York (2013), doi:10.1145/2527317.2527324

4. Biham, E.: A Fast New DES Implementation in Software. In: Biham, E. (ed.) FSE 1997. LNCS, vol. 1267, pp. 260–272. Springer, Heidelberg (1997)
5. Blömer, J., Guajardo, J., Krummel, V.: Provably Secure Masking of AES. In: Handschuh, H., Hasan, M.A. (eds.) SAC 2004. LNCS, vol. 3357, pp. 69–83. Springer, Heidelberg (2005)
6. Boscher, A., Handschuh, H.: Masking Does Not Protect Against Differential Fault Attacks. In: FDTC, 5th Workshop on Fault Detection and Tolerance in Cryptography, pp. 35–40. IEEE-CS, Washington, DC (2008), doi:10.1109/FDTC.2008.12
7. Bringer, J., Chabanne, H., Le, T.-H.: Protecting AES against side-channel analysis using wire-tap codes. J. Cryptographic Engineering 2(2), 129–141 (2012)
8. Carlet, C.: Boolean Functions for Cryptography and Error Correcting Codes: Chapter of the monography. In: Crama, Y., Hammer, P. (eds.) Boolean Models and Methods in Mathematics, Computer Science, and Engineering, pp. 257–397. Cambridge University Press (2010), Preliminary version available at http://www.math.univ-paris13.fr/carlet/chap-fcts-Bool-corr.pdf
9. Carlet, C., Danger, J.-L., Guilley, S., Maghrebi, H., Prouff, E.: Achieving side-channel high-order correlation immunity with Leakage Squeezing. Journal of Cryptographic Engineering, 1–15 (2014), doi:10.1007/s13389-013-0067-1
10. Carlet, C., Guillot, P.: A New Representation of Boolean Functions. In: Fossorier, M., Imai, H., Lin, S., Poli, A. (eds.) AAECC 1999. LNCS, vol. 1719, pp. 94–103. Springer, Heidelberg (1999)
11. Coron, J.-S.: Higher Order Masking of Look-up Tables. Cryptology ePrint Archive, Report 2013/700 (2013), http://eprint.iacr.org/
12. Coron, J.-S., Goubin, L.: On Boolean and Arithmetic Masking against Differential Power Analysis. In: Paar, C., Koç, Ç.K. (eds.) CHES 2000. LNCS, vol. 1965, pp. 231–237. Springer, Heidelberg (2000)
13. Debraize, B.: Efficient and provable Secure Methods for Switching from Arithmetic to Boolean Masking. In: Prouff, E., Schaumont, P. (eds.) CHES 2012. LNCS, vol. 7428, pp. 107–121. Springer, Heidelberg (2012)
14. Goubin, L., Patarin, J.: DES and Differential Power Analysis. In: Koç, Ç.K., Paar, C. (eds.) CHES 1999. LNCS, vol. 1717, pp. 158–172. Springer, Heidelberg (1999)
15. M. Joye, M. Tunstall.: Fault Analysis in Cryptography. Springer (March 2011), http://joye.site88.net/FAbook.html, doi: 10.1007/978-3-642-29656-7, ISBN 978-3-642-29655-0
16. Mangard, S., Oswald, E., Popp, T.: Power Analysis Attacks: Revealing the Secrets of Smart Cards. Springer (December 2006), http://www.springer.com/, ISBN 0-387-30857-1
17. Messerges, T.S.: Securing the AES Finalists Against Power Analysis Attacks. In: Goos, G., Hartmanis, J., van Leeuwen, J., Schneier, B. (eds.) FSE 2000. LNCS, vol. 1978, pp. 150–164. Springer, Heidelberg (2001)
18. Moradi, A.: Statistical tools flavor side-channel collision attacks. In: Pointcheval, D., Johansson, T. (eds.) EUROCRYPT 2012. LNCS, vol. 7237, pp. 428–445. Springer, Heidelberg (2012)
19. NIST/ITL/CSD. Advanced Encryption Standard (AES). FIPS PUB 197 (November 2001), http://csrc.nist.gov/publications/fips/fips197/fips-197.pdf
20. Prouff, E., Rivain, M.: A Generic Method for Secure SBox Implementation. In: Kim, S., Yung, M., Lee, H.-W. (eds.) WISA 2007. LNCS, vol. 4867, pp. 227–244. Springer, Heidelberg (2007)
21. Rivain, M., Dottax, E., Prouff, E.: Block Ciphers Implementations Provably Secure Against Second Order Side Channel Analysis. In: Nyberg, K. (ed.) FSE 2008. LNCS, vol. 5086, pp. 127–143. Springer, Heidelberg (2008)

22. Rivain, M., Prouff, E.: Provably Secure Higher-Order Masking of AES. In: Mangard, S., Standaert, F.-X. (eds.) CHES 2010. LNCS, vol. 6225, pp. 413–427. Springer, Heidelberg (2010)

23. Tunstall, M., Mukhopadhyay, D., Ali, S.: Differential Fault Analysis of the Advanced Encryption Standard Using a Single Fault. In: Ardagna, C.A., Zhou, J. (eds.) WISTP 2011. LNCS, vol. 6633, pp. 224–233. Springer, Heidelberg (2011)

24. Tunstall, M., Whitnall, C., Oswald, E.: Masking Tables - An Underestimated Security Risk. IACR Cryptology ePrint Archive, 2013:735 (2013)

25. University of Sydney. Magma Computational Algebra System, http://magma.maths.usyd.edu.au/magma/

26. Vadnala, P.K., Großschädl, J.: Algorithms for Switching between Boolean and Arithmetic Masking of Second Order. In: Gierlichs, B., Guilley, S., Mukhopadhyay, D. (eds.) SPACE 2013. LNCS, vol. 8204, pp. 95–110. Springer, Heidelberg (2013)

27. Veyrat-Charvillon, N., Medwed, M., Kerckhof, S., Standaert, F.-X.: Shuffling against Side-Channel Attacks: A Comprehensive Study with Cautionary Note. In: Wang, X., Sako, K. (eds.) ASIACRYPT 2012. LNCS, vol. 7658, pp. 740–757. Springer, Heidelberg (2012)

28. Waddle, J., Wagner, D.: Towards Efficient Second-Order Power Analysis. In: Joye, M., Quisquater, J.-J. (eds.) CHES 2004. LNCS, vol. 3156, pp. 1–15. Springer, Heidelberg (2004)

29. Ye, X., Eisenbarth, T.: On the Vulnerability of Low Entropy Masking Schemes. In: CARDIS. LNCS. Springer, Berlin (November 2013)

A   Proofs of Security Property Claimed in Theorem 2: Resistance against jth-order ($j < d_{\mathcal{C}} = d_{\mathcal{D}}^{\perp}$) in the Case of Monovariate Side-Channel Attacks

We denote in this appendix by Ψ the function that encodes x, i.e., $\Psi(x) = xG \in \mathbb{F}_2^n$. In ODSM, $\Psi(x)$ is manipulated masked by some $d \in \mathcal{D}$ (see Eq. (1)). The indicator of $\mathcal{D}$ is noted $f : \mathbb{F}_2^n \to \mathbb{F}_2$, in the sense that:

$$\forall d \in \mathbb{F}_2^n, \quad f(d) = 1 \iff d \in \mathcal{D} .$$

Said differently, $f(d) = 1 \iff \exists y \in \mathbb{F}_2^{n-k}$ s.t. $yH = d$.

For the rest of the security analysis, we resort to statistics. Thus, we use the following notations: capital letters (e.g., D) are random variables, small letters (e.g., d) are realizations, and calligraphic letters (e.g., $\mathcal{D}$) are representing the support of random variables.

Obviously, a monovariate first-order attack fails is the mask D is balanced. As motivated by monovariate high-order attacks coined by Moradi [18] and Carlet et al. [9] the attacker needs to create combinations between the bits of Z. Consequently, we model the attacker as a pseudo-Boolean function $\Phi : \mathbb{F}_2^n \to \mathbb{R}$ of a given numerical degree j in the bits of Z. For example, Φ can be the power j of the Hamming weight (as in zero-offset attacks). The leakage model can be, in general, any affine function of the bits of Z. This simply means that there is no "glitch" nor "cross-couping". This case is usual for software platforms.

So, when $j = 2$, the function Φ can model the product of two bits. This model captures the probing attacks, as with j probes, the attacker can build any polynomial of degree j in the sensible variables.

Proposition 3 (*jth-order security condition on the masks coding*). *Let $\Phi : \mathbb{F}_2^n \to \mathbb{R}$ a leakage function of numerical degree j, an arbitrary $\Psi : \mathbb{F}_2^k \to \mathbb{F}_2^n$ and a mask D uniformly distributed in a code $\mathcal{D}$, with f the indicator of $\mathcal{D} \subset \mathbb{F}_2^n$. Then the leakage $\Phi(\Psi(X) \oplus D)$ resists a monovariate attack if $\mathcal{D}$ is a code of dual distance $j + 1$.*

This Proposition 3 is the accurate rephrasing of Theorem 2. We aim now at proving them. In Proposition 3, the condition of jth-order security is: for all Φ of numerical degree smaller than or equal to j, $\mathbb{E}\left[\Phi(\Psi(X) \oplus D)|X = x\right]$ does not depend on $x \in \mathbb{F}_2^k$. This is rewritten as the condition:

$$\text{Var}\left[\mathbb{E}\left[\Phi(\Psi(X) \oplus D)|X\right]\right] = 0 \ . \tag{14}$$

Indeed, in this case, any correlation attack fails: indeed, there is no linear dependency between the leakage $\Phi(\Psi(X) \oplus D)$ and the sensitive variable X.

Now, the expectation $\mathbb{E}\left[\Phi(\Psi(X) \oplus D)|X = x\right]$ is taken on the mask D random variable only, because $\Psi(X)$ depends only on X. So we have:

$$\mathbb{E}\left[\Phi(\Psi(X) \oplus D)|X = x\right] = \sum_{d \in \mathcal{D}} \frac{1}{\text{Card}[\mathcal{D}]} \Phi(\Psi(x) \oplus d)$$

$$= 2^{-(n-k)} \sum_{d \in \mathbb{F}_2^n} f(d)\Phi(\Psi(x) \oplus d)$$

$$= 2^{-(n-k)} \left(f \otimes \Phi\right)\left(\Psi(x)\right) \ .$$

So, the countermeasure is jth-order secure if and only if $\left(f \otimes \Phi\right)\left(\Psi(x)\right)$ does not depend on x. Therefore, a sufficient condition for resistance against jth-order attacks is that $f \otimes \Phi(z)$ does not depend on $z \in \mathbb{F}_2^n$ (irrespective of function Ψ).

Let g a pseudo-Boolean function $\mathbb{F}_2^n \to \mathbb{R}$. We call $\hat{g}$ the Fourier transform of g, i.e., $\hat{g}(z) = \sum_a g(a)(-1)^{a \cdot z}$. We have: ($g$ is constant) $\iff \forall z \neq 0$, $\hat{g}(z) = 0 \iff \hat{g} \propto \delta$, the Kronecker symbol.

Let us apply this result to $g = f \otimes \Phi$. The Fourier transform turns a *convolution product* into a *product*, i.e., $\widehat{f \otimes \Phi}(z) = \hat{f}(z)\hat{\Phi}(z)$. To prove that:

$$\hat{f}\hat{\Phi} = 0 \ , \tag{15}$$

let us introduce the following useful Lemma 1.

Lemma 1. *Let P be a pseudo-Boolean function $P : \mathbb{F}_2^n \to \mathbb{R}$ of numerical degree $d^\circ(P)$ [8,10]. Then, $\forall z \in \mathbb{F}_2^n$, $w_H(z) > d^\circ(P) \implies \hat{P}(z) = 0$.*

Proof. Any pseudo-Boolean function can be written uniquely as a multilinear polynomial $P(y_1, \cdots, y_n) = \sum_{I \subseteq \mathcal{P}(\llbracket 1,n \rrbracket)} a_I y^I$, where $\mathcal{P}(\llbracket 1,n \rrbracket)$ is the set of all subsets of interval $[\![1, n]\!]$, a_I is a real coefficient, and y^I is an abbreviation for $\prod_{i \in I} y_i$. By definition, the numerical degree $d^\circ(P)$ of P is the maximal degree of each monomial, *i.e.* $d^\circ(P) = \max\{\mathsf{Card}[I] \text{ s.t. } a_I \neq 0\}$. By linearity of the Fourier transform, $\widehat{P}(z) = \sum_{I \subseteq \mathcal{P}([\![1, n]\!])} a_I \widehat{M_I}(z)$, where $M_I :$ $y \in \mathbb{F}_2^n \mapsto y^I$. Let us prove that $\forall z \in \mathbb{F}_2^n$, $w_H(z) > \mathsf{Card}[I] \implies \widehat{M_I}(z) = 0$. Let z such that $w_H(z) > \mathsf{Card}[I]$. Thus z has at least one non-zero coordinate outside I. As all the coordinates in M_I are equivalent, we can assume (without loss of generality), that this coordinate is the last one. We note $y = (y', y_n)$, where $y' = (y_1, \cdots, y_{n-1}) \in \mathbb{F}_2^{n-1}$ and $y_n \in \mathbb{F}_2$. Thus, $\widehat{M_I}(z) = \sum_{y' \in \mathbb{F}_2^{n-1}} \sum_{y_n \in \mathbb{F}_2} y^I (-1)^{y \cdot z} = \sum_{y' \in \mathbb{F}_2^{n-1}} (y', 1)^I (-1)^{y' \cdot (z_1, \cdots, z_{n-1})} (1 + (-1)) = 0$. As, by definition, any monomial M_I has numerical degree $d^\circ(M_I) \leq d^\circ(P)$, we also have $\widehat{P}(z) = \sum_{I \subseteq \mathcal{P}([\![1, n]\!])} a_I \times 0 = 0$. □

Based on Lemma 1, we give hereafter the proof of Proposition 3 / Theorem 2.

Proof. (Proof of Proposition 3) So, to prove that $\widehat{f}\,\widehat{\Phi} = 0$, we start by applying Lemma 1. As Φ is of numerical degree j, $\widehat{\Phi}(z) = 0$ for $w_H(z) > j$. So, the masking is jth-order secure if $\forall z \in \mathbb{F}_2^n$, $0 < w_H(z) \leq j$, $\widehat{f}(z) = 0$. By definition, this means that f is jth-order correlation-immune (j-CI in brief). This is equivalent to saying the $\mathcal{D}$ is of dual distance $d_{\mathcal{D}}^\perp = j + 1$.

Irrespective of the way the sensitive variable $X \in \mathbb{F}_2^k$ is mapped (by function Ψ) onto $\mathbb{F}_2^n$, a sufficient condition for security against zero-offset attacks [28] of orders $1, 2, \cdots, j$ is that the mask D be distributed uniformly in $\mathcal{D}$, a code of dual distance $j + 1$. Said differently, the lowest order j of a successful zero-offset attack is equal to the dual distance of $\mathcal{D}$.

As $\mathcal{D} = \mathcal{C}^\perp$, we have that $d_{\mathcal{D}}^\perp = d_{\mathcal{C}}$ (see Proposition 1). □

B   Example of Matrices for the ODSM on AES

The generator matrix G of $\mathcal{C}$ is written in systematic form in Eq. (16). This matrix is the direct result of the two following Magma [25] commands:

```
K := FiniteField( 2 );
BestKnownLinearCode( K, 16, 8 );
```

The matrix H (see also Eq. (16)) is a basis of $\mathcal{C}^\perp$, obtained by the following command of GNU/Pari: $H = \mathtt{matker(G)}\tilde{\ }$. As $G = [I_k \| M]$ is in systematic form, Proposition 2 can be readily applied to check whether the lines of G and of H, together, form a basis of $\mathbb{F}_2^{16}$. It happens that indeed, $I_8 \oplus MM^\mathsf{T}$ has rank 8, and so $\mathcal{C}^\perp$ is the supplementary of $\mathcal{C}$.

$$G = \begin{pmatrix} 1\,0\,0\,0\,0\,0\,0\,0 & 1\,0\,0\,1\,1\,1\,1\,0 \\ 0\,1\,0\,0\,0\,0\,0\,0 & 0\,1\,0\,0\,1\,1\,1\,1 \\ 0\,0\,1\,0\,0\,0\,0\,0 & 1\,1\,0\,0\,1\,1\,0\,0 \\ 0\,0\,0\,1\,0\,0\,0\,0 & 0\,1\,1\,0\,0\,1\,1\,0 \\ 0\,0\,0\,0\,1\,0\,0\,0 & 0\,0\,1\,1\,0\,0\,1\,1 \\ 0\,0\,0\,0\,0\,1\,0\,0 & 1\,1\,1\,1\,0\,0\,1\,0 \\ 0\,0\,0\,0\,0\,0\,1\,0 & 0\,1\,1\,1\,1\,0\,0\,1 \\ 0\,0\,0\,0\,0\,0\,0\,1 & 1\,1\,0\,1\,0\,1\,1\,1 \end{pmatrix}, \quad H = \begin{pmatrix} 1\,0\,1\,0\,0\,1\,0\,1 & 1\,0\,0\,0\,0\,0\,0\,0 \\ 0\,1\,1\,1\,0\,1\,1\,1 & 0\,1\,0\,0\,0\,0\,0\,0 \\ 0\,0\,0\,1\,1\,1\,1\,0 & 0\,0\,1\,0\,0\,0\,0\,0 \\ 1\,0\,0\,0\,1\,1\,1\,1 & 0\,0\,0\,1\,0\,0\,0\,0 \\ 1\,1\,1\,0\,0\,0\,1\,0 & 0\,0\,0\,0\,1\,0\,0\,0 \\ 1\,1\,1\,1\,0\,0\,0\,1 & 0\,0\,0\,0\,0\,1\,0\,0 \\ 1\,1\,0\,1\,1\,1\,0\,1 & 0\,0\,0\,0\,0\,0\,1\,0 \\ 0\,1\,0\,0\,1\,0\,1\,1 & 0\,0\,0\,0\,0\,0\,0\,1 \end{pmatrix}. \tag{16}$$

The matrices involved in $z = xG \oplus yH \mapsto x$ and $z \mapsto y$ (see Eq. (3) and (4)) are given in Eq. (17).

$$G^{\mathsf{T}}(GG^{\mathsf{T}})^{-1} = \begin{pmatrix} 0\,0\,1\,1\,1\,0\,0\,1 \\ 0\,0\,1\,0\,0\,1\,0\,1 \\ 1\,1\,1\,1\,1\,0\,1\,0 \\ 1\,0\,1\,0\,1\,1\,0\,0 \\ 1\,0\,1\,1\,1\,1\,1\,0 \\ 0\,1\,0\,1\,1\,1\,1\,1 \\ 0\,0\,1\,0\,1\,1\,1\,1 \\ 1\,1\,0\,0\,0\,1\,1\,0 \\ 0\,1\,0\,1\,1\,0\,1\,0 \\ 1\,1\,0\,0\,0\,1\,0\,1 \\ 0\,1\,1\,0\,0\,0\,1\,0 \\ 0\,0\,1\,1\,0\,0\,0\,1 \\ 1\,1\,0\,0\,1\,0\,0\,1 \\ 1\,0\,0\,0\,1\,1\,0\,0 \\ 1\,0\,0\,1\,0\,1\,1\,1 \\ 0\,1\,1\,1\,0\,0\,1\,0 \end{pmatrix}, \quad H^{\mathsf{T}}(HH^{\mathsf{T}})^{-1} = \begin{pmatrix} 0\,1\,0\,0\,1\,1\,1\,0 \\ 1\,1\,1\,0\,1\,0\,0\,1 \\ 0\,0\,1\,1\,0\,0\,0\,1 \\ 1\,0\,0\,1\,0\,0\,1\,1 \\ 1\,0\,0\,0\,1\,1\,0\,0 \\ 0\,1\,0\,0\,0\,1\,1\,0 \\ 1\,0\,1\,0\,0\,0\,1\,1 \\ 0\,1\,0\,1\,1\,0\,1\,0 \\ 1\,1\,1\,0\,0\,0\,1\,1 \\ 1\,0\,1\,1\,0\,1\,0\,0 \\ 1\,1\,0\,1\,1\,0\,1\,0 \\ 0\,1\,1\,0\,1\,1\,0\,1 \\ 0\,0\,1\,1\,1\,1\,0\,1 \\ 0\,1\,0\,1\,1\,0\,1\,1 \\ 1\,0\,1\,0\,0\,1\,1\,0 \\ 1\,0\,0\,1\,1\,1\,0\,1 \end{pmatrix}. \tag{17}$$

Recall that the `xtime` function of AES [19, Sec. 4.2.1] is the multiplication by X in $\mathbb{F}_2^8$, seen as the finite field $\mathbb{F}_{2^8} \equiv \mathbb{F}_2[X]/(X^8 + X^4 + X^3 + X + 1)$. It is a linear function, generated from this $k \times k$ (i.e., 8×8) matrix L:

$$L = \begin{pmatrix} 0\,0\,0\,1\,1\,0\,1\,1 \\ 1\,0\,0\,0\,0\,0\,0\,0 \\ 0\,1\,0\,0\,0\,0\,0\,0 \\ 0\,0\,1\,0\,0\,0\,0\,0 \\ 0\,0\,0\,1\,0\,0\,0\,0 \\ 0\,0\,0\,0\,1\,0\,0\,0 \\ 0\,0\,0\,0\,0\,1\,0\,0 \\ 0\,0\,0\,0\,0\,0\,1\,0 \end{pmatrix}. \tag{18}$$

The masked `xtime` function can be computed using Eq. (8). The generating matrix L' is $n \times n$ (i.e., 16×16):

$$L' = \begin{pmatrix} 1\,1\,0\,0\,1\,0\,1\,1 & 1\,1\,0\,1\,0\,0\,1\,0 \\ 0\,0\,1\,0\,1\,1\,1\,1 & 1\,1\,1\,0\,1\,1\,0\,0 \\ 0\,0\,1\,1\,0\,1\,0\,1 & 0\,1\,0\,0\,0\,0\,1\,1 \\ 1\,1\,1\,1\,1\,1\,1\,1 & 0\,1\,1\,1\,0\,0\,1\,0 \\ 1\,1\,0\,1\,0\,0\,0\,1 & 0\,1\,0\,1\,0\,0\,1\,1 \\ 1\,1\,1\,0\,0\,1\,0\,1 & 1\,1\,0\,0\,1\,0\,1\,0 \\ 0\,1\,1\,1\,0\,0\,1\,1 & 0\,0\,1\,1\,0\,0\,1\,0 \\ 0\,1\,0\,1\,0\,0\,0\,0 & 1\,1\,1\,1\,1\,1\,1\,0 \\ 1\,1\,1\,0\,1\,1\,1\,0 & 0\,0\,1\,0\,0\,1\,0\,1 \\ 0\,1\,0\,1\,0\,1\,0\,0 & 1\,0\,0\,1\,1\,0\,1\,1 \\ 1\,0\,1\,0\,0\,1\,1\,0 & 1\,1\,1\,1\,1\,0\,0\,1 \\ 0\,1\,0\,1\,0\,0\,1\,1 & 1\,0\,0\,1\,0\,1\,1\,1 \\ 0\,1\,0\,0\,0\,0\,0\,0 & 0\,1\,0\,0\,0\,1\,1\,1 \\ 1\,0\,0\,0\,1\,1\,1\,1 & 1\,1\,1\,1\,0\,1\,0\,1 \\ 1\,0\,1\,0\,0\,0\,1\,0 & 0\,0\,1\,0\,1\,0\,0\,1 \\ 1\,0\,0\,1\,0\,1\,1\,0 & 0\,1\,1\,1\,0\,0\,1\,0 \end{pmatrix}. \tag{19}$$

New Countermeasures against Fault and Software Type Confusion Attacks on Java Cards

Guillaume Barbu and Christophe Giraud

Oberthur Technologies
Cryptography & Security Group
4, allée du Doyen Georges Brus, 33 600 Pessac, France
{g.barbu,c.giraud}@oberthur.com

Abstract. Attacks based on type confusion against Java Card platforms have been widely studied in the literature over the past few years. Until now, no generic countermeasure has ever been proposed to cover simultaneously and efficiently direct and indirect type confusions. In this article we bridge this gap by introducing two different schemes which cover both type confusions. First, we show that an adequate random transformation of all the manipulated data on the platform according to their type can bring a very good resistance against type confusion exploits. Secondly, we describe how a so-called Java Card Virtual Machine *Abstract Companion* can allow one to detect all type confusions between integers and Objects all across the platform. While the second solution stands as a strong but resource-demanding mechanism, we show that the first one is a particularly efficient memory/security trade-off solution to secure the whole platform.

Keywords: Java Card, Countermeasures, Fault Injection, Combined Attacks.

1 Introduction

Putting Java into memory constrained embedded systems such as smartcards was not an easy bet. However, since its introduction in 1996, the Java Card technology has been successively adopted in all environments of the smartcard industry, from mobile telecommunication to banking and pay-tv, proving both the need for such a standard and the security level that can be reached on these platforms.

Actually, Java Cards can be considered as more secure than native cards due to the additional controls performed by the Java Card Runtime Environment. Among these, we can cite for instance the check of array boundaries or the application firewall ensuring the isolation between the different applications hosted by the card. In order to challenge the intrinsic security mechanisms of the platform, the notion of *ill-formed applications* has emerged. Ill-formed applications are obtained by modifying the binary representation of a Java Card

D. Naccache and D. Sauveron (Eds.): WISTP 2014, LNCS 8501, pp. 57–75, 2014.

application[1] in order to escape certain language rules or particular checks [1–5]. Hopefully, such logical attacks can be counteracted by the use of a *ByteCode Verifier* (BCV) [6, §4.9.2] which aims at ensuring that an application is conformed to the Java Card specifications [7–9]. Nevertheless, an attacker having hands on an open platform may not necessarily execute the BCV, unless it is embedded within the platform, as mandated for instance for the high-end Java Card *Connected* Edition [10–13] but rarely found on *Classic* platforms.

A few years after the publication of these logical attacks, the idea to combine malicious applications with fault injections emerged [14]. Firstly, *Fault Attacks* were known to affect the security of embedded cryptographic implementations, either asymmetric or symmetric [15–17]. But as stated in [18–20], these attacks can actually target any function implemented on embedded devices, which naturally includes Java Card internal routines. Nowadays, the main mean of disturbing an embedded chip is to use light beams [21] or electromagnetic pulses [22]. The so-called *Combined Attacks* aim at allowing a malicious but well-formed application (i.e. that passes the BCV) to bypass certain security features of Java Cards by using fault attacks. Since 2009, several Combined Attacks have been published to attack vital points of a Java Card such as the application firewall, the operand stack or the garbage collector [23–30].

In this paper, after recalling the main software and combined attacks, we analyze the countermeasures against type confusion presented so far in the literature. As a result of this analysis, we show not only that none of the proposed countermeasures can detect all kind of type confusions but also that some attack paths are not covered at all, even when combining these countermeasures. This statement is the motivation for our study towards a platform-wide approach to type confusion detection. We propose in the following two different solutions allowing one to cover the entire JCRE. The first one involves random transformations and comes with almost no memory overhead while offering *only* a probabilistic (although very close to 100 %) security level. On the other hand, the second proposal, entitled the Java Card Virtual Machine Abstract Companion, comes with a certain memory overhead while providing a very strong and deterministic security level. As we will see, these solutions allow to counteract all the identified attack paths and do not require any profound modification of existing Java Card implementations.

Section 2 introduces the different flavours of type confusions that can be encountered in the literature. Section 3 briefly describes the different countermeasures published so far and analyzes their benefits and flaws. Section 4 presents the two approaches we define and discuss their effectiveness and efficiency.

2   Type Confusion on Java Cards

Either achieved by a Software or Combined Attack, a type confusion can have various origins. The following gives a classification for these origins and an

---

[1] The .CAP file for Converted APplet, obtained from the standard .CLASS file generated by the Java compiler.

example of a practical attack for each class. The two first classes concern software attacks based on ill-formed or ill-verified applications which imply that the attacker can load any application on the platform. The three other classes consider a combination of software and fault injection attacks that only require that the attacker can load verified applications. Finally, this section will present another classification for the attacks which may appear less specific but will better suit the remainder of our analysis.

Software Attack: Ill-Formed Application (SA-IFA). In the case one is able to load any application onto the card without executing the BCV, one can freely load a corrupted binary file representing an ill-formed application that does not comply to the Java Card language rules.

In particular, it is well known that it is not possible to manipulate directly the length of an array of byte after its instantiation in Java. A typical attack would then consist in loading the corrupted binary file representing the code depicted in List. 1.1 as proposed in [2].

Listing 1.1. Example of an SA-IFA

```
public class Fake { short len = (short) 0x7FFF; }

byte[] bArray = new byte[10];
Fake f = bArray;
// Subsequent manipulations of f.len allow to modify bArray's
// length
```

By modifying the length of the array, one may be able to access data out of its bounds and then to get a dump of the card.

Another classical example of an SA-IFA consists in setting the reference of a given object through an integer value (List. 1.2), which is prohibited by the language and leads to an error during the verification process. Indeed, modification of the .CAP file is mandatory here since any Java compiler would raise an error on such Java sources.

Software Attack: Ill-Verified Application (SA-IVA). Another way of having an ill-typed application loaded into the card is to use a particular library already on-card and to feed the BCV with an erroneous export file for this library[2]. Again, this would allow one to escape the language rules and in particular those concerning type safety.

An example of such an attack abusing the sharing mechanism (derived from that described in [2]) is presented in List. 1.3. Using the corrupted export file, the BCV will pass and the byte array sent by the Client will be used as a short array by the Server.

---

[2] This file will be used as the definition of the library by the off-card verification process.

Listing 1.2. Example of an SA-IFA (2)

```
// Receive reference through the APDU buffer
int reference = getValue(apduBuffer);

// Assign it to the object instance
myObject = reference;
// The above line can be obtained for instance by compiling:
// reference = reference;
// myObject = myObject;
// And replacing the unwanted bytecodes by NOPs in the CAP
```

Listing 1.3. Example of an SA-IVA

```
// Server CAP file: Server uses short []
public interface MyInterface extends Shareable {
    void accessArray(short[] array); }

// Server EXP file: Server assumes byte []
public interface MyInterface extends Shareable {
    void accessArray(byte[] array); }

// Client CAP file: Client assumes byte []
public interface MyInterface extends Shareable {
    void accessArray(byte[] array); }
```

By accessing a byte array as a short array, one may be able to access twice as much data as it should be allowed to, getting here again a partial dump of the card.

Combined Attack: Data Disruption (CA-DD). The different ways to combine software and fault attacks mainly differ in the effect of the fault injection. Firstly, we consider that the attacker can modify the data manipulated by the application.

Such an attack can for example consist in creating numerous instances of a given class B and attempt to corrupt the reference of an instance of another class A so that it actually points to one instance of class B. This attack was firstly described on standard Java platforms in [31] and adapted on Java Card platforms in [32]. List. 1.4 recalls it briefly. By modifying the reference of $b.a1$ and by manipulating the short value $b.a1.s1$, one can access an instance field she should not.

Combined Attack: JC Application Code Disruption (CA-JCACD). It is also possible for an attacker with fault injection capabilities to target directly the code of her own Java Card application. This option was for instance used

Listing 1.4. Example of a CA-DD

```
public class A { short s1, s2, s3, s4; }
public class B { A a1, a2, a3, a4; }

// Create as many instances of class B as possible
B b0000 = new B(); B b0001 = new B(); ... B b00FF = new B(); ...

// Create one instance of class A
A a = new A();

// A perturbation of the reference of a will most likely make it
// point to an instance of class B
a.s1++;        // actually increments the reference of b.a1
```

in [23] to return a value that will be used as the reference of a *Key* object by forcing a bytecode instruction to 0, corresponding to the bytecode *NOP* (for No OPeration), as recalled in List. 1.5.

Listing 1.5. Example of a CA-JCACD

```
Key getKey(short index)
{
    // The if-statement is coded as: 1D 1077 6D08
    // Forcing to 0 the instruction bspush (10) results in coding
    // the following statement:
    //     return index;
    if (index<0x77)
        return keys[index];
    else
        return null;
}
```

In another kind of application code disruption, we can also refer to the work by Bouffard *et al.* [25] which shows that the perturbation of a branch instruction (a *goto_w* at the end of a for-loop to be specific) can lead to the execution of arbitrary instructions stored in a static array of byte.

Combined Attack: JCVM Code Disruption (CA-JCVMCD). Another kind of disruption that can lead to a type confusion is the perturbation of the execution of the JCVM itself.

An example of such an attack was presented in [24] where the *checkcast* instruction, which is meant to verify dynamically the validity of explicit type casting, was disrupted to provoke a type confusion. The authors exploit then this fault to take advantage of the specific features of the Java Card 3 *Connected Edition* platform, yet it can totally be used on *Classic* Editions as shown in List. 1.6.

Listing 1.6. Example of a CA-JCVMCD

```
public class A { C c; }
public class B { short s;}

A a = new A();
// Explicit casting to B forces the compiler to generate a
// checkcast instruction which can be disrupted
B b = (B) (Object) a;
// Subsequent manipulation of b.s allow to modify c's reference
b.s = sRef;
```

Table 1 sums up the different attack classes and states the effectiveness of the only countermeasure initially present to counteract these attacks. All along this article we will enrich this table in order to assess previous works as well as the propositions presented in the remainder.

Table 1. Efficiency of the ByteCode Verifier versus the different classes of attack leading to type confusion

	SA-IFA	SA-IVA	CA-DD	CA-JCACD	CA-JCVMCD
ByteCode Verifier	Yes	Yes, with correct .EXP files	No	No	No

Furthermore, beyond this classification we also denote that two different kinds of type confusion can occur on the platform:

- Direct type confusion : As in List. 1.5, direct type confusion consists in directly using an object reference as an integer value (or *vice versa*).
- Indirect type confusion : As in List. 1.4 and 1.6, indirect type confusion consists in using an object reference as an integer value (or *vice versa*) through two object instance fields.

One should also note that except the confusions involving arrays, all attacks are based on an integer-to-Object type confusion which allows to manipulate object references. We will pay a particular interest to this specific kind of type confusion in following sections.

3   A Survey of Previous Works

This section gives a brief overview of different solutions enabling to counteract some type confusion attacks presented in the literature. As previously stated, we focus in the remainder on type confusions between integer values and object references. For each of the presented work, we refer the reader to the original articles for a detailed description.

3.1   Redundant Stack Checks

Description. In [27] Barbu *et al.* introduce an element within the Java Card runtime frame of execution allowing them to check the integrity of the data read and written (i.e. pushed onto and popped from) the operand stack. Indeed, given that any data pushed onto the operand stack is meant to be popped from the operand stack at a certain point, they exhibit an invariant relation permitting to somehow check the operand stack integrity.

Analysis. The proposed countermeasure actually procures a protection against type confusion based on operand disruption. However this method fails to detect an error if the operand stack is not directly targeted, which limits its overall effectiveness.

3.2   The Typed Stack

Description. In [33], Dubreuil *et al.* proposed to enhance the robustness of Java Card platforms against type confusions thanks to the use of a typed operand stack. Their proposal consists in dynamically splitting the operand stack into two parts dedicated to integer values on the one hand and to object references on the other hand as depicted in Figure 1.

Analysis. As claimed by the authors, this countermeasure is very efficient in detecting direct type abuse such as the one described in List. 1.5 where an integer value is returned as a reference to a *Key* object. Indeed, since the integer would be pushed on one side of the stack, trying to pop a reference from the other side of the stack would result in a stack underflow error. It is also worth noticing that the cost for this countermeasure at the JCVM level is really negligible since only an additional pointer is required to keep track of both the integer-top-of-stack and the reference-top-of-stack.

However, the authors also claim that the typed stack allows to counteract attacks like that presented in Section 2, based on an indirect type confusion. This turns out to be incorrect since in this case the confusion occurs within an object instance field, i.e. away from both sides of the operand stack. Besides, not only this attack is not detected by the typed stack but it also allows one to circumvent the security brought by the typed stack. Indeed, once an indirect type confusion has been achieved, executing any type confusion just require an additional step through the involved instance fields to avoid the check enforced by the typed stack without any additional fault injection.

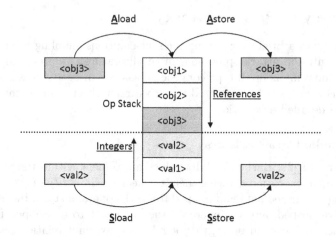

Fig. 1. The typed stack

3.3 Integrity Checks

Description. In [32], Lancia proposed to add integrity checks within object instances in order to detect possible disruptions of instance fields and thus to prevent type confusions due to data disruptions (CA-DD).

Analysis. Obviously, such a countermeasure is only meant to avoid CA-DD attacks and will not detect any of the other attacks previously described. Furthermore, the cost of this mechanism both in terms of memory footprint and execution time should not be neglected.

3.4 Typewise Masking

Description. Further proving the industrial interest in type confusion attacks, Girard *et. al* filed a patent [34] in which they propose a typewise masking scheme randomizing the effects of a successful type confusion. Their idea consists in applying a transformation to data manipulated in RAM (i.e. local variables and instruction operands) depending on their primitive type by associating one different random number to each type: *integer, boolean, character, reference*, other (*double, ...*). In order to be able to execute operations on these data, the mentioned transformations need to come with their reciprocals, such as Exclusive OR/Exclusive OR and Addition/Substraction for instance. The authors argue that succeeding in a type confusion, an attacker would only be able of manipulating random variables and would consequently not threaten the security of the card.

Analysis. If such a technique is actually efficient at countering the attack described in List. 1.2 (the value stored in *myObject* would indeed be random), a small modification of the malicious code is sufficient to render it useless. For instance, the boolean masking can be circumvented by executing the sequence

myObject = reference ^ null; and the additive masking by the sequence
myObject = reference + null;. Furthermore, an attack such as presented in
List. 1.4 would not be thwarted. We detail the attacks on [34] in Appendix A.

3.5 Limitations of State-of-the-Art Countermeasures

Table 2 sums up the efficiency of the different countermeasures presented so far
with regards to the attacks introduced in Section 2. Analysing Tab. 1, one can

Table 2. Efficiency of published countermeasures versus the different classes of attack
leading to type confusion

	SA-IFA	SA-IVA	CA-DD	CA-JCACD	CA-JCVMCD
ByteCode Verifier [6]	Yes	Yes, with correct .EXP files	No	No	No
Stack Invariant [27]	No	No	Yes	No	No
Typed Stack [33]	Yes	Yes	No	Partial	Partial
Field Integrity [32]	No	No	Partial	No	No
Typewise Masking [34]	No	No	No	No	No

immediately see that none of the solutions proposed so far can withstand all the
identified attack scenarios. Furthermore, we can see that even a combination of
different countermeasures offers only a partial coverage of the attack paths.

Indeed Tab. 3, showing the behaviours of the state-of-the-art methods with
regards to whether the type confusion is direct (DTC) or indirect (ITC), better
reflects the limitations of the proposed countermeasures.

Again, it is obvious that none of the state-of-the-art countermeasures fully
cover the identified threats, and even combining the different countermeasures,
one does not reach a complete security, particularly because of indirect-type-
confusion-based Combined Attacks. Section 4 introduces two embodiments of a
platform-wide approach to prevent both direct and indirect type confusion.

4 A Platform-Wide Approach to Type Confusion Detection

As we have seen, the main drawback of the different countermeasures presented
so far is that they focus on one particular part of the JCRE. Therefore each
solution fails to detect the type confusion or its exploitation as soon as it occurs
out of the scope of the protected area. In order to detect such flaws, one needs
to propagate the type information within the whole runtime environment.

Table 3. Efficiency of published countermeasures versus the different classes of attack leading to type confusion

	SA-DTC	SA-ITC	CA-DTC	CA-ITC
ByteCode Verifier [6]	Yes	Yes	No	No
Stack Invariant [27]	No	No	Partial	No
Typed Stack [33]	Yes	No	Yes	No
Field Integrity [32]	No	No	No	Partial
Typewise Masking [34]	No	No	No	No

4.1   Random Transformation of Object References

In this section we intend to propose a very memory-efficient method that does not aim at detecting the type confusion itself but rather at preventing an attacker from using integer-to-Object confusion with an overwhelming probability.

Everything Is NOT an Object. As highlighted in Section 2, a particularly attractive capacity endowed by an integer-to-Object type confusion is to use a kind of C-like pointer arithmetic on object references. It is indeed generally easy for an attacker to perform such operations since object references are usually affected linearly, cf. [32]. Therefore once one reference is obtained through the initial type confusion, she can increment/decrement it to access potentially all other object instances.

The base idea of our proposal is that the number of object instantiated on a platform is rather small in practice. Assuming object references are coded on N-bit words, we argue that only a small fraction of these values are actually used. We then have a large number of references that do not point to any object instance.

Definition 1. *Let $\mathcal{M}$ be the set of values returned by the implementation of the bytecode instruction* new *for all created object instances and $\mathcal{N}$ be the set of all possible N-bit reference values.*

According to Def. 1, all values in $\mathcal{N} \backslash \mathcal{M}$ are undefined references. Given that these undefined references should never be used by the JCRE, we can easily imagine that a strong security action is taken whenever an application attempts to access it. The security of our scheme relies on this last statement that the platform does not allow an attacker to repeat access attempts endlessly (i.e. until she meets success) as well as on the order of magnitude between the size of the two sets $\mathcal{N}$ and $\mathcal{M}$.

The Random Transformation Scheme. In order to prevent the attacker from gaining access on the reference allocation mechanism and more precisely on the values of the references, we propose to define a secret random transformation scheme to randomly inject the values of $\mathcal{M}$ in $\mathcal{N}$, such a transformation being specific for each card. Therefore, the probability that the attacker gains access to an unknown reference will be relative to the ratio $\frac{\#\mathcal{M}}{\#\mathcal{N}}$.

The following describes how this can easily be achieved by applying a random affine function to each and every reference[3].

Definition 2. *Let $f : X \to a \cdot X + b \bmod p$, with p the largest prime number such that $p \leq 2^N - 1$ and a and b two random numbers drawn in $[1, p[$.*

Property 1. One should note that f is a bijective function from $\mathbb{F}_p$ to $\mathbb{F}_p$ since $gcd(a, p) = 1$ ensures that $\forall a \in \mathrm{GF}(p)^*, \exists i_a = a^{-1} \bmod p$ such that $f^{-1}(Y) = (Y - b) \cdot i_a \bmod p$.

The following shows that it is possible to use such a function f to randomise object references while preserving the compatibility with all instructions of the standard Java Card instruction set.

Proposition 1. *If*

- *for all created object instance with reference X, the JCRE transforms X into $Y = f(X)$, and*
- *for all manipulated integer value S, the JCRE transforms S into $T = S \oplus c$ (with c a random number drawn in $[1, p[$),*

then every Java Card standard instruction can be executed by reversing the transformation.

Proof. Each instruction of the instruction set manipulates either

a reference: *in this case the JCRE can use $X = (Y - b) \cdot a^{-1} \bmod p$;*
an integer: *in this case the JCRE can use $S = T \oplus c$;*
an untyped: *in this case the JCRE does not need to evaluate the data being manipulated since dup* and pop* instructions only duplicate or discard operands regardless of their type.*
no data: *obviously in this case nothing needs to be done.*

$\square$

Proposition 2. *If*

- *for all created object instance with reference X, the JCRE transforms X into $Y = f(X)$, and*
- *for all manipulated integer value S, the JCRE transforms S into $T = S \oplus c$,*

then the probability P that an attacker setting the reference of an object to an arbitrary value actually sets a valid object reference is as low as:

$$P = \frac{\#\mathcal{M}}{p-1} \tag{1}$$

---

[3] Note however that any bijective function $f : \mathcal{N} \to \mathcal{N}$ would suit our purpose.

even in the case where the attacker is able to read a stored reference through an integer local variable or instance field.

Proof. Let S be the integer value set by the attacker. The JCRE will actually store $T = S \oplus c$, with c a random value unknown from the attacker. Therefore even in the case where S is known to be the image by f of a valid reference, the stored integer T can be considered as a random variable.

Now given a random value $T \in [0, p[$, the probability P that it corresponds to one of the #$\mathcal{M}$ images of function f applied on an existing reference can be straightforwardly computed to obtain the stated result.   □

We assume that short values are used in practice. Therefore, we let $N = 16$ and $p = 65\,521$ in the rest of this section.

Analysis. According to this scheme, an attacker attempting to set the reference of an object would trigger a security action with a certain probability depending on the number of valid references the platform supports. Fig. 2 gives an estimation of the number of valid references depending on the memory available for Java objects and the average size of an object instance on the platform.

We depict in Fig. 3 the success rate of an integer-to-Object confusion depending on the number of valid references. As we can see, an attacker attempting to set the reference of an object would trigger a security action with an overwhelming probability in most practical cases. For instance, the attack detection probability reaches 96.9% if we consider $2\,048$ objects simultaneously instantiated. Provided this security action is sufficiently severe, we can then conclude that the security level ensured by this proposition is satisfying, although only theoretically probabilistic. However, it is only fair to recall that this method detects integer-to-Object type confusions but only randomizes the other-way-round confusion. Yet this latter appears much less concerning from a security point of view.

Now considering the memory footprint penalty, it is excellent since it requires 5 words to be stored only: the three random parameters a, b and c, the value $a^{-1} \bmod p$ and the prime p. Regarding the time penalty, executing the affine function costs one multiplication, one addition and one modular reduction on N-bit words, that is to say 5 clock cycles per f evaluation on components using an efficient assembly language.

Finally, it can be mentioned that unlike the proposal of Girard *et al.* presented in Section 3.4, our scheme does not use the same transformation for integers and references, which prevent it from suffering the same flaws.

4.2   The JCVM Abstract Companion

Section 4.1 has shown an efficient probabilistic way to reflect the type of manipulated data. In a second embodiment of the global approach for type safety, we propose to run together with the JCVM what we call an *Abstract Companion*. The aim of this JCVM Abstract Companion is to duplicate the behaviour of the

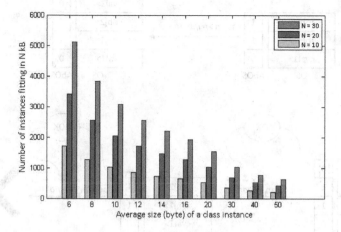

Fig. 2. Number of valid reference depending on available memory and average object instance size on the platform

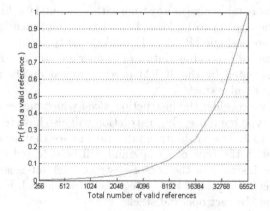

Fig. 3. Success rate of a confusion Vs Number of valid reference on the platform

JCVM but manipulating only boolean values reflecting the type (i.e. whether it is a reference or an integer) of the data simultaneously manipulated by the JCVM, hence the *Abstract* qualifier.

In order to implement this companion, one only needs to take care of three different structures: the operand stack, the local variables table and the instance fields. The modification to apply to the JCVM are detailed hereafter.

The Abstract Operand Stack. The operand stack is the central element of the JCRE. Indeed it is the data structure where all parameters and returned values of the bytecode instructions are pushed-on and popped-out. Concerning the operand stack, the most straightforward and efficient technique to keep track of

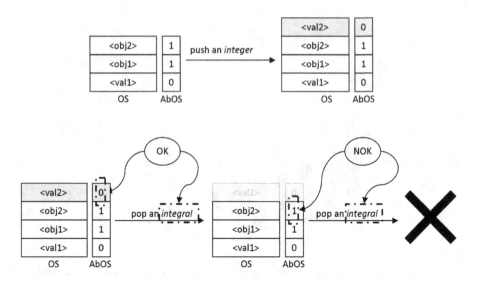

Fig. 4. The abstract stack

the type of the top-of-stack value at any time with a minimal modification of both the JCVM and the applets to be loaded consists in implementing an abstract operand stack where a single bit (0 or 1) reflects the type (integer or reference respectively) of the corresponding data in the operand stack. Consequently, all instructions implemented by the JCVM need to repeat on the abstract stack their action on the regular stack.

For instance, if we consider the instruction *aload* which pushes onto the stack a local variable of type reference, this instruction will also have to set the top-of-abstract-stack bit to 1. Then it is straightforward to see that an operation that is not consistent with the type of an operand will be detected by the abstract operand stack. For instance, if the top-of-abstract-stack bit is set to 1, any instruction operating on a data of type integer will be rejected. Fig. 4 illustrates the principle of the abstract operand stack.

It is worth noticing that the abstract operand stack is fully compliant with all standard instructions, unlike the typed stack proposed in [33] which does not support untyped instructions: *dup**, *pop**. Yet this comes at the price of a superior cost in memory footprint. Our method requires $2^{\lceil log(max\_stack\_size) \rceil}/2^8$ bytes (considering the general case where memory is byte-addressable) whereas the method of Dubreuil *et al.* only requires one additional word (say two bytes) but comes at the price of rewriting all incompatible operations in each and every Java Card applet loaded on the platform.

The Abstract Local Variable Table. Regarding the local variable table, a very similar approach can be used. At first, one can think of assigning each cell a particular type, for instance at the first access to this cell. However, the fact that a single cell of the table may be used to store different local variables in the framework of a single method execution forces us to be less restrictive.

We therefore propose to define a bitwise abstract local variable table that is updated each time a local variable is stored and checked against the type of the bytecode instruction whenever a variable is loaded. For instance, executing the bytecode instruction *sstore_1* will reset bit 1 of the table to 0 and if the bytecode instruction *aload_1* is subsequently executed then an error would be raised since the value 1 would be expected at bit 1 of the abstract local variable table.

Abstract Trusted Instances. Finally, the type of the fields of all objects instantiated on the platform need to be verified. For that purpose, we suggest to define what we call an abstract trusted instance for each class loaded on the platform. This trusted instance can be store in Non-Volatile Memory together with the class definition. Its structure shall be identical to that of future instance of this class, except that each field is represented with one bit set either to 0 or 1 depending on whether the field is of type integer or reference.

As for the previous structure, at runtime, any access to the field of a given class instance should be checked against this class trusted abstract instance and execution should continue only if this check deems successful.

Analysis. The JCVM Abstract Companion is no more than a way of keeping track of the type information all along the execution of an application. Its representation is compact as can be since we use only the bit of information that is necessary to hold the boolean statement saying whether a data is of type reference or not (save the possible space lost due to byte-addressable memory). Furthermore, it appears suitable for any JCVM since it does not rely on any specific implementation choices and we believe that it should not require major modifications for any JCVM's implementation to support it. However, we add to each of the described structure an area of size of the order of $log(S_i)$ bytes,

Table 4. The different classes of attack leading to type confusion

	SA-DTC	SA-ITC	CA-DTC	CA-ITC
ByteCode Verifier [6]	Yes	Yes	No	No
Stack Invariant [27]	No	No	Partial	No
Typed Stack [33]	Yes	No	Yes	No
Field Integrity [32]	No	No	No	Partial
Typewise Masking [34]	No	No	No	No
Random Transformation [§4.1]	Yes with $P \sim 97\%$	Yes with $P \sim 97\%$	Yes with $P \sim 97\%$	Yes with $P \sim 97\%$
Abstract Companion [§4.2]	Yes	Yes	Yes	Yes

with S_i the size of these structures. The cost in terms of memory footprint of this solution is therefore non-negligible.

4.3 Summary

Tab. 4 sums up the results obtained with the proposed method and compares them to the countermeasures presented in Section 3. As we can see both our proposals achieve a better coverage regarding direct and indirect type confusion from integer to reference.

5 Conclusion

In this article, we have pointed out through a comprehensive analysis of the state-of-the-art that several attack paths involving type confusion presented in the literature have never been fully covered. This lack is mainly due to the fact that all proposed countermeasures mainly focused on one specific area, either the operand stack or instance fields. Starting from this point, we have shown that a generic platform-wide approach is possible and we have proposed two particular schemes implementing this approach. The first one, based on a card-specific random transformation, provides a probabilistic security against integer to reference type confusion (also across the whole platform). Nevertheless, it was shown that the probability of success for an attacker is extremely low and that this technique can be implemented at a very low cost. On the other hand, the JCVM Abstract Companion has been shown as a resource-demanding but very effective security mechanism since it is meant to detect each and every type confusion between integers and Objects across the whole platform.

References

1. Witteman, M.: Java Card Security. Information Security Bulletin 8, 291–298 (2003)
2. Mostowski, W., Poll, E.: Malicious Code on Java Card Smartcards: Attacks and Countermeasures. In: Grimaud, G., Standaert, F.-X. (eds.) CARDIS 2008. LNCS, vol. 5189, pp. 1–16. Springer, Heidelberg (2008)
3. Séré, A., Iguchi-Cartigny, J., Lanet, J.L.: Automatic Detection of Fault Attack and Countermeasures. In: Proceedings of the 4th Workshop on Embedded Systems Security, WESS 2009, pp. 1–7 (2009)
4. Hogenboom, J., Mostowski, W.: Full Memory Attack on a Java Card. In: 4th Benelux Workshop on Information and System Security, Louvain-la-Neuve, Belgium (2009)
5. Iguchi-Cartigny, J., Lanet, J.L.: Developing a Trojan Applet in a Smart Card. Journale on Computers and Virology 6, 343–351 (2010)
6. Lindholm, T., Yellin, F.: Java Virtual Machine Spec. 2nd edn. Addison-Wesley, Inc. (1999)
7. Oracle Corp.: Virtual Machine Spec. – Java Card Plateform, Version 3.0.4 Classic Ed. (2011)

8. Oracle Corp.: Application Programming Interface, Java Card Platform, Version 3.0.4 Classic Ed (2011)
9. Oracle Corp.: Runtime Environment Spec. Java Card Platform, Version 3.0.4 Classic Ed. (2011)
10. Sun Microsystems Inc.: Virtual Machine Spec. – Java Card Plateform, Version 3.0.1 Connected Ed. (2009)
11. Sun Microsystems Inc.: Application Programming Interface, Java Card Platform, Version 3.0.1 Connected Ed. (2009)
12. Sun Microsystems Inc.: Java Servlet Spec., Java Card Platform, Version 3.0.1 Connected Ed. (2009)
13. Sun Microsystems Inc.: Runtime Environment Spec., Java Card Platform, Version 3.0.1 Connected Ed. (2009)
14. Barbu, G.: Fault Attacks on Java Card 3 Virtual Machine. In: e-Smart 2009 (2009)
15. Bellcore: New Threat Model Breaks Crypto Codes. Press Release (1996)
16. Boneh, D., De Millo, R.A., Lipton, R.J.: On the Importance of Checking Cryptographic Protocols for Faults. In: Fumy, W. (ed.) EUROCRYPT 1997. LNCS, vol. 1233, pp. 37–51. Springer, Heidelberg (1997)
17. Piret, G., Quisquater, J.-J.: A Differential Fault Attack Technique against SPN Structures, with Application to the AES and KHAZAD. In: Walter, C.D., Koç, Ç.K., Paar, C. (eds.) CHES 2003. LNCS, vol. 2779, pp. 77–88. Springer, Heidelberg (2003)
18. Giraud, C., Thiebeauld, H.: A Survey on Fault Attacks. In: Smart Card Research and Advanced Applications VI – CARDIS 2004, pp. 159–176. Kluwer Academic Publishers (2004)
19. Bar-El, H., Choukri, H., Naccache, D., Tunstall, M., Whelan, C.: The Sorcerer's Apprentice Guide to Fault Attacks. IEEE 94, 370–382 (2006)
20. Vertanen, O.: Java Type Confusion and Fault Attacks. In: Breveglieri, L., Koren, I., Naccache, D., Seifert, J.-P. (eds.) FDTC 2006. LNCS, vol. 4236, pp. 237–251. Springer, Heidelberg (2006)
21. Skorobogatov, S., Anderson, R.: Optical Fault Induction Attack. In: Kaliski Jr., B.S., Koç, Ç.K., Paar, C. (eds.) CHES 2002. LNCS, vol. 2523, pp. 2–12. Springer, Heidelberg (2003)
22. Quisquater, J.J., Samyde, D.: Eddy Current for Magnetic Analysis with Active Sensor. In: e-Smart 2002 (2002)
23. Vetillard, E., Ferrari, A.: Combined Attacks and Countermeasures. In: Gollmann, D., Lanet, J.-L., Iguchi-Cartigny, J. (eds.) CARDIS 2010. LNCS, vol. 6035, pp. 133–147. Springer, Heidelberg (2010)
24. Barbu, G., Thiebeauld, H., Guerin, V.: Attacks on Java Card 3.0 Combining Fault and Logical Attacks. In: Gollmann, D., Lanet, J.-L., Iguchi-Cartigny, J. (eds.) CARDIS 2010. LNCS, vol. 6035, pp. 148–163. Springer, Heidelberg (2010)
25. Bouffard, G., Iguchi-Cartigny, J., Lanet, J.L.: Combined Software and Hardware Attacks on the Java Card Control Flow. In: Prouff, E. (ed.) CARDIS 2011. LNCS, vol. 7079, pp. 283–296. Springer, Heidelberg (2011)
26. Barbu, G., Thiebeauld, H.: Synchronized Attacks on Multithreaded Systems - Application to Java Card 3.0. In: Prouff, E. (ed.) CARDIS 2011. LNCS, vol. 7079, pp. 18–33. Springer, Heidelberg (2011)
27. Barbu, G., Duc, G., Hoogvorst, P.: Java Card Operand Stack: Fault Attacks, Combined Attacks and Countermeasures. In: Prouff, E. (ed.) CARDIS 2011. LNCS, vol. 7079, pp. 297–313. Springer, Heidelberg (2011)

28. Bouffard, G., Lanet, J.-L.: The Next Smart Card Nightmare, Logical Attacks, Combined Attacks, Mutant Applications and Other Funny Things. In: Naccache, D. (ed.) Quisquater Festschrift. LNCS, vol. 6805, pp. 405–424. Springer, Heidelberg (2012)

29. Barbu, G., Hoogvorst, P., Duc, G.: Application-Replay Attack on Java Cards: When the Garbage Collector Gets Confused. In: Barthe, G., Livshits, B., Scandariato, R. (eds.) ESSoS 2012. LNCS, vol. 7159, pp. 1–13. Springer, Heidelberg (2012)

30. Barbu, G.: On the Security of Java Card Platforms against Hardware Attacks. PhD thesis, Télécom ParisTech – Institut Télécom (2012)

31. Govindavajhala, S., Appel, A.: Using Memory Errors to Attack a Virtual Machine. In: IEEE Symposium on Security and Privacy, pp. 154–165. IEEE Computer Society (2003)

32. Lancia, J.: Java Card Combined Attacks with Localization-Agnostic Fault Injection. In: Mangard, S. (ed.) CARDIS 2012. LNCS, vol. 7771, pp. 31–45. Springer, Heidelberg (2013)

33. Dubreuil, J., Bouffard, G., Lanet, J.L., Cartigny, J.: Type classification against fault enabled mutant in java based smart card. In: ARES, pp. 551–556. IEEE Computer Society (2012)

34. Girard, P., Gonzalvo, B.: Making Secure Downloaded Application in Particular in a Smart Card. Publication Number: FR2266222 - US7168625, Gemplus (2003)

A   Attacking Typewise Masking

In Section 3.4, we claim that the typewise masking can be easily circumvented by a slight modification of the malicious application involved. In the following we detail the execution of the initial and modified malicious line of code for both the additive and boolean masking schemes, together with the evolution of the content of the operand stack. We refer to the object type and integer type masks as M_A and M_I respectively.

Additive Masking.

Initial malicious code: `myObject = reference;`

Executed Bytecode	*Operand Stack*
`iload <reference>`	$[reference + M_I]$
`astore <myObject>`	$[-]$

Consequently, the value stored in `myObject` is actually set to the random value: $reference + M_I - M_A$ and the attack is either thwarted or detected.

Modified malicious code: `myObject = reference + null;`

Executed Bytecode	*Operand Stack*
`aconst_null`	$[0 + M_A]$
`iload <reference>`	$[M_A, reference + M_I]$
`iadd`	$[((M_A - M_I) + ((reference + M_I) - M_I)) + M_I]$
	$[M_A + reference]$
`astore <myObject>`	$[-]$

Consequently, the value stored in myObject is actually set to the targeted value: *reference* and the attacker can carry on.

Boolean Masking.

Initial malicious code: myObject = reference;

Executed Bytecode	Operand Stack
iload <reference>	$[reference \oplus M_I]$
astore <myObject>	$[-]$

Consequently, the value stored in myObject is actually set to the random value: $reference \oplus M_I \oplus M_A$ and the attack is either thwarted or detected.

Modified malicious code: myObject = reference ^ null;

Executed Bytecode	Operand Stack
aconst_null	$[0 \oplus M_A]$
iload <reference>	$[M_A, reference \oplus M_I]$
ixor	$[((M_A \oplus M_I) \oplus ((reference \oplus M_I) \oplus M_I)) \oplus M_I]$ $[M_A \oplus reference]$
astore <myObject>	$[-]$

Again, the value stored in myObject is actually set to the targeted value: *reference* and the attacker can carry on.

A Pre-processing Composition
for Secret Key Recovery on Android Smartphone

Yuto Nakano[1], Youssef Souissi[2], Robert Nguyen[2], Laurent Sauvage[2],
Jean-Luc Danger[2], Sylvain Guilley[2], Shinsaku Kiyomoto[1], and Yutaka Miyake[1]

[1] KDDI R&D Laboratories Inc.
2-1-15 Ohara, Fujimino, Saitama 356-8502, Japan
{yuto,kiyomoto,miyake}@kddilabs.jp
[2] Secure-IC S.A.S.
37-39, rue Dareau 75014 Paris, France
{youssef.souissi,robert.nguyen,laurent.sauvage,
jean-luc.danger,sylvain.guilley}@secure-ic.com

Abstract. Simple Side-Channel Analyses (SSCA) are known as techniques to uncover a cryptographic secret from one single spied waveform.
Up to now, these very powerful attacks have been illustrated on simple
devices which leakage was obvious. On more advanced targets, such as
high-end processors of smartphones, a simple visual analysis of the waveforms might not be sufficient to read the secret at once. In this paper, we
detail and explain how a composition of time-frequency pre-processings
manages to extract the relevant information from one signal capture of
an asymmetric cryptographic operation (RSA and ECC) running on an
Android system. The lesson is that side-channel countermeasures must
be applied even on advanced platforms such as smartphones to prevent
secret information theft through the electromagnetic (EM) waveforms.

Keywords: Simple Side-channel Attack, Time-frequency Pre-processing,
Asymmetric Cryptography, RSA, ECC, Android smartphone.

1 Introduction

Side-channel attacks (SCA) are becoming more and more serious threats to secure systems as the latter can be broken even if the underlying cryptographic
algorithms are mathematically secure. In fact, these non-invasive attacks consist in exploiting the physical properties (e.g. electromagnetic, power, acoustic
or time leakage) of a device when running some cryptographic process, in order to recover a sensitive information. The idea of power consumption based
SCA was first introduced by Kocher [16]. Then, other side-channels have been
exploited such as electromagnetic (EM) emanations [10], which are a more powerful source of leakage and can be performed without a physical contact to the
device. Basically, SCA can be classified into *advanced* and *simple* attacks. Advanced SCA require a lot of waveforms to be statistically analysed. In some
recent scientific papers (*e.g.* [3]), this kind of SCA is also called *vertical* attack

D. Naccache and D. Sauveron (Eds.): WISTP 2014, LNCS 8501, pp. 76–91, 2014.
© IFIP International Federation for Information Processing 2014

as the analysis focuses on the statistical behaviour of one (or some) time samples over many acquired waveforms. In spite of their effectiveness, in some real world situations, advanced SCA might not be applicable. As a matter of fact, the acquisition of many waveforms for the analysis is not possible because of the physical protections and software limitations (*e.g.* filters, sensors, number of trials to enter a password, etc) made to protect the target device. Besides, for some cryptographic RSA or ECC based protocols (*e.g.* key session generation like DH, RSA and ECDH protocols; or digital signature like ECDSA) or some protected implementations, the secret is generated only once. Thus, the attack must deal with only one single waveform. For this purpose, Simple SCA (SSCA) have been developed to work on such restrictive situations. SSCA are also called *horizontal* attacks as they exploit the information provided by the whole time samples within the waveform. Basically, the SSCA is usually performed over the time domain [25,4,14,8,16]. The frequency domain can be used to perform a noise-filter as a first step in the analysis in order to identify the secret patterns in the time domain as a second step. In the same context, it is shown that vertical SCA can be applied separately over each domain. As a matter of fact, Aboulkassimi et al. [1] proposed two different vertical SCA on PDA mobile device: the first attack, called Spectral Density Approach (SDA), aims at performing a vertical attack (correlation analysis) based on the power spectrum density representation (*i.e.* frequency domain) to overcome the problem of waveforms misalignment; and the second attack, called Template Resynchronisation Approach (TRA), consists in performing a correlation vertical attack over the time domain after resynchronising the waveforms.

From the signal processing theory viewpoint, the information content is the same in both domains, but its representation is not. This has a special flavour for side-channel analysis. In fact, the combination of both domains (*i.e.* time-frequency analysis) should provide better description of the secret leakage. More importantly, signal processing theory has provided us with powerful tools that can be used for this purpose, like the Short-Time Fourier Transform (STFT or spectrogram) and wavelet transforms. However, despite their great efficiency, the usage of these tools is not democratised for SCA. To our best knowledge, in the general context of SCA, very few scientific papers and reports [24] [11] [12] [22] have analysed the side-channel leakage from its time-frequency representation: in [24], Vuagnoux proposed to spy the electromagnetic (EM) activity of computer keyboards based on independent pre-processings. In fact, they used the STFT just as first and independent step to visualise the overall EM activity. The extraction of the secret itself is performed thanks to another tool that is a frequency filter applied directly on the non-noisy baseband waveforms. In addition to this, an anechoic room is used to obtain a good success rate. The time-frequency side-channel analysis has been also addressed by Gebotys et al. in [11]. They proposed a vertical attack, called DSA, on an AES-192bit (Advanced Encryption Standard) and ECC-192bit implementation-based PDA mobile device. Technically, the attack is mainly based on the computed spectrograms of acquired waveforms. However, a lot of EM waveforms (around 1100) are necessary to recover the secret key. Similarly to [1], the main idea behind DSA is to get round the problem of misaligned waveforms. In [12], Genkin et al. have recently proposed an improved acoustic SCA on RSA-4096bit implementation, based on the spectrograms of acoustic leakages, emitted at very low frequencies. It is noteworthy that the proposed attack requires many acoustic waveforms, based on chosen ciphertexts, and follows several steps (*e.g.* waveforms classification, etc) to recover the RSA secret key. Besides, Souissi et al. in [22], have described several side-channel applications (vertical and horizontal SCA) based only on wavelet transforms. However, they briefly showed the power of such tool in SSCA context. Note that, in our paper, we will focus on the merits of Short-Time Fourier transform that is faster and easier to compute than wavelet transform.

Our Contributions. In this paper, our contributions are four-fold:

1. We propose a composition of a time-frequency SSCA to localise and characterise the secret leakage. By contrast to [11] [1], the proposed attack is **horizontal** and requires only **one single** EM measurement to recover the whole secret. Such attack is suitable for real implementations of asymmetric cryptography.
2. We show how classic SSCA, like Wiener and average mobile filtering, are unable to localise the secret patterns within a sample RSA waveform.
3. We perform the proposed SSCA on a modern device that is an Android smartphone clocked at 832 MHz. In this context, some publications pointed out the possibilities of SCA on smartphones and PDAs [11] [1] [15]. Kenworthy and Rohatgi [15] analysed side-channel vulnerabilities of RSA-Chinese Remainder Theorem (CRT) and elliptic curve point multiplication. They showed that the private key of both cryptosystems can be recovered from a single EM waveform using a specific equipment. Actually, an Icom IC-R7000 VHF-UHF receiver is used to demodulate the baseband waveform. The main issue, not addressed by the authors, is the way to find out the most appropriate frequency bandwidth related to the secret leakage. Moreover, note that this characterisation requires many measurements. On the other hand, the method we propose, instantaneously provides such characterisation, using software pre-processing on a single baseband (or raw) waveform. Our approach is more flexible as it is not limited by the range of frequencies to analyse that is necessary to be verified by the features of the demodulator equipment. Obviously, it is a real challenge to deal with such modern devices. Indeed, in the literature, we found that some studies (*e.g.* [26]) failed to mount a complete SSCA on smartphones.
4. We target asymmetric cryptographic algorithms. Indeed, we show how to break the security of basic RSA and ECC-based Android applications. More importantly, we note that we did not target home made applications. In fact, the targets are the cryptographic functions provided by JCE the default library of Android that is the most commonly used by the developers community.

2   A Pre-processing Composition for Secret Recovery

2.1   SSCA Types and Tools: Overview

In the literature, SSCA come basically with four types of analysis according to the implementation difficulty level, the used tools and the noise nature. Before going further, it is noteworthy that two kinds of noise can be considered: the measurement noise that is caused by surrounded electronic components and external environment; and the algorithmic noise that is generated by the whole activity of the target circuit except of course the one that is related to the secret. Now, the four types of SSCA can be described as follows:

1. *SSCA First Type*: it is the simplest one as it is based only on a visual detection of the secret patterns. Such type of analysis is possible only when the useful information is not perturbed by the noise [16]. It is generally applied on fully controlled platforms often used for demonstration or academic purposes.

2. *SSCA Second Type*: it involves the usage of pre-processing tools. This SSCA basically deals with the measurement noise in order to make easier the visual detection of secret patterns. In the real world (*i.e.* when performing the attack on real devices), acquired waveform is usually noisy. Hence, pre-processing is essential. We note that the core idea behind this paper mainly turns around this type of SSCA. In what follows, we list commonly used techniques:
   - Frequency filtering (High & Low pass filters),
   - Time linear & non-linear filtering (e.g. Wiener or Kalman filtering [23]),
   - High order statistics [17],
   - Threshold-based Wavelets transforms [7] [22].

   Generally, when acquired EM waveforms are very noisy, the extraction of the secret key is a challenging task as the sensitive leakage is not properly localised. Indeed, in such situation, those techniques usually fail to recover the secret.

3. *SSCA Third Type*: it statistically analyses (*e.g.* linear correlation, time samples combination, collision analysis, etc) the whole time information within the waveform in order to extract the secret [4] [14] [8]. Such SSCA type is useful to efficiently target some protected implementations like blinding RSA.

4. *SSCA Fourth Type*: it combines both pre-processing and statistical analysis. These SSCA are generally used to deal with noisy and protected real world implementations.

2.2   Theoretical Background: DFT, STFT and Noise-Filtering

In this section, we recall some theoretical definitions and basics necessary to properly understand the proposed attack. From the signal processing viewpoint, the acquired EM waveform can be represented as a sequence of N discrete time samples. We denote by $\{y[0], y[1], ..., y[N-1]\}$ such sequence. Hence, the discrete Fourier transform (DFT) returns N frequency components that can be written as follows (Eq.1):

$$Y[k] = \sum_{n=0}^{N-1} y[n] \, \omega_N^{kn}, \tag{1}$$

where $\omega_N = e^{-j\frac{2\pi}{N}} = \cos(\frac{2\pi}{N}) - j\sin(\frac{2\pi}{N})$ and $k = \{0, 1, ..., N-1\}$ is the frequency index. For the sake of clarity, the DFT can be represented in a matrix form such that (Eq.2):

$$\begin{bmatrix} Y[0] \\ Y[1] \\ Y[2] \\ \vdots \\ Y[k] \end{bmatrix} = \begin{bmatrix} 1 & 1 & 1 & \cdots & 1 \\ 1 & \omega_N^1 & \omega_N^2 & \cdots & \omega_N^{(N-1)} \\ 1 & \omega_N^2 & \omega_N^4 & \cdots & \omega_N^{2(N-1)} \\ \vdots & \vdots & \vdots & \ddots & \vdots \\ 1 & \omega_N^{(N-1)} & \omega_N^{2(N-1)} & \cdots & \omega_N^{(N-1)^2} \end{bmatrix} \times \begin{bmatrix} y[0] \\ y[1] \\ y[2] \\ \vdots \\ y[k] \end{bmatrix}. \tag{2}$$

According to Eq.2, the DFT allows us to characterise the periodicity of elementary activities within the analysed sequence. Indeed, from the SSCA point of view, the idea being that the waveform is exhaustively compared to different sinusoidal waves. In practice, DFT can be very useful in telling us about the number of most significant patterns in the EM waveform. However, the DFT is not able to detect time varying activities as it provides an averaged value of the frequency over the whole time samples in the sequence. For this purpose, the Short-Time Fourier Transform (STFT) proposes to apply the DFT over a windowed version of the sequence. Indeed, the sequence is segmented into successive time intervals (windows) of fixed length $L \leq N$. Then, the DFT is computed over each window. This way the frequency information is time-localised. Consequently, the STFT can be expressed as follows:

$$Y[k, t_0] = \sum_{n=0}^{L-1} y[t_0 + n] \cdot s[n] \cdot e^{-j\frac{2\pi kn}{L}}, \tag{3}$$

where, k is the frequency index, s is the sliding window and t_0 is the time reference index related to s. It is noteworthy that, the window size determines the time and frequency resolution. As the window size is fixed, a good frequency resolution is obtained to the detriment of a good time resolution, especially when the used window is large. In practice, we slide the window by one time sample to enhance the time resolution. Eventually, the STFT can be seen as a two-dimensional representation showing the information over both, the time and the frequency scales. This way, the STFT allows differentiating the elementary activities of the target component. This means that the STFT is able to deal with the algorithmic noise.

Now, in order to deal with the measurement noise, any basic noise-filtering (*e.g.* mobile average smoother, Wiener filter, Kalman filter, low pass filter, linear regression, etc) can be used. In our attack, we use the simplest noise-filter that is the mobile average. Let l be the window size of such filter. Thus the filter simply consists in computing the arithmetic mean of all subsequent time intervals, each of length l.

2.3 Composition Scheme and Steps

Based on the previous definitions, we introduce our proposed SSCA tool that performs the analysis based on a composition scheme. We remind the reader that our attack requires only one single EM waveform. Basically, as shown in Fig. 1, the composition scheme is composed of 3 chained pre-processing blocks:

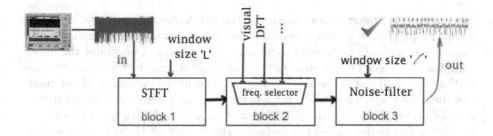

Fig. 1. An illustration of the pre-processing composition scheme

1. **Block 1: Time-Frequency Localisation.** The first step consists in computing the STFT over the baseband waveform. In the SSCA context, the usage of this tool is justified for multiple reasons:
   - The sliding STFT allows the analysis to keep the **time** component of the signal. As the SSCA is based on demarcation of the sequential pattern, the study of time is mandatory.
   - The **frequency** component created by STFT allows the analysis to forge a local frequency signature. This signature is very relevant as the processes are always performed in a circular manner, with periodic loops. This is true at both application level, especially in cryptography, or at implementation level, especially in software. Inside a loop the activity pattern is specific, hence allowing to discriminate the pattern for SSCA. This way, as stated before, the algorithmic noise would be properly analysed.
2. **Block 2: Frequency Bandwidth Selection.** The second step aims at selecting the frequency area of interest, where the secret leakage exists. This can be performed through a simple visual analysis, especially when the internal activities had been efficiently decorrelated by the STFT. Alternatively, advanced techniques like DFT, clustering or probability density estimation can be used. The idea being that we should able to start characterising the secret patterns (*e.g.* periodicity, frequency, classes, shape, etc).
3. **Block 3: Noise-Filtering.** The third step, definitely removes the measurement noise. Therefore, the full characterisation of the secret patterns becomes an easy task.

3 Real Case Study: RSA / ECC Key Recovery on Android Smartphone

3.1 SSCA on Android Environment: Key Points

In the following, we discuss the key points to properly mount an SSCA on Android smartphone: first, we describe the measurement requirements to properly access the Android smartphone; second we tackle the most important difficulties which arise when targeting such device; and third we outline the possible software modifications of the Android system that might be performed by an attacker to enhance his malicious analysis.

Access to the Smartphone. Basically, the SSCA measurement bench is composed of a PC-Target system (or client-server system) and a measurement device (an oscilloscope and an antenna) to record EM waveforms. Concerning the minimum features needed in the oscilloscope, four points should be taken into consideration: the sampling frequency, the memory depth, the placement of antennas and the trigger which provides a reference timing point necessary to synchronise waveforms. Most of recent smartphones are equipped with high speed processors to offer higher performance. For instance, the default CPU clock frequency of the handset we use is set to 832 MHz. This means we need an oscilloscope which is capable to sample at least 3 Gsample/s (i.e., 3×10^9 samples per seconds) in order to get an acceptable EM measurement for SSCA. Additionally, note that increasing the sampling frequency might create a problem with a memory depth. Besides, the attacker is also conducted to identify which type of antenna should be used and how to place it. In practice, the localisation of the secret leakage can be simply performed by sweeping the antenna all over the backside of the smartphone. The most appropriate location can be precisely recovered by performing an EM cartography. The EM cartography consists of two steps: observing the EM field while sweeping the antenna over the device and then mapping the EM level to each position. The higher the EM level is in the cartography, the more the leakage is at the corresponding position.

Now, we consider the last important factor: the trigger signal which is necessary to identify the start/end of the target process. This also allows aligning acquired EM traces. Regarding SSCA, as only a single waveform is required for the analysis, the trigger is less critical than for vertical SCA that require perfectly aligned waveforms. In our study, we will show how the first block in the proposed composition scheme (*i.e.* the STFT) can be an efficient solution for triggering. In the case of smartphones, the existing problem relies on the way the trigger is generated. Unlike testing boards (*e.g.* the SCA-Standard Evaluation Board (SASEBO) [21]), smartphones do not have I/O ports for sending/receiving control signals. Aboulkassimi et al. [1] proposed to generate a pulse trigger based on read/write queries sent to the SD card system. In our experiments we realised that such method is fast and efficient to localise in time the target cryptographic process. Moreover, we tested another solution which is less invasive and easier to mount in real world attack situations. In fact, it consists in spying in real time the activity of running processes, and activating a serial trigger (through the USB connector) only when the target application is called by the system. More precisely, when the flag associated with the target application is written in the Android log file system that can be checked using Android ADB tool [2].

Factors That Can Make SSCA Difficult

1. **Just in Time Compiler**
   The Just In Time Compile (JIT) aims to compile on-the-fly the Android bytecode into native machine instructions. This significantly enhances the performance of the Dalvik Virtual Machine that is in charge of executing Android applications. From the side-channel point of view, the activity of the JIT compiler might slightly influence the analysis as reported by Aboulkassimi et al. in [1]. In practice, the impact of the JIT can be seen through the first executions of an iterative process. For instance, in the case of a basic RSA process, the JIT activity may impact the first patterns related to the secret key bits manipulation. As only the first patterns are affected, this does not harm the overall efficiency of the SCA. Besides, even if some few secret bits are guessed incorrectly, some techniques [5] allows recovering the entire secret key.

2. **Garbage Collector**
   The Garbage Collector (GC) can be defined as the process in charge of cleaning the memory (e.g. heap) by deleting unused Java objects. It is basically activated at random times by the processor when running user or Android system applications. This might create a problem for SSCA as it is not trivial to deal with the undesired activity generated by the GC. The GC is normally deactivated during the execution of native elementary processes. For instance, we observed that OpenSSL native cryptographic library is never perturbed by the GC. This is not the case for pure non-native libraries. However, in this case, when the GC is called, it is still easy to characterise its activity and remove it especially when the EM antenna or probe is properly placed. During our experiments, we also noticed that when using hybrid libraries[1] the GC might be called by the system, but will never impact (or interrupt) the native calls.

3. **Multi-core Processor.** In order to provide higher performances for users, handsets with multi-core processors are now the mainstream of smartphones. Unlike the single-core processors, multi-core processors distribute tasks to other existing cores so that they can be efficiently completed. In fact, during the cryptographic operation, the process might be moved from one core to another due to system interruptions. It might be also executed in parallel by several cores for the sake of performance. Therefore, this might rise EM acquisition problems. In practice, to deal with issue, one may acquire the

---

[1] A hybrid library, like the JCE default Android library, is basically designed with a non-native language that makes recurrent calls to native primitives, like for instance to the modular arithmetic functions of OpenSSL.

waveforms as following two ways: either try to stay focused on the core executing the targeted implementation by placing a tiny antenna over the right decoupling capacitor; or capture the whole activity with a single and large antenna placed over the target processor. In our case, this did not impact our analysis as we targeted a mono-core processor based smartphone.

Software Modifications for Better EM Acquisition

1. **Under-Clocking the CPU.** The higher the CPU clock frequency is, the higher the resolution of the oscilloscope is required. In case that the clock frequency is too high and the oscilloscope is unable to acquire enough samples to cover the necessary leakage, the attacker can decrease the CPU clock frequency for a better acquisition. Basically, lowering clock frequency is not always necessary. In fact, in our experiments we kept the original CPU clock frequency of 832 MHz.
2. **Lowering Radio Emission.** When many applications are running on the Android smartphone, in particular that ones which are responsible for ensuring radio and cell communications, the noise generated might have a considerable impact on the effectiveness of SSCA. In such situation, the attacker may reduce the level of noise by turning on the airplane mode available on most smartphones. We note that, in our experiments we show how our SSCA is still efficient even if the airplane mode is turned off.

3.2   Target Cryptographic Android Implementations

There are several cryptographic libraries compatible with the Android environment such as Java Crypto Extension (JCE) [19], OpenSSL [18], Bouncy Castle [6], Crypto++ [9], RELIC [20] and so on.

At first we intended to exhaustively evaluate the security of all libraries when RSA and ECC are being executed. Then we realised that most of libraries, particularly the non-native ones, are mainly based on the same low level native primitives to perform arithmetic calculations on big integers, necessary for asymmetric cryptography. This can be verified by checking the source code of libraries or more easily by analysing the real time processor activity through the debugging Trace View Android tool [13]. We note that the comparison of these libraries is out of the scope of this paper.

Now, for the sake of generality and clarity, we will focus only on the most commonly used library that is the default JCE Android library. Actually, JCE provides the essential cryptographic primitives to manage security within an application. Its basic API packages are *java.math*, *javax.crypto* and *java.security*. Note that these APIs call the arithmetic primitives of the *OpenSSL* native library, such as modular squaring and multiplying, that have been already ported to Android system. Moreover, these APIs include a lightweight version of *Bouncy Castle* library that provides ready high level functions to execute, for instance, an elliptic curve point multiplication.

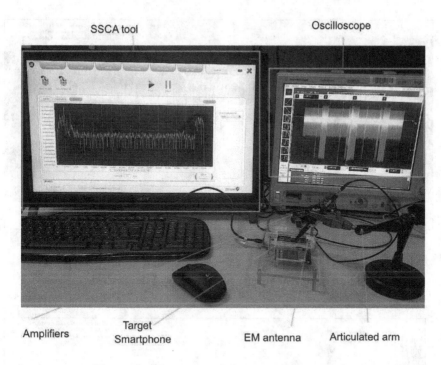

Fig. 2. An illustration of the measurement bench

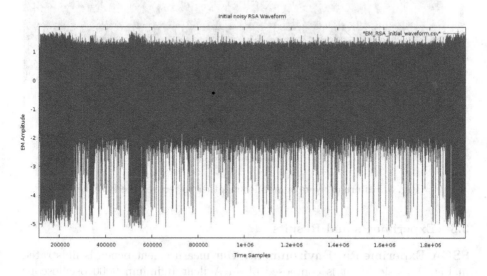

Fig. 3. Initial noisy RSA EM waveform

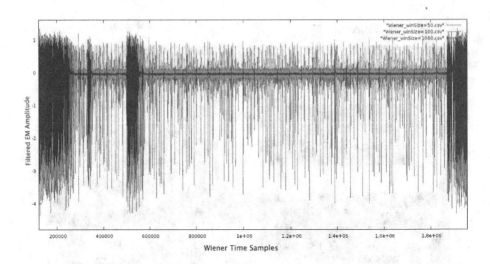

Fig. 4. Failure of Wiener filter to recover the RSA key

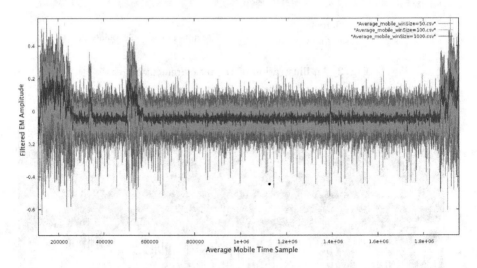

Fig. 5. Failure of average mobile smoother to recover the RSA key

3.3   Experiments and Results

SSCA Experimental Environment. Our measurement bench is illustrated in Fig. 2. Basically, it is composed of an Agilent Infiniium 9000 oscilloscope with a bandwidth of 2.5 GHz, a maximal memory depth of 123 mega samples, a maximal sample rate of 20 giga samples per seconds; antenna of the HZ-15 kit from Rohde & Schwarz and a 30 dB amplifier.

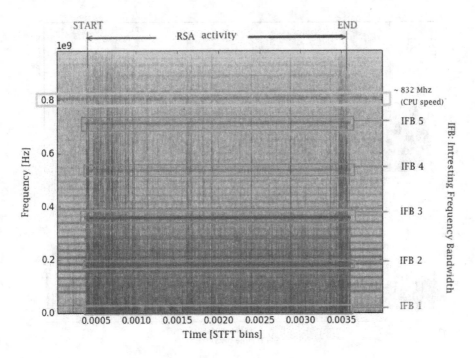

Fig. 6. STFT based 2D-localisation of the RSA activity

The communication between our SSCA tool, referred to as *Smart-SIC Analyzer*[2], and the smartphone is ensured by the TCP/IP protocol. Note that the attack can be performed over different ways of communication (i.e. USB, Wifi, etc).

RSA Key Recovery. The targeted RSA implementation is the right-to-left binary exponentiation variant: the sequence of operations (*i.e.* multiply and square) are dependent on the private key. Therefore, from the SSCA viewpoint, the idea being that we could identify the multiply-square pattern when the corresponding bit of the private key is '1', and only square pattern when the corresponding bit of the key is '0'. The RSA baseband waveform as it is acquired by the oscilloscope is shown in Fig. 3. We note that for the sake of clarity, in this example we have chosen a small RSA key that is 0xAF0AE3 (hexadecimal form). Clearly, the RSA activity is totally hidden by the noise, which makes classic SSCA inefficient. Indeed, in our experiments, we tested the most commonly used techniques (Wiener filtering and Average mobile smoothing) to extract the useful leakage from such noisy waveform. The results are illustrated by Fig. 4 and Fig. 5. We exhaustively tested many window sizes (*i.e.* the input parameter *l*). For the sake of convenience only the results for window sizes 50, 100 and 1000 are shown in both figures. Obviously, the localisation of the secret patterns is

---

[2] http://secure-ic.com/smart-sic-analyzer

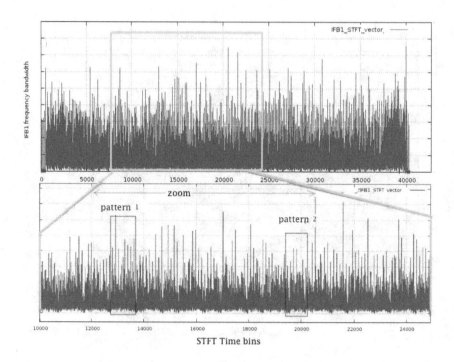

Fig. 7. IFB1 vector when extracted from the STFT matrix

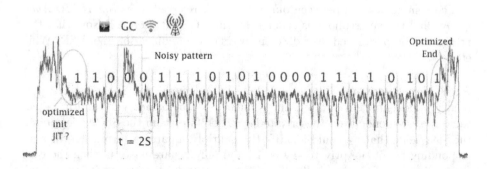

Fig. 8. Key recovery of RSA right-to-left binary exponentiation

not possible when applying these techniques directly on the baseband waveform. Indeed, these techniques are usually used to remove only the measurement (or Gaussian) noise which is not sufficient in our case, as we should deal also with the algorithmic noise. In what follows, we will show the efficiency of our proposed method when applied on the same EM waveform. The Fig. 6 is an illustration of the STFT when applied on the RSA baseband waveform. Three important points can be directly deduced from this representation:

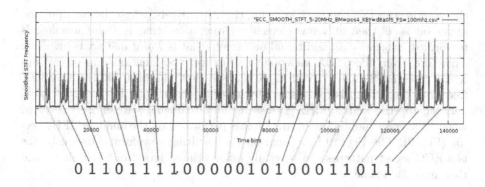

Fig. 9. An illustration of smoothed ECC activity

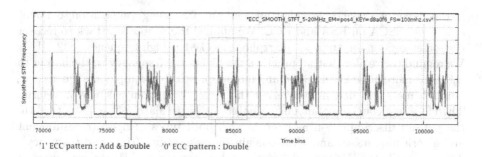

Fig. 10. Zoom on smoothed ECC activity

- The time-localisation of the RSA activity (start/end time identification).
- The recovery of the CPU activity around 832 MHz.
- The frequency-localisation of five interesting activities (i.e. the most leaking sources) located into different frequency bandwidths, termed by Interesting Frequency Bandwidth (IFB) in the figure. Numerically, IFBs are float vectors that can be extracted from the STFT matrix to be analysed.

After having visually analysed the five IFB vectors, we noticed that IFB1 vector ([10 MHz–40 MHz]) is likely to reveal the secret RSA patterns. The extracted IFB1 vector is illustrated by Fig. 7. Interestingly, it is possible to identify a very noisy sequence of patterns located in the same time interval of the RSA process. More precisely, two forms of patterns can be revealed and that are likely to be related to the activity of Square and Multiply RSA operations. Now when applying a basic smoother, like the mobile average smoothing filter, the secret RSA patterns are clearly identified as shown in Fig. 8. Besides, we noticed the presence of some noisy patterns, which are likely to be caused by the JIT or the cellular communications.

ECC Key Recovery. Our target here is a basic ECC implementation, more precisely its elliptic curve point multiplication operation. The challenge is to characterise the ECC activity knowing that, iteratively, when the manipulated secret bit is '0' then only one elementary operation, that is *Point doubling* is performed; otherwise an additional operation, that is *Point adding*, is involved. Therefore, from the SSCA viewpoint one expect the identification of two different patterns. Similarly to RSA, we realised that, the most interesting STFT frequency bandwidth is represented by lower frequencies (IFB1 vector) located between 10 MHz and 20 MHz. The secret bits (0xD8A0F6) are entirely revealed when an average mobile smoothing filter is performed on the analysed IFB1 vector (Fig. 9). The Fig. 10 is a zoom on the resulting waveform. Obviously, the two ECC secret patterns can be easily differentiated based on their shape and their execution time.

4   Conclusion and Perspectives

In this paper, we have proposed an efficient pre-processing composition to mount a powerful SSCA on RSA and ECC. We applied the proposed attack to recover the secret keys on an Android smartphone clocked at high frequency (832 MHz). We remind the reader that, in practice, the higher the frequency is, the harder to attack as more noise is generated and more sophisticated equipments are needed. Our scheme succeeded in recovering the secret keys from a single waveform. Therefore, we conclude that our technique is particularly efficient to perform the pattern discrimination as it deals with both types of noise (measurement and algorithmic noise) and both domain representations (time and frequency). The proposed attack is applied directly on baseband traces. Hence, we expect to further enhance our analysis with a Software-Defined Radio (SDR) demodulator. Future work will be applying our attack to the devices with the CPUs of higher frequency and multi cores.

References

1. Aboulkassimi, D., Agoyan, M., Freund, L., Fournier, J., Robisson, B., Tria, A.: ElectroMagnetic analysis (EMA) of software AES on Java mobile phones. In: WIFS, pp. 1–6. IEEE (2011)
2. Android Debug Bridge, http://developer.android.com/tools/help/adb.html
3. Bauer, A., Jaulmes, E., Prouff, E., Wild, J.: Horizontal and vertical side-channel attacks against secure RSA implementations. In: Dawson, E. (ed.) CT-RSA 2013. LNCS, vol. 7779, pp. 1–17. Springer, Heidelberg (2013)
4. Bauer, A., Prouff, E., Jaulmes, É., Wild, J.: Horizontal Collision Correlation Attack on Elliptic Curves. In: Lange, T., Lauter, K., Lisoněk, P. (eds.) SAC. LNCS, vol. 8282. Springer, Heidelberg (2014)
5. Boneh, D., Durfee, G., Frankel, Y.: An Attack on RSA Given a Small Fraction of the Private Key Bits. In: Ohta, K., Pei, D. (eds.) ASIACRYPT 1998. LNCS, vol. 1514, pp. 25–34. Springer, Heidelberg (1998)
6. Bouncy Castle project. Bouncy Castle Crypto APIs, http://www.bouncycastle.org/documentation.html

7. Charvet, X., Pelletier, H.: Improving the DPA Attack using Wavelet Transform. In: Physical Security Testing Workshop, http://csrc.nist.gov/groups/STM/cmvp/documents/fips140-3/physec/papers/physecpaper14.pdf

8. Clavier, C., Feix, B., Gagnerot, G., Roussellet, M., Verneuil, V.: Horizontal correlation analysis on exponentiation. IACR Cryptology ePrint Archive, Report 2010/394 (2010), http://eprint.iacr.org/2010/394

9. Crypto++ Library, http://www.cryptopp.com/

10. Gandolfi, K., Mourtel, C., Olivier, F.: Electromagnetic analysis: Concrete results. In: Koç, Ç.K., Naccache, D., Paar, C. (eds.) CHES 2001. LNCS, vol. 2162, pp. 251–261. Springer, Heidelberg (2001)

11. Gebotys, C.H., Ho, S., Tiu, C.C.: EM Analysis of Rijndael and ECC on a Wireless Java-Based PDA. In: Rao, J.R., Sunar, B. (eds.) CHES 2005. LNCS, vol. 3659, pp. 250–264. Springer, Heidelberg (2005)

12. Genkin, D., Shamir, A., Tromer, E.: RSA key extraction via low-bandwidth acoustic cryptanalysis. Cryptology ePrint Archive, Report 2013/857 (2013)

13. Google Inc. Profiling with Traceview and dmtracedump, http://developer.android.com/tools/debugging/debugging-tracing.html

14. Heyszl, J., Ibing, A., Mangard, S., Santis, F.D., Sigl, G.: Clustering Algorithms for Non-Profiled Single-Execution Attacks on Exponentiations. IACR Cryptology ePrint Archive, Report 2013/438 (2013), http://eprint.iacr.org/2013/438

15. Kenworthy, G., Rohatgi, P.: Mobile Device Security: The case for side channel resistance, http://mostconf.org/2012/papers/21.pdf

16. Kocher, P.C., Jaffe, J., Jun, B.: Differential Power Analysis. In: Wiener, M. (ed.) CRYPTO 1999. LNCS, vol. 1666, pp. 388–397. Springer, Heidelberg (1999)

17. Le, T.H., Clédiere, J., Serviere, C., Lacoume, J.L.: Noise Reduction in Side Channel Attack Using Fourth-Order Cumulant. IEEE Transactions on Information Forensics and Security (4), 710–720

18. OpenSSL Project. OpenSSL library documentation, http://www.openssl.org/related/binaries.html

19. Oracle Corporation. JAVA JCE documentation, http://docs.oracle.com/javase/6/docs/technotes/guides/security/crypto/CryptoSpec.html

20. RELIC library (UNICAMP), https://code.google.com/p/relic-toolkit/

21. Research Center for Information Security (RCIS). Side-channel Attack Standard Evaluation Board (SASEBO), http://www.rcis.aist.go.jp/special/SASEBO/index-en.html

22. Souissi, Y., Aabid, A.E., Debande, N., Guilley, S., Danger, J.-L.: Novel Applications of Wavelet Transforms based Side-Channel Analysis. Non-Invasive Attack Testing Workshop (2011), http://csrc.nist.gov/news_events/non-invasive-attack-testing-workshop/papers/01_Souissi.pdf

23. Souissi, Y., Guilley, S., Danger, J.-L., Mekki, S., Duc, G.: Improvement of power analysis attacks using Kalman filter. In: ICASSP, pp. 1778–1781. IEEE (2010)

24. Vuagnoux, M., Pasini, S.: Compromising electromagnetic emanations of wired and wireless keyboards. In: Proceedings of the 18th Conference on USENIX Security Symposium, SSYM 2009, Berkeley, CA, USA, pp. 1–16. USENIX Association (2009)

25. Walter, C.D.: Sliding Windows Succumbs to Big Mac Attack. In: Koç, Ç.K., Naccache, D., Paar, C. (eds.) CHES 2001. LNCS, vol. 2162, pp. 286–299. Springer, Heidelberg (2001)

26. Zenger, C., Paar, C., Lemke-Rust, K., Kasper, T., Oswald, D.: SEMA of RSA on a Smartphone. B.Sc. (from March 01, 2011 to October 17, 2011) report, http://www.yumpu.com/en/document/view/19636241/sema-of-rsa-on-a-smartphone

Usable Privacy for Mobile Sensing Applications

Delphine Christin[1,2], Franziska Engelmann[3], and Matthias Hollick[3]

[1] University of Bonn, Friedrich-Ebert-Allee 144, 53113 Bonn, Germany
[2] Fraunhofer FKIE, Fraunhoferstr. 20, 53343 Wachtberg, Germany
christin@cs.uni-bonn.de
[3] Technische Universität Darmstadt
Mornewegstr. 32, 64293 Darmstadt, Germany
firstname.lastname@seemoo.tu-darmstadt.de

Abstract. Current mobile applications gather an increasing amount of data about the users and their environment. To protect their privacy, users can currently either opt out of using the applications or switch off their mobile phones. Such binary choices, however, void potential benefit for both users and applications. As an alternative, finer control over their privacy could be given to users by deploying privacy-preserving mechanisms. However, it is unclear if users are able to perform the necessary configuration of such schemes. In this paper, we therefore investigate to which degree users can understand the underlying mechanisms as well as the resulting trade-offs in terms of, e.g., privacy protection and battery consumption. To this end, we have conducted a user study involving 20 participants based on user interfaces especially designed for this purpose. The results show that our participants would prefer deciding on the consequences and leave the system parameterizing the underlying mechanism.

1 Introduction

With over 6 billion subscriptions worldwide [14], mobile phones are ubiquitous and their technological advances have led to the emergence of millions of novel applications. However, most mobile applications require the collection of a wealth of information about the users [10]. This not only includes their current locations, but also data gathered by the sensors embedded in their mobile phones. For example, accelerometers can serve to monitor users' activity, while microphones can be leveraged to infer users' context. The information collected by the mobile phones can be further combined with, e.g., past users' search queries, agenda, or mails, in order to improve the application services and anticipate their next queries as proposed in Google Now [1]. Through the utilization of these applications, users' privacy is hence seriously put at risk.

Efforts to make the collection of location information transparent to the users have been recently undertaken, e.g., in the iOS 7 Beta 5 version [21] where users can consult their most frequently visited locations and the corresponding stay duration. While such transparency may increase user awareness about potential privacy issues, this still does not contribute to protect their privacy. On the

D. Naccache and D. Sauveron (Eds.): WISTP 2014, LNCS 8501, pp. 92–107, 2014.

contrary, mobile phones fallen into wrong hands may reveal when users are usually not at home and thus help potential burglars. The most frequent solution offered to the users is to either disable such applications or even switch off their mobile phones in order to protect their privacy. Consequently, no fine-granular solutions exist. Such solutions could not only benefit to the users, but also to the applications. In other domains, it has been shown that providing control to users over their data and privacy protection increase their trust in the system [13]. Instead of completely opting out, privacy-conscious users may still benefit from limited application features, thus still providing information to the application but in a way that respects their privacy.

In this paper, we therefore investigate the feasibility of giving users control over their privacy protection and allow them to customize it according to their personal preferences. To this end, we select a noise monitoring application, in which users collect sound levels with their mobile phones. The collected sensor readings are then consolidated to build noise pollution maps. We further integrate the path jumbling scheme proposed in [7] into the noise monitoring application. In particular, our contributions are as follows:

1. We design privacy interfaces to provide users control over the underlying privacy-preserving mechanism and thus over their privacy protection. We base our design on a thorough analysis of the considered mechanism and its functional requirements. Simultaneously, our objective is to cater for *comprehension, transparency,* and *simplicity* in order to provide user interfaces with a high degree of usability.
2. We evaluate our proof-of-concept implementation by means of a user study involving 20 participants. In our study, the participants tested and evaluated the different privacy interfaces by completing both a guided and a free task, in which they had to configure the mechanism according to given settings and their personal preferences, respectively. The study highlights that most participants appreciated the additional control offered, but some of them were still overstrained by the overall complexity.

The paper is organized as follows. We first introduce and analyze the underlying privacy-preserving scheme in Sec. 2, before presenting our design drivers and design decisions in Sec. 3 and 4, respectively. We detail the results of our user study in Sec. 5 and summarize existing work in Sec. 6, before making concluding remarks in Sec. 7.

2   The Path Jumbling Concept

We assume that users are registered to a noise monitoring application. Their mobile phones automatically collect sensor readings, i.e., noise levels. The sensor readings are stamped with the collection time and location information. In order to protect their privacy, users leverage the collaborative path-hiding mechanism proposed in [7] instead of directly reporting the sensor readings to the application server. This means that their mobile phones swap their sensor readings when they are in physical proximity in order to break the association between the spatiotemporal context of the sensor readings and the user's identity.

Different strategies to exchange the sensor readings between users have been introduced in [7]. Users can swap all their sensor readings using the *realistic strategy*, while they can exchange a random number of them with the *random-unfair* and *random-fair* strategies. In the *random-fair* strategy, the users exchange the same number of sensor readings. As a result, the selection of an exchange strategy requires to balance the trade-offs between the expected jumbling degree (i.e., the percentage of exchanged versus own collected sensor readings), the reporting overhead (e.g., when users get more sensor readings as they initially collected and exchanged), and the degree of trust in other users (i.e., exchanging fewer sensor readings with less trusted users).

Depending on the user-meeting pattern, users may not be able to always exchange their sensor reading with others. In this case, the sensor readings can be either reported to the application or stored until the next encounter(s). In the former case, the original paths followed by users will be revealed to the application as the sensor readings could not be jumbled, while it will introduce additional latency for the application in the latter case. Depending on the application scenario, low latency may be preferred to allow a timely delivery of the collected sensor readings. Users can hence select and parameterize one of the following reporting strategies: *time-based*, *exchange-based*, and *metric-based*. Each strategy determines a particular condition needed to be fulfilled in order to trigger the reporting of the sensor readings to the application server.

In summary, users should be able to choose among the proposed exchange and reporting strategies based on the trade-offs between trust, overhead, reporting latency, and jumbling degree according to their preferences.

3   Design Drivers

In this paper, we aim at providing user interfaces that allow users to configure the path jumbling scheme presented in Sec. 2. Our first design driver is to increase the users' *consciousness* about potential privacy threats in mobile sensing applications as recommended in [20] in order to motivate the necessity of configuring and applying such a privacy-preserving scheme. Additionally, we intend to provide *control* to the users. They should be able to: (a) select one exchange strategy among the realistic, random-unfair, and random-fair strategies, (b) select a user reputation threshold above which users will be considered trustworthy enough to initiate an exchange of sensor readings, (c) select one reporting strategy among the time-based, exchanged-based, and metric-based strategies and customize the respective parameter. Once the path jumbling mechanism has been configured, users should be able to review the selected parameterization and consult the potential consequences. This caters for both *transparency* and *comprehension*. Through the whole configuration process, users should be assisted by different dialogues to support their comprehension of the overall mechanism. Furthermore, the required interactions should be kept to a minimum in order to enable fast configuration and reconfiguration and limit the burden for the users.

4   Designed Privacy Interfaces

Based on the drivers detailed in Sec. 3, we have designed and implemented the following privacy interfaces. Our proof-of-concept implementation is based on the iOS operating system (version 5.1). Our privacy interfaces are integrated into a noise monitoring application we called "Noisecapture". Similar to those proposed in [4] and [19], the application captures sound samples and extracts the corresponding noise levels. As illustrated in Fig. 1(a), users can access the application results in form of statistics or maps. When users select the *"Privacy"* option, an informative text about the nature of the collected data and the associated risks for their privacy is first displayed in order to increase user awareness (see Fig. 1(b)). A second view shown in Fig. 1(c) then explains the purpose and basic principles of the path jumbling concept. For both views, we have attempted to reduce the length of the texts to a minimum using as simple as possible wording and illustrate it with different icons to catch users' attention. Both descriptive views are only displayed when users access the privacy interfaces for the first time, except if the users explicitly require help using the corresponding button. The same principle is applied for the remaining interfaces: novice users are assisted by dialogues that explain the different process steps. Each dialogue follows the same structure and includes the goal of the current step, details about the mechanism to configure, and an explanation about the importance of configuring it.

In what follows, we detail the designed interfaces implementing the requirements defined in Sec. 3 and including the dialogues especially designed for novice users. We cluster these interfaces according to the following steps: (a) exchange strategy selection, (b) reputation-based user selection, (c) reporting strategy selection, and (d) setting review. Users can navigate through these steps either

(a) Entry point of the noise monitoring application

(b) Informative view on data collection

(c) Informative view on the path jumbling concept

Fig. 1. Screenshots of the introductory interfaces

(a) Introductory dialogue on the exchange strategies   (b) Main screen to select the exchange strategy   (c) Details about the realistic exchange strategy

Fig. 2. Screenshots of the interfaces dedicated to the selection of the exchange strategies

sequentially using the upper navigation bar or individually select the numbered views in the lower navigation bar.

4.1 Exchange Strategy Selection

If the dialogues are enabled, users first access an introduction on the exchange strategies illustrated in Fig. 2(a). Next, they can choose one of the proposed exchange strategies using the second screen displayed in Fig. 2(b). If the dialogues are disabled, users directly access this second screen. Each strategy is accompanied by an icon illustrating its main principle and a short description. By selecting the blue arrow, users obtain additional details about the corresponding exchange strategy (see Fig. 2(c)). These details include a rating of the strategy according to the resulting jumbling degree, overhead, and trust in other users and whether the strategy is more beneficial to the users (thumb-up icon), to the application (thumb-down icon), or both of them (thumb-middle icon). The more green crosses, the better the rating. While only the details of the realistic exchange strategies are displayed in Fig. 2, similar detail views are available for both random-fair and random-unfair exchange strategies. Consequently, users can see the consequences of the different exchange strategies and which parties benefit most from its application at a glance.

4.2 Reputation-Based User Selection

After having selected the exchange strategy to apply, users can first inform themselves on the selection of users to exchange sensor readings with based on their reputation (see Fig. 3(a)). The reputation level is computed based on peer-based ratings about past exchanges as detailed in [8] and reflects the users' readiness to cooperate in this scheme. For example, dropping sensor readings or exchanging incorrect ones will result in low reputation scores. Users can choose the minimum reputation other users should have to initiate an exchange with them using the interface depicted in Fig. 3(b). The reputation level is computed based on peer-based ratings about past exchanges as detailed in [8]. The reputation levels are coded using a 5-star scale, each star differing in both size and color. The biggest green star is associated to the highest reputation level, while the smallest red star is for the smallest reputation level. By selecting a low reputation level, users take the risks that their sensor readings may not be reported to the application server by the concerned exchange partners. On the other side, the number of potential exchange partners may be limited when selecting a high reputation level.

(a) Introductory dialogue on the reputation-based user selection

(b) Main screen to select the minimum users' reputation to exchange with

Fig. 3. Screenshots of the interfaces dedicated to the selection of users

4.3 Reporting Strategy Selection

Similarly to the exchange strategy selection, users first obtain basic information on the reporting principles as shown in Fig. 4(a) when using the dialogue-based configuration. Otherwise, they can directly select the desired reporting strategy in the screen represented in Fig. 4(b). Additionally, they can parameterize the selected reporting strategy according to their preferences. For example, they can determine the reporting frequency for the time-based reporting strategy, the number of exchanges for the exchange-based reporting strategy, the distance between the original paths, or the minimum jumbling percentage for the metric-based reporting strategies. Fig. 4(c) illustrates the parameterization of the minimum jumbling percentage. By moving the slider, the shares of personal and jumbled data are adjusted according to users' preferences.

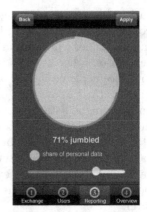

(a) Introducing dialogue on the reporting strategies   (b) Main screen to select the reporting strategy   (c) Configuration of the jumbling threshold

Fig. 4. Screenshots of the interfaces dedicated to the reporting strategies

4.4 Setting Review

After the configuration of the path jumbling mechanism, users can consult an overview of their selected settings and learn about the potential consequences as illustrated in Fig. 5. In Fig. 5(a), users can review which exchange strategy, reputation level for other users, and reporting strategy they have chosen in the upper part of the screen. In the lower part, they can see an estimation of the jumbling degree and the reputation level that could be reached when applying these settings. Moreover, the implications of their selection are displayed in a second view depicted in Fig. 5(b). In this view, users can see at a glance the influence of their settings with respect to privacy, trust in other users, reporting latency, and data completeness based on the different colors and associated icons. Data completeness refers to the reporting of consecutive sensor readings to the server. The better the completeness, the better the data processing at the server side, as results in the same area are available. By clicking on each cell, users can obtain additional information about potential risks and change the associated settings if those do not match their personal conception. Alternatively, they can navigate to the corresponding interface using the lower navigation bar.

4.5 Summary

By using the designed interfaces, users can *control* the path jumbling mechanism and take *informed* decisions based on the different proposed dialogues. Users can hence control both the exchange and the report of the sensor readings. They can also review their settings and their potential implications, thus catering for *transparency*. If the settings do not correspond to their personal conception, users can directly access them and update them.

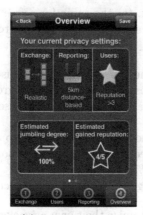

(a) Setting overview   (b) Setting consequences

Fig. 5. Screenshots of the interfaces dedicated to the review of the selected settings

5 Evaluation of the Designed Privacy Interfaces

In order to evaluate the usability of the privacy interfaces presented in Sec. 4, we have performed an empirical user study. Our study was advertised on different student forums at our university. In total, 20 participants volunteered to test and evaluated the designed interfaces. The participants were rewarded for their contribution with refreshments, no monetary remunerations were offered. In this section, we present the participants' demographics and provide details about the study settings, before commenting the obtained results.

5.1 Demographics

Our participant sample is composed of 20 undergraduate students aged between 20 and 25 years ($\mu=22.7$, $\sigma=1.87$). They were predominantly male ($n=12$) and their fields of study were as follows: electrical engineering (30%), natural sciences (30%), computer science (25%), and humanities (15%). 62% of the participants owned a smartphone, among which 23% owned at least one iOS-based device. Their average experience level with such devices was rated with a score 4.25 with $\sigma=1.58$ on a scale from one (beginner) to seven (expert). While our sample may not be representative for the whole population, we especially targeted this group of participants as they are more susceptible to contribute to mobile sensing applications than other socio-demographic categories as shown in [6].

5.2 Study Settings

The study was performed under supervised laboratory conditions. We distributed to each participant an iPhone 4 configured with the privacy interfaces detailed in Sec. 4. Additionally, each participant had a leaflet written in English including: (a) a brief introduction to mobile sensing applications and related privacy issues, (b) instructions for a guided task, (c) the same for a free task, and (d) a questionnaire. In the guided task, we asked the participants to conduct the following main steps:

1. Identify the strategy that requires the lower trust in other users and select the exchange strategy that guarantees the best jumbling degree,
2. Choose the reputation level that will allow them to exchange sensor readings with every encountered user,
3. Set the time-based and distance-based reporting strategies to a threshold of two days and 6 km, respectively. Select the metric-based reporting strategy and set the jumbling threshold to 75%,
4. Review the chosen settings and change those categorized as critical.

Next, the participants could freely customize their own privacy settings in the free task. In order to investigate their understanding of the existing trade-offs and the helpfulness of the review step, we first asked them to indicate whether their settings would benefit the application or their privacy protection. In average, the completion of the study took approximately one hour per participant.

5.3   Results

In this section, we present the results of our user study, including both our observations as well as the participants' answers to the distributed questionnaire. We first focus on the comprehensibility of the proposed dialogues, before addressing the different interfaces related to the selection of the exchange strategy, the minimum user reputation, the reporting strategy, and the setting review, respectively. We finally examine user acceptance.

Dialogue Comprehensibility. After having read the first introductory dialogues displayed in Fig. 1, the users answered a set of multiple choice questions about potential risks to their privacy caused by contributions to mobile sensing applications, the basic principle of the path jumbling mechanism, and the objective of the proposed interfaces. Based on these dialogues, 90% of the participants correctly answered all questions, meaning that they fully understood the motivation for these interfaces and the key principle of the underlying privacy-preserving mechanism. The remaining participants had a majority of correct answers, but did not select all possible correct answers.

Additionally, we submitted the following different statements to the participants: "*The first view [in Fig. 1(b)] helped me to understand the risks of mobile sensing applications*" (#1), "*The second view [in Fig. 1(c)] helped me to understand the goals of these privacy interfaces*" (#2), "*The second view clearly described what I had to do next*" (#3), and "*The second view clearly described the goal of the next step*" (#4). The participants rated them using a seven point Likert scale. A score of 1 indicates a strong disagreement with the statement, 4 is neutral, and 7 indicates a strong agreement. Figure 6(a) shows the minimum, quartiles, and maximum scores attributed to these statements. With the

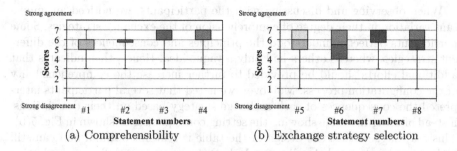

(a) Comprehensibility   (b) Exchange strategy selection

Fig. 6. Minimum, quartiles, and maximum score attributed to the statements focused on the comprehensibility and the exchange strategy selection

exception of one participant, all participants agreed with the proposed statements. This confirms that the first views contribute to the comprehensibility of the privacy threats, the motivations behind the interfaces, as well as the different steps of the configuration process. Globally, the second view about the path jumbling concept obtained better scores than the first view describing the potential privacy threats. Participants may be more willing to have a detailed information about possible risks when contributing to such applications, as participant P_3 commented that "you should also indicate what providers can do with your personal data: location tracking, habit analysis,...".

Exchange Strategy Selection. In a second step, we asked the participants to rate the interfaces designed for the selection of the exchange strategies introduced in Fig. 2. With the exception of three participants, all participants agreed that "*the icons appropriately illustrate the exchange strategies*" (#5), and "*selecting an exchange strategy is easy*" (#6), as shown in Fig. 6(b). Moreover, they found that "*the table describing the pros and cons of the exchange strategies is clearly structured*" (#7), and it "*helped [them] to find the exchange strategy that best fits [their] preferences*" (#8).

Concerning the disagreeing participants, the participant P_2 did not find the proposed icons appropriate (#5), but did not comment on how to improve them. For #8, the participant P_4 strongly disagreed as he preferred using the textual descriptions rather than the summary table "[...] because they provide more information". In comparison, the participant P_{20} thought that the table is not useful as "reporting strategies can change the pros and cons of the exchange strategies again". Her reasoning is due to a confusion between the achieved jumbling degree and the jumbling-based reporting strategy. Despite these three strong disagreements, the scores selected by the participants however remain positive. By comparing the results of #5 to #8, the scores given to #6 are globally lower. Based on our observations, this difference may not be exclusively due to the design of the main interface (see Fig. 2(b)), but also to the navigation complexity between the interface itself and both the introductory dialogues (see Fig. 1) and the table displaying the setting consequences (see Fig. 5(b)).

When observing and discussing with the participants, we noticed an important variation in their degree of comprehension of the exchange strategies. Some participants perfectly understood the principles and consequences of the different strategies, whereas others had only a vague idea. Hence, this indicates that additional efforts should be provided to further increase the comprehensibility of the configuration process. Moreover, we noted that several participants interpreted the consequences of each exchange strategy based on their descriptions, instead of using the table showing the setting consequences as shown in Fig. 5(b). This may suggest that the design of the table is still not optimal and can still be improved to better help all users. In both cases, understanding and selecting an exchange strategy was time-consuming and required concentration. While we attempted to keep the amount of text to the minimum, our observations showed that other alternatives should be found to reduce the burden for the users. For example, videos or cartoons, could be investigated in the future.

Reputation-Based User Selection. Based on their experience in the guided and free tasks, the participants next evaluated both the dialogue (cf. Fig. 3(a)) and the main interface (cf. Fig. 3(b)) used to set the minimum reputation level that other users should have to initiate an exchange with them. As shown in Fig. 7(a), the distribution of the scores attributed to the corresponding statements are slightly higher than for the previous results. Most participants agreed that "*the illustration clearly indicates the minimum reputation score of [their] exchange partners should have*" (#9). Moreover, "*the combination of color and size of the stars [helped them] to recognize the corresponding reputation score*" (#10) and "*the text [helped them] to understand the characteristics of the users having the respective reputation score*" (#11). This means that the participants are more positive about the control provided to select the minimum reputation level for their exchange partners than that for the exchange strategy selection.

Most participants were able to understand and explain the consequences of exchanging data with users having either low or high reputation scores. For example, P_3 explained the implications of choosing very high reputation scores as follows: "The network of exchange partners shrinks as you are excluding many [users] this way". Participants having initial doubts indicated that the text had been useful to select the appropriate reputation level. P_3, however, commented that the labeling could be improved as "[it] is not intuitively clear what means low and high". Again, P_{10} particularly disagreed on #9 and #10. While he understood the interface objective as shown by his comments, the reputation attribution remained unclear to him.

Reporting Strategy Selection. The participants next rated the interfaces dedicated to the selection of the reporting strategy detailed in Fig. 4. By comparing the obtained results shown in Fig. 7(b) with those for the exchange strategy selection in Fig. 6(b), we can observe that the participants found that the respective icons better illustrate the reporting strategies (#12) than the exchange strategies (#5). Moreover, fewer participants strongly agreed that "*selecting a reporting strategy is easy*" (#13) compared to the exchange strategy selection (#6). This may be due

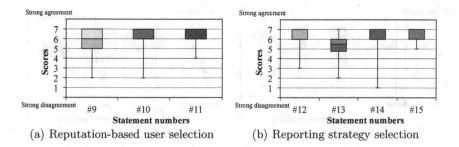

Fig. 7. Minimum, quartiles, and maximum score attributed to the statements focused on the reputation-based user selection and the reporting strategy selection

to the additional interaction required to customize the reporting strategy parameter, e.g., the reporting frequency in the time-based reporting strategy. At the same time, more participants globally agreed with this statement based on a comparison of the first quartiles. Our observations show that the degree of comprehension not only varied between participants as for the exchange strategy selection, but also between strategies. According to our expectations, the time-based reporting strategy was relatively easy to understand while the distance-based reporting strategy was the most difficult. With the exception of P_2, all participants, however, rated *"the animations used to configure the metrics of the reporting strategies are comprehensible"* (#14) and *"the animations used to configure the metrics of the reporting strategies are illustrative"* (#15) with a score of either six or seven. This means that the proposed interactions were appreciated by the participants, but the navigation and the overall comprehension could be generally improved.

Setting Review. Fig. 8(a) shows that all participants agreed that *"information on [their] configuration are clearly arranged in the overview"* (#16). A wide spread of scores is however observed for #17 about the intuitiveness of the scrolling between the overview and consequence table introduced in Fig. 5(a) and Fig. 5(b), respectively. Our observations confirm that participants had difficulty to find the consequence table because of the implemented sideways scrolling. As a result, the sideways scrolling should be replaced by a more transparent interaction in order to address this issue. Moreover, almost all participants claimed to have understood the objective of the consequence table as shown by the score distribution of #18. Some participants, however, needed to read the provided explanations in order to fully understand it. While most participants agreed that the color mapping *"helped them to quickly recognize critical aspects of [their] settings"* (#19), some of them indicated that the color mapping could be improved to provide additional levels, instead of the current binary classification between critical and uncritical. The participant having attributed the lowest score commented that *"it is not always clear what the colors mean"* (P_5). These encouraging results are confirmed by our observations, as most participants needed only one to two attempts to correctly modify their settings when those were

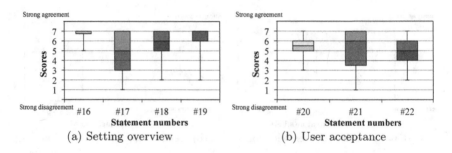

(a) Setting overview   (b) User acceptance

Fig. 8. Minimum, quartiles, and maximum score attributed to the statements focused on the setting overview and the user acceptance

identified as critical. Few participants were even able to immediately identify which strategy and parameter needed to be changed.

User Acceptance. We finally investigated the participants' acceptance and show the results in Fig. 8(b). With the exception of one participant, all participants globally agreed that *"the concept of path jumbling is easy to understand"* (#20). This is not fully aligned with our observations, as some participants required additional information from the study supervisor. Overall, the more technical backgrounds the students had, the easier it was for them to provide fast and precise answers. However, there were some exceptions. For example, a student in physics performed better than one in mechatronic. Additional efforts are hence still needed to improve the overall scheme comprehensibility. Asked if *"[they] would like to configure the mechanism [themselves] if an application would offer it"* (#21), 50% of the participants strongly agreed, despite the observed time and concentration required. The remaining remained neutral or disagreed, thus showing that the proposed control and associated interfaces did not gain the full acceptance of our participants. Those participants however indicated that *"[they] would rather like to directly adjust the consequences according to [their] preferences than configuring the mechanism in detail"* (#22) by selecting higher scores compared to #21. However, the participants having strongly agreed with #21 indicated to be less interested in controlling the mechanism as compared to selecting the consequences.

In summary, the majority of our participants understood the path jumbling mechanism and configured it wisely. This shows that potential users are able to excerpt fine-granular control over the protection of their privacy. Some of them considered their privacy and the associated control as important, but were overwhelmed by all scheme details. They would prefer only deciding on the consequences and leave the system parameterizing the underlying mechanism.

By putting the configuration of the privacy settings in the foreground and conducting the study in a laboratory setting, we were able to evaluate our design decisions based on the participants' comments and reactions. However, the chosen methodology cannot fully capture normal user behaviors. We hence plan to conduct an additional long-term study in order to investigate, i.e., whether and how privacy settings are updated over time under real-world conditions and how many interactions do the users actually need in absence of guidance.

6 Related Work

In recent years, designing privacy interfaces and analyzing privacy concerns and behaviors have attracted increasing attention in a wide range of application domains. Generic guidelines to design privacy user interfaces have been provided in [20,22] and recommendations to avoid common pitfalls have been made in [16]. Moreover, enhanced privacy interfaces for online social networks have been proposed, e.g., in [18], while the impact of the related information exposure on privacy concerns and behaviors have been investigated in [2,17]. Additionally, interfaces for peer-to-peer file sharing systems and website privacy policies have been designed and evaluated in [12] and [11], respectively. In the former, existing interfaces have been leveraged, whereas new concepts, such as the Privacy Bird, have been introduced in the latter. Users' privacy decisions have also been examined in picture sharing applications [3]. These solutions, however, focus on application domains orthogonal to participatory sensing applications.

Concerning mobile sensing applications, few user studies have been conducted. Users' privacy concerns contributing to a mobile sensing application have been explored in [15], while the authors of [5] have analyzed how users understand, choose, and feel comfortable with different location privacy-preserving schemes. No dedicated user interfaces have, however, been proposed. This work shares more similarities with our previous work [9], in which different privacy interfaces allow users to select the granularity degree at which their sensor readings are released. Similarly to this work, a user study based on a proof-of-concept implementation have been conducted. Their focuses however differ. In [9], we explore the users' preferences in terms of visualization of privacy settings, while we build upon this work and focus on investigating to which degree users can understand and configure complex technical schemes to protect their privacy.

7 Conclusions

We have designed and implemented privacy interfaces that provide control over a privacy-preserving scheme to users of mobile sensing applications. By using our interfaces, users can select and customize different strategies according to their personal preferences. We have evaluated our interfaces by means of a user study involving 20 participants and shown that most of our participants were able to comprehend the underlying mechanism and the associated trade-offs based on our interfaces despite their complexity. While some users would prefer an assisted version where the system would configure the settings based on their chosen consequences, others would be ready to invest time and manually configure each setting according to their preferences. In addition to providing insights about future design improvements, the outcomes of our study therefore demonstrate that users have more than a binary choice between either renouncing to their privacy or not using the application at all, thus laying the first stones on the path to usable and controllable privacy protection for mobile applications.

Acknowledgments. The authors would like to thank the participants of the user study. This work was supported by CASED (`www.cased.de`).

References

1. Google Now. The right informaiton at just the right time, `http://www.google.com/landing/now/` (accessed in August 2013)
2. Acquisti, A., Gross, R.: Imagined Communities: Awareness, Information Sharing, and Privacy on the Facebook. In: Danezis, G., Golle, P. (eds.) PET 2006. LNCS, vol. 4258, pp. 36–58. Springer, Heidelberg (2006)
3. Ahern, S., Eckles, D., Good, N.S., King, S., Naaman, M., Nair, R.: Over-exposed? Privacy Patterns and Considerations in Online and Mobile Photo Sharing. In: Proceedings of the SIGCHI Conference on Human Factors in Computing Systems (CHI), pp. 357–366 (2007)
4. Bilandzic, M., Banholzer, M., Peev, D., Georgiev, V., Balagtas-Fernandez, F., De Luca, A.: Laermometer: A Mobile Noise Mapping Application. In: Proceedings of the 5th ACM Nordic Conference on Human-Computer Interaction (NordiCHI), pp. 415–418 (2008)
5. Brush, A., Krumm, J., Scott, J.: Exploring End User Preferences for Location Obfuscation, Location-based Services, and the Value of Location. In: Proceedings of the 12th ACM International Conference on Ubiquitous Computing (Ubicomp), pp. 95–104 (2010)
6. Christin, D., Büchner, C., Leibecke, N.: What's the Value of Your Privacy? Exploring Factors That Influence Privacy-sensitive Contributions to Participatory Sensing Applications. In: Proceedings of the IEEE Workshop on Privacy and Anonymity for the Digital Economy, LCN Workshop (2013)
7. Christin, D., Guillemet, J., Reinhardt, A., Hollick, M., Kanhere, S.S.: Privacy-preserving Collaborative Path Hiding for Participatory Sensing Applications. In: Proceedings of the 8th IEEE International Conference on Mobile Ad-hoc and Sensor Systems (MASS), pp. 341–350 (2011)
8. Christin, D., Pons-Sorolla, D.R., Hollick, M., Kanhere, S.S.: TrustMeter: A Trust Assessment Framework for Collaborative Path Hiding in Participatory Sensing Applications. In: Proceedings of the 9th IEEE International Conference on Intelligent Sensors, Sensor Networks and Information Processing (ISSNIP) (2014)
9. Christin, D., Reinhardt, A., Hollick, M., Trumpold, K.: Exploring User Preferences for Privacy Interfaces in Mobile Sensing Applications. In: Proceedings of 11th ACM International Conference on Mobile and Ubiquitous Multimedia (MUM). pp. 14:1–14:10 (2012)
10. Christin, D., Reinhardt, A., Kanhere, S.S., Hollick, M.: A Survey on Privacy in Mobile Participatory Sensing Applications. Journal of Systems and Software 84(11), 1928–1946 (2011)
11. Cranor, L.F., Guduru, P., Arjula, M.: User Interfaces for Privacy Agents. ACM Transactions on Computer-Human Interacteration (TOCHI) 13, 135–178 (2006)
12. Good, N.S., Krekelberg, A.: Usability and Privacy: A Study of Kazaa P2P Filesharing. In: Proceedings of the SIGCHI Conference on Human Factors in Computing Systems (CHI), pp. 137–144 (2003)

13. Hansen, M., Fischer-Hübner, S., Pettersson, J., Bergmann, M.: Transparency Tools for User-controlled Identity Management. In: Proceedings of the 17th eChallenges Conference (e-2007), pp. 1360–1367 (2007)
14. International Communication Union: The World in 2013: ICT Facts and Figures, http://www.itu.int (accessed in May 2013)
15. Klasnja, P., Consolvo, S., Choudhury, T., Beckwith, R., Hightower, J.: Exploring Privacy Concerns about Personal Sensing. In: Tokuda, H., Beigl, M., Friday, A., Brush, A.J.B., Tobe, Y. (eds.) Pervasive 2009. LNCS, vol. 5538, pp. 176–183. Springer, Heidelberg (2009)
16. Lederer, S., Hong, I., Dey, K., Landay, A.: Personal Privacy Through Understanding and Action: Five Pitfalls for Designers. Personal Ubiquitous Computing 8(6), 440–454 (2004)
17. Lipford, H., Besmer, A.: Users' (Mis)Conceptions of Social Applications. In: Proceedings of the 36th Graphics Interface Conference (GI), pp. 63–70 (2010)
18. Lipford, H., Besmer, A., Watson, J.: Understanding Privacy Settings in Facebook with an Audience View. In: Proceedings of the 1st Conference on Usability, Psychology, and Security (UPSEC), pp. 1–8 (2008)
19. Maisonneuve, N., Stevens, M., Niessen, M.E., Steels, L.: NoiseTube: Measuring and Mapping Noise Pollution with Mobile Phones. In: Proceedings of the 4th International Symposium on Information Technologies in Environmental Engineering (ITEE), pp. 215–228 (2009)
20. Patrick, A.S., Kenny, S.: From Privacy Legislation to Interface Design: Implementing Information Privacy in Human-Computer Interactions. In: Dingledine, R. (ed.) PET 2003. LNCS, vol. 2760, pp. 107–124. Springer, Heidelberg (2003)
21. Warzel, C.: This Is What It Looks Like When Your Phone Tracks Your Every Move, http://www.buzzfeed.com (accessed in August 2013)
22. Yee, K.-P.: User Interaction Design for Secure Systems. In: Deng, R., Qing, S., Bao, F., Zhou, J. (eds.) ICICS 2002. LNCS, vol. 2513, pp. 278–290. Springer, Heidelberg (2002)

A Secure Genetic Algorithm for the Subset Cover Problem and Its Application to Privacy Protection

Dan Bogdanov[1], Keita Emura[2], Roman Jagomägis[1], Akira Kanaoka[3],
Shin'ichiro Matsuo[2], and Jan Willemson[3]

[1] Cybernetica, Mäealuse 2, 12618 Tallinn, Estonia
{dan,lighto,janwil}@cyber.ee
[2] National Institute of Information and Communications Technology,
4-2-1 Nukui-Kitamachi, Koganei, Tokyo 184-8795, Japan
{smatsuo,k-emura}@nict.go.jp
[3] Toho University, 2-2-1 Miyama, Funabashi, Chiba
akira.kanaoka@is.sci.toho-u.ac.jp

Abstract. We propose a method for applying genetic algorithms to confidential data. Genetic algorithms are a well-known tool for finding approximate solutions to various optimization and searching problems. More specifically, we present a secure solution for solving the subset cover problem which is formulated by a binary integer linear programming (BIP) problem (i.e. a linear programming problem, where the solution is expected to be a 0-1 vector). Our solution is based on secure multi-party computation. We give a privacy definition inspired from semantic security definitions and show how a secure computation system based on secret sharing satisfies this definition. Our solution also achieves security against timing attacks, as the execution of the secure algorithm on two different inputs is indistinguishable to the observer. We implement and benchmark our solution on the SHAREMIND secure computation system. Performance tests show that our privacy-preserving implementation achieves a 99.32% precision within 6.5 seconds on a BIP problem of moderate size. As an application of our algorithm, we consider the problem of securely outsourcing risk assessment of an end user computer environment.

Keywords: privacy, secure multi-party computation, genetic algorithms.

1 Introduction

1.1 Background

Secure computation is a well-known cryptographic tool, where parties can jointly compute a function without revealing their own inputs. The two-party setting was introduced by Yao [34], and a more general case, secure multi-party computation (SMC), was introduced by Goldreich, Micali, and Wigderson [18].

D. Naccache and D. Sauveron (Eds.): WISTP 2014, LNCS 8501, pp. 108–123, 2014.

SMC is recognized as a useful tool and several applications have been proposed, e.g. privacy-preserving data mining [26], testing disjointness of private datasets [35], applications to on-line marketplaces [13], private stable matching [33], genome-wide association studies [24], etc. Especially, due to the recent concern against cyber security incidents, it is desirable to share protection/attack knowledge, whereas such information is usually sensitive. In such a case, SMC comes into effect, e.g., privacy-preserving sharing of network monitoring data has been considered [10].

In theory, any function can be computed by garbled circuits [34] with oblivious transfer schemes which require heavy costs. However, it is a challenging task to implement an efficient SMC system, since even a simple comparison or scalar product circuit can require a few seconds to complete [29] on standard hardware.

Fully homomorphic encryption (FHE) is a new and promising technique [15]. However, the current implementations of FHE are impractical. For example, Gentry and Halevi have implemented the original Gentry's FHE scheme in [16]. In their implementation, a single bootstrapping operation (which is needed to get the complete homomorphic operation) requires at least 30 minutes (for the large setting). A FHE scheme proposed by Brakerski, Gentry, and Vaikuntanathan (which is known as FHE without bootstrapping) has also been implemented for the evaluation of the AES circuit [17]. However, one AND operation requires from 5 to 40 minutes, making the system impractical.

1.2 Our Contribution

In this paper, we focus on solving optimization problems on confidential information. Our approach is to adapt genetic algorithms (GAs)—well-known algorithms for computing approximate solutions of the underlying problems—to SMC. GAs are inherently heuristic and are not guaranteed to produce the globally optimal result, nevertheless, they have been proven to yield results good enough for practical use. Since performance overhead added by introducing SMC is remarkable, finding good trade-offs between performance and some other parameters is an interesting research question. GA provides an interesting trade-off between precision and performance—something that has not been extensively treated in the existing literature for SMC algorithms.

We begin by defining privacy in a client-server data processing scenario. Our definition is similar to semantic security definitions for cryptosystems. We then present one secure computation setting that achieves the desired privacy goals. This setting is based on secure multiparty computation using additively homomorphic secret sharing. One of the main challenges that we tackle is security against timing attacks—our privacy definition requires that even the different executions of the secure program are indistinguishable from each other. Stating it otherwise, the program execution flow should not depend on the input data. This is a non-trivial restriction on the implementation of optimization algorithms.

We show how to securely solve (weighted) subset cover problems (SCP) formulated by binary integer linear programming (BIP) problems. We present a

BIP algorithm that satisfies our privacy definition, providing indistinguishability of any two algorithm executions. We implemented this algorithm on the SHAREMIND SMC system [8,6]. We provide benchmarking results from several algorithm executions with different parameters.

Finally, we consider an application of our SMC to capture the following scenario: a user who has a confidential input vector would like to solve some optimization problem in a outsourcing manner. As a concrete application, we show that our SMC can be applied for outsourced risk evaluation system [32], where it can be used to propose countermeasures that the user should deploy to reduce risks without releasing its private local information (e.g., OS/software/hardware versions).

1.3   Related Work

Sakuma and Kobayashi [30] have proposed a secure GA for solving the distributed traveling salesman problem (TSP) in the privacy preserving manner. However, their solution uses an additively homomorphic public key encryption (e.g., the Paillier public key encryption scheme [28]) in two-party setting. Also, their approach uses Edge Assembly Crossover and is hence specific to TSP and can not directly be used to solve SCP or BIP problems.

SMC based on the Shamir secret sharing scheme was proposed by Ben-Or, Goldwasser, and Wigderson [5], and secret sharing schemes are recognized as a useful tool for constructing SMC. There are several security definitions of SMC that have been considered. In the semi-honest model, adversaries follow the protocol, but they try to extract useful information, whereas in the malicious model, adversaries can have full control over some parties who may deviate from the protocol. Recently, degradation of both security and corruptions has been considered in [22], where different security guarantees can be achieved depending on the actual number of corrupted parties. Moreover, a mixed adversary structure, where some of the parties are corrupt actively and some passively has also been recently studied [23].

As an intermediate security level between passive and active, covert adversaries can be considered [12,20,19]. In this setting the parties are willing to actively cheat, but only if they are not caught.

In addition to SHAREMIND [6], several SMC frameworks have been constructed so far, e.g., FairplayMP [4], VMCrypt [27], TASTY [21], SEPIA [11]. There are also other secure computation systems based on different techniques like searchable encryption, e.g. BLIND SEER [1] and CryptDB [2].

2   Privacy-Preserving Computations

2.1   Defining Privacy for the User

Consider a distributed computation system with the following parties. $\mathcal{C}$ is the user who needs to solve a problem and uses the help of the server $\mathcal{S}$ to do that.

Protocol 1. Abstract protocol for server-assisted problem-solving

Data: $\mathcal{C}$ has its problem instance $e \in E$.
Result: $\mathcal{C}$ gets a solution m from the solution space M.
1 $\mathcal{C}$ *classifies its inputs and sends them to the server*:
2    $e_C \leftarrow$ CLASSIFY(e)
3    $\mathcal{C}$ sends e_C to $\mathcal{S}$
4 $\mathcal{S}$ *solves the instance using the appropriate routine* r_C:
5    $m_C = r_C(e_C)$
6    $\mathcal{S}$ sends m_C to $\mathcal{C}$
7 $\mathcal{C}$ *declassifies the solution*:
8    $m \leftarrow$ DECLASSIFY(m_C)

However, the server should not learn anything about the particular problem instance, hence we will introduce a classification mechanism that $\mathcal{C}$ can use before sending the problem out. Then $\mathcal{S}$ will solve the problem in a classified manner, and will send a similarly secured result back to $\mathcal{C}$.

For generality, we do not describe our model in the context of a particular data protection primitive such as encryption. Instead, we categorize data into *classified* and *public* categories. Classified values are confidential and must remain secret from the $\mathcal{S}$ during the computation. The *classification function* CLASSIFY() converts the public value x into its classified form. The declassification function DECLASSIFY() converts a classified value to a public one. A pair of classification and declassification functions is *sound*, if

$$\forall x \text{ DECLASSIFY(CLASSIFY}(x)) = x \,.$$

Protocol 1 presents this general setting from the perspective of the user. We assume that $\mathcal{C}$ has access to efficient classification and declassification functions.

The core of Protocol 1 is the classified computation routine r_C, taking the classified problem instance e_C as input and generating the solution m_C as output. The corresponding unclassified version of the solution routine is defined as

$$r(e) = \text{DECLASSIFY}(r_C(\text{CLASSIFY}(e)) \,.$$

We have two security requirements for the private problem solving system in Protocol 1—correctness, and oblivious execution. For *correctness*, we require that when $\mathcal{C}$ learns $m = r(e)$ at the end of the process, then m is a solution to the original problem instance.

The solution routine is *oblivious*, if $\mathcal{S}$ does not learn anything about e during the solving process. Note that we assume that $\mathcal{S}$ follows Protocol 1 and provides $\mathcal{C}$ with an output.

We will now give a privacy definition for the solution routine. The definition follows the real-or-random approach used in IND-CPA-style proofs (see Figure 1). We will let the attacker choose the input e and later observe the transcript of the protocol consisting of the output e_C of the initial CLASSIFY step and subsequent application of r_C. We will denote the transcript corresponding to input e as Transcript(e). Note that by letting the adversary choose the problem instance e we actually allow him to do more than we would assume in reality, where he would be a mere observer of the messages. In the accompanying random world in Figure 1, the adversary is given a transcript produced on uniformly chosen random input e', and a task of distinguishing between the two worlds.

The function Transcript(e) is defined by the underlying implementation methodology. For example, if the system is implemented by a fully homomorphic encryption scheme, Transcript(e) comprises of all the values that S sees, whereas if the system is implemented by k-out-of-n secret sharing (as will be done in Protocol 2), Transcript(e) comprises of the values seen by up to k servers that make up S. Moreover, the power of the adversary $\mathcal{A}$ is also defined according to the underlying implementation methodology. E.g., for fully homomorphic encryption, $\mathcal{A}$ should be a probabilistic polynomial-time (PPT) adversary, whereas for a secret sharing scheme, $\mathcal{A}$ is allowed to have unconditional power. As Definition 1 is an abstract privacy definition independent of the underlying technology, we need a more specific definition for each implementation. An example of an adapted privacy definition is given in Section 2.2.

$$\mathcal{G}_{\text{real}}^{\mathcal{A}}$$
$$\left[\begin{array}{l} e \leftarrow \mathcal{A} \\ \textbf{return } \mathcal{A}(\textsf{Transcript}(e)) \end{array} \right.$$

$$\mathcal{G}_{\text{rnd}}^{\mathcal{A}}$$
$$\left[\begin{array}{l} e \leftarrow \mathcal{A} \\ e' \xleftarrow{U} E \\ \textbf{return } \mathcal{A}(\textsf{Transcript}(e')) \end{array} \right.$$

Fig. 1. Privacy definition games for secure risk evaluation

Definition 1. *The secure solution routine in Protocol 1 is private, if for the security games in Figure 1,*

$$\Pr\left[\mathcal{G}_{\text{real}}^{\mathcal{A}} = 1\right] = \Pr\left[\mathcal{G}_{\text{rnd}}^{\mathcal{A}} = 1\right] \;.$$

According to Definition 1, we require the constructions for CLASSIFY and r_C to be such that an adversary cannot learn anything about the input e of $\mathcal{C}$ by seeing e_C or executing $r_C(e_C)$. We note that the adversary can not have access to the declassification oracle, as it would then be trivial to break privacy. The particular secure computation technique used for implementing the solution routine will have to provide constructions for CLASSIFY, DECLASSIFY and r_C so that this assumption holds.

2.2   A Threshold Version of the Privacy Definition

In Section 2.1 we gave a definition for privacy, but omitted details on how to achieve it. In this section, we will describe how to satisfy this definition using secret sharing and secure multi-party computation. Alternatively, one could build

---

Protocol 2. Server-assisted problem-solving using SMC

Data: $\mathcal{C}$ has its problem instance $e \in E$.

Result: $\mathcal{C}$ gets a solution m from the solution space M.

1 $\mathcal{C}$ *shares its problem instance and sends shares to the solving servers*:

2   $(e_1, \ldots, e_n) \leftarrow \mathsf{Share}(e)$

3   $\mathcal{C}$ sends e_i to $\mathcal{S}_i$

4 Each $\mathcal{S}_i$ *participates in SMC to find the solution*:

5   $(m_1, \ldots, m_n) = r(e_1, \ldots, e_n)$

6   $\mathcal{S}_i$ sends m_i to $\mathcal{C}$

7 $\mathcal{C}$ *reconstructs the solutions from shares*:

8   $m \leftarrow \mathsf{Reconstruct}(m_1, \ldots, m_n)$

---

a secure problem solving system using, for example, homomorphic encryption, garbled circuits or trusted hardware.

SMC requires that we implement the routine as a distributed system, but the same holds for most other cryptographic techniques. Fully homomorphic encryption could be used to create a single-server solution in theory, but currently known protocols are very inefficient in practice [16]. Trusted hardware that provides data protection and anti-tamper guarantees would also be a suitable tool for implementing r_C. However, such hardware is still not widely available.

We give an updated privacy definition that allows the problem solving system to be distributed between n parties $\mathcal{S}_1, \ldots, \mathcal{S}_n$. First, we define the CLASSIFY and DECLASSIFY functions using secret sharing [31]. To classify a value s, we compute its shares $s_1, \ldots, s_n$ using the sharing function of the chosen secret sharing scheme and send s_i to $\mathcal{S}_i$. Similarly, to declassify a value, each $\mathcal{S}_i$ must send its share of the value to $\mathcal{C}$. The updated protocol is given as Protocol 2.

We use the threshold notion in our security assumption. Namely, we assume that no more than k nodes in the problem-solving system $\mathcal{S}$ are corrupted by the adversary. In the context of Definition 1 based on the games in Figure 1 this means that the Transcript available to the adversary will consist of the views of up to k nodes.

To prove that the adversary cannot distinguish between the real and random game, we need to show that in the Transcript, the adversary cannot distinguish 1) the shares of its chosen input from the shares of random input, and 2) the computations performed on these shared inputs. In the next section we will present one specific instantiation of all the required components allowing for the required security proofs.

2.3 The Sharemind Secure Multi-party Computation Platform

In order to implement the components CLASSIFY, DECLASSIFY and r_C, we need to instantiate the abstract secret sharing and share computing engine with a concrete one. For the purposes of this paper, we chose the SHAREMIND framework for implementing privacy-preserving computations [6]. SHAREMIND supports the operations that we require for our risk analysis task and the protocols are universally composable, simplifying our privacy proof. SHAREMIND was chosen for its performance and rapid application development tools [7,9]. Also, we could obtain the software implementation of SHAREMIND for conducting practical experiments.

In its current implementation, SHAREMIND uses three computing nodes (also called *miners*) working on additively shared 32-bit unsigned integers. To share a value $x \in \mathbb{Z}_{2^{32}}$, two random elements $x_1, x_2 \in \mathbb{Z}_{2^{32}}$ are generated and the third (uniquely determined) value $x_3 \in \mathbb{Z}_{2^{32}}$ is selected so that $x_1 + x_2 + x_3 \equiv x \bmod 2^{32}$. This is essentially the definition for the CLASSIFY operation. The corresponding DECLASSIFY operation is even simpler – the three shares just need to be added modulo 2^{32}.

In order to implement the private problem solving function r_C we need a number of primitive protocols for addition, multiplication, compare-exchange, etc. The specifications of these protocols and the security proofs can be found in [9,25].

All the SHAREMIND protocols have been designed to withstand a passive attacker who is able to monitor the communications of one computing node out of three. For such an attacker, the Transcript of the protocol will not differ from a random Transcript. More formally, we are using the definition of perfect simulatability given in [6].

Definition 2. *We say that an SMC protocol is perfectly simulatable if there exists an efficient universal non-rewinding simulator S that can simulate all protocol messages to any real-world adversary $\mathcal{A}$ so that for all input shares, the output distributions of $\mathcal{A}$ and $S(\mathcal{A})$ coincide.*

It is additionally proved in [6] that if a perfectly simulatable protocol is appended by a perfectly secure resharing step, we obtain a perfectly secure protocol. Using this result, the paper [9] proves that all the fundamental protocols (multiplication, share conversion, bit extraction, equality, division) used by the current SHAREMIND engine are secure against one passive adversary. Furthermore, due to universal composability of perfectly secure elementary operations, all the fundamental protocols also remain universally composable. This implies that higher level protocols (such as sorting) retain the property of having the Transcript indistinguishable from the random one. Hence the requirements of Definition 1 are satisfied as long as no intermediate results are declassified. Achieving this presumes that the protocols implemented are data-agnostic, that is, the program flow of the algorithm does not depend on its inputs. Unfortunately, not all efficient algorithms are data-agnostic and we need to select or design algorithms based this quality. In the following section we will present one approach to implementing a data-agnostic private optimization problem solving function.

3   Privacy-Preserving Optimization Problem Solving

In this Section, we will concentrate on the cheapest subset covering problem. Formally, let $\mathcal{Z} = \{z_1, z_2, \ldots, z_m\}$ be a set of m elements, and let $X_1, X_2, \ldots, X_n \subseteq$

$\mathcal{Z}$ be a collection of available subsets of $\mathcal{Z}$. Let us also have a target set $T \subseteq \mathcal{Z}$ and our aim is to select some X_{i_j} out of the given collection so that the selected sets would cover T, i.e.

$$T \subseteq \bigcup_j X_{i_j} . \tag{1}$$

Additionally, let every set X_i have an associated cost c_i; then our optimization goal is

$$\sum_j c_j \to \min . \tag{2}$$

We will represent the covering restrictions in terms of the incidence matrix $A = (a_{ij})_{i,j=1}^{m,n}$ given by

$$a_{ij} = \begin{cases} 1 & \text{if } z_i \in X_j, \text{ and} \\ 0 & \text{otherwise.} \end{cases}$$

We represent the target set T by its characteristic vector $\mathbf{t} = (t_1, t_2, \ldots, t_m)^T$ where $t_i = 1$ indicates that $z_i \in T$. As the output, we are required to produce another 0-1 vector $\mathbf{x} = (x_1, x_2, \ldots, x_n)^T$, where $x_j = 1$ indicates that the set X_j was selected.

Then the condition (1) translates to

$$A \times \mathbf{x} \geq \mathbf{t} \tag{3}$$

and the optimization goal (2) becomes

$$\mathbf{c} \cdot \mathbf{x} = \sum_{j=1}^{n} c_j \cdot x_j \to \min,$$

where $\mathbf{c} = (c_1, c_2, \ldots, c_n)^T$.

Out of the data given to the algorithm, the matrix A and the cost vector $\mathbf{c}$ are assumed to be public, but the vectors $\mathbf{t}$ and $\mathbf{x}$ must remain oblivious. Formulated as such, we have a standard binary integer programming problem (BIP) that have been well-studied and can be solved by branch-and-bound type of algorithms like Balas Additive Algorithm [3].

However, in order to efficiently prune the search tree, such methods need to make decisions on control bits, and their runs differ on different input data. This behaviour is unwanted in a privacy-preserving algorithm, as the running time of the program could be used to infer details about the private inputs.

Hence, we decided not to choose a branch-and-bound algorithm and take a totally different approach. In this paper, we implement a genetic algorithm for solving the underlying BIP problem. This approach has several advantages. First, we do not have to leak any bits, since the control flow does not depend on the private inputs. Second, a genetic algorithm can be made to run for a predefined number of iterations or a predefined amount of time. On the other hand, genetic algorithms are inherently heuristic and are not guaranteed to produce

---

Algorithm 3. Basic genetic algorithm

Data: Characteristic vector $t \in \{0,1\}^m$; incidence matrix $A \in \{0,1\}^{m \times n}$; vector
$c \in (\mathbb{Z}_{2^{32}})^n$ expressing the costs of subsets
Result: A set of k candidate solutions
1   Generate a random generation $(x_1, x_2, \ldots, x_k)$
2   **while** *there is time to compute* **do**
3   │   For each pair of individuals x_i and x_j produce their offspring by *crossover*
4   │   For some offspring *mutate* some of their bits
5   │   Sort the offspring pool by the *fitness* $c \cdot x$
6   │   Choose k fittest for the new generation $(x_1, x_2, \ldots, x_k)$.
7   **end**
8   **return** $(x_1, x_2, \ldots, x_k)$

---

the globally optimal result. Nevertheless, they have been proven to yield results good enough for practical use.

Genetic algorithms work on *generations* of individuals. In our case, the individuals are 0-1 vectors x_i corresponding to the candidate countermeasure suites. Each generation has k individuals where k is a system-wide configurable parameter. Computation proceeds in iterations, where both the input and output of each iteration is a k-element generation. The general structure of the routine is presented in Algorithm 3.

There are several implementation details to fill in in the basic algorithm. We have to choose the size of the generation, crossover strategy and mutation strategy. Since these parameters depend on each other non-linearly, making the optimal choices is a highly non-trivial task.

For our demo application we ran tests with the size of the generation set to $k = 8, 12, 16, 23, 32$, and for the number of iterations $g = 5, 10, 20$. We applied uniform crossover and mutated the bits of individuals also randomly with the probability 2^{-s}. The last two choices were made because of the need to hide the control flow. Next to the uniform crossover, another frequently used strategy is one- or two-point crossover. However, selecting a few random cutting points has no straightforward implementation in the oblivious setting. At the same time, uniform selection between the parent genes is rather easy to achieve by generating random selection vectors and performing n oblivious choices for each candidate offspring. Similar reasoning applies to the mutation operation as well. In order to flip the bits of individuals with probability 2^{-s}, we can generate s random bit vectors and multiply them bitwise. In our experiments we set $s = 4$ giving 6.25% of probability for any bit to be flipped.

The pool of candidates for the next generation consists of k members of the previous generation plus $\binom{k}{2}$ of their offspring. Since technically, it is simpler to sort 2^t elements, some of the offspring are discarded to get the closest power of two for the pool size. E.g. when $k = 8$, we get the original pool size $8 + \binom{8}{2} = 36$ and we drop 4 of them to get down to 32. For $k = 12, 16, 23, 32$, we sort arrays of size $64, 128, 256, 512$, respectively.

In order to select the k fittest individuals, i.e. the candidate covers with the smallest cost, several steps need to be taken. First, for every candidate vector we need to verify the matrix inequality in Equation 3, and if it is not satisfied, we obliviously assign a very high cost to this vector. Next, we need to sort all the candidate vectors by the costs. Full sorting is a rather expensive operation, and it is not really needed for the purposes of genetic algorithms. Hence, we decided to implement Swiss tournament sorting. It is known that this sorting method works better in both ends on the sorted array, whereas the middle part is not guaranteed to be linearly ordered [14]. In our case, we obliviously evaluate as much of the Swiss tournament sorting network as is needed for finding the top k elements. However, our experiments show that compared to full sorting, the degradation of the precision of the whole genetic algorithm is rather small, but the gain in computing time is significant.

To conclude the Section, we state and prove the main theorem of the paper.

Theorem 1. *Algorithm 3 is private in the sense of Definition 1.*

Proof. The proof relies on two main building blocks – privacy of the primitive operations and preservation of the privacy property through composition.

In order to implement Algorithm 3, only two primitive operations are needed – addition and multiplication.

Indeed, generating a random initial bitvector for the first generation is a trivial local operation. Crossover can be implemented by multiplying s random bitvectors and then applying oblivious choice as specified in [8]. Mutation operation also needs a biased random vector which can be generated as in the case of crossover, and then applying an XOR operation that can be implemented as

$$a \, \mathrm{XOR} \, b = a + b - 2ab.$$

Fitness computation is a simple dot product which only needs addition and multiplication. For sorting, a greater-than primitive and a compare-exchange block are needed. Suitable constructions are found in [8] and [25]. Note that Swiss tournament sorting can be implemented as a sorting network and is hence data agnostic, i.e. the control flow does not depend on the actual values.

Addition of values is a local operation and trivially satisfies Definition 1. A suitable multiplication together with the accompanying privacy proof is given in [9]. The necessary compositionality theorems are given in [6]. This completes the proof.

Next, we will present a concrete application scenario for our optimization framework.

4 Application Scenario: Secure Service Provisioning Framework

Our example scenario builds on top of the problem of outsourcing risk assessment computations. In [32] Takahashi *et al.* have proposed the concept of a risk visualisation and alerting framework. The framework consists of four components.

The **user system** contains the platform and applications utilized by the user requesting access to an online service. We assume that the user system connects to services over a network and can collect information about its software, hardware and network connection. The **service provider** is providing users with a service over a network. Each service provider can set security requirements for using the service.

The **security authority** collects information about threats to software, hardware and networking systems and the respective countermeasures to compile a knowledge base. This knowledge base is used by the **risk evaluation system** (RES) to help the user system in selecting appropriate countermeasures for securing online transactions.

When a user decides to access an online service, the user system compiles a description of its environment and sends it to the risk evaluation system together with the security expectations. The risk evaluation system determines the security threats that could affect the user's transaction and proposes countermeasures that the user should deploy to reduce risks.

The service provision framework is illustrated in Figure 2. We refer to [32] for more details.

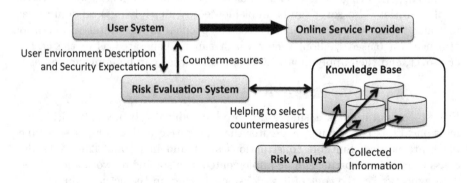

Fig. 2. The secure service provision framework

While the use of this framework enhances the security of online transactions that the user performs, a naïve implementation does so at the expense of privacy, since the user is forced to disclose the information about its vulnerability status to a third, potentially untrusted party.

However, this problem can be solved by applying our secure subset cover computation routine. In terms defined in Section 3, we may view $\mathcal{Z} = \{z_1, z_2, \ldots, z_m\}$ as the set of possible threats against the user system. The sets X_i correspond to the possible countermeasures, where $z_j \in X_i$ (i.e. $a_{ij} = 1$) means that the measure X_i is efficient against the threat z_j. The input characteristic vector t then refers to all the threats relevant for the particular user, and the output vector **x** describes a set of countermeasures that, in collection, mitigate all the threats and are together as cheap as the system was able to find within given time. In order to complete real performance tests, we built a model problem, the parameters of which can be found in Appendix A.

Note that our test vectors do not reflect any real environment, and are provided for benchmarking purposes only. The actual parameter values may vary between different real setups and need to be re-evaluated as a part of real risk analysis process. This work remains out of the scope of the current paper.

5   Practical Results

We implemented the risk evaluation system on the SHAREMIND system. We created a data importer that was used to load the knowledge base into a SHAREMIND installation. We then developed the described genetic algorithm in the SECREC programming language that is used to implement SHAREMIND applications. We implemented the oblivious top-k as a new protocol in SHAREMIND for optimization purposes. We then created a testing application that let SHAREMIND evaluate the risks on all possible inputs according to the used knowledge base. We also computed all the optimal solutions using Sage and the GNU Linear Programming Kit and used the results as reference values to evaluate the correctness of the private implementation.

The SHAREMIND system was deployed on three computers running on a local network. The computers contain 12 CPU cores and 48 gigabytes of RAM. However, during experiments we saw that at most two cores per machine were being fully used and the memory usage of SHAREMIND did not grow over 150 megabytes. It is reasonable to assume such resources, as the Risk Evaluation System will be deployed centrally, on high-performance hardware.

For our performance tests, we selected $m = 10$ threats and $n = 16$ countermeasures together with their correspondences and costs as described in Appendix A. We ran the tests for generation sizes $k = 8, 12, 16, 23, 32$ and number of generations $g = 5, 10, 20$. For each of the pairs of these values, we determined the percentage of correctly computed optimal costs out of $2^{10} = 1024$ possible input vectors. We also measured the average execution time. The results are displayed in Table 1.

Table 1. Accuracy and running time of the privacy-preserving genetic algorithm for g generations of size k

	$g = 5$	$g = 10$	$g = 20$
$k = 8$	3.71% (3711 ms)	45.21% (7187 ms)	78.22% (14167 ms)
$k = 12$	18.75% (4220 ms)	79.39% (8186 ms)	92.87% (16120 ms)
$k = 16$	55.66% (4733 ms)	95.61% (9247 ms)	99.51% (18291 ms)
$k = 23$	89.55% (5420 ms)	99.80% (10546 ms)	99.90% (21008 ms)
$k = 32$	99.32% (6440 ms)	100.00% (12702 ms)	100.00% (25164 ms)

We see that in already under 6.5 seconds it is possible to achieve near-perfect performance of the algorithm, and that increasing the size of the generation helps to obtain better precision with much lower cost in time compared to increasing the number of generations.

6   Conclusions and Future Works

After the first introduction of the SMC concept in early 1980s, continuous research efforts have been carried out to take this concept to practical applications. The current paper also contributes to this research.

One of the main problems when trying to implement practical SMC systems is the prohibitive performance overhead. This paper considers one possible trade-off to address this problem, namely relaxing the precision requirements in order to achieve better running time of the algorithms. One setting where such a trade-off makes sense are the optimization problems. Even then, not all the optimization methods are suitable for implementing using SMC mechanisms. Most notably, the method should be data-agnostic.

In this paper, we considered weighted subset covering problems and constructed a genetic algorithm to solve them. We implemented this algorithm on top of the SHAREMIND SMC engine and benchmarked on the model problem of secure outsourced risk analysis. Our results show that on moderate size problems, genetic algorithm running on SHAREMIND can have excellent precision in reasonably fast running time, with many possible trade-offs.

Genetic algorithms are by far not the only method for solving optimization problems. It is an interesting future research target to develop privacy-preserving versions of other well-known approaches (gradient descent, simulated annealing, ant colony optimization, etc.).

On the other hand, weighted subset covering problem is rather general and it has many other possible application areas (e.g. determining suitable treatment for a patient without revealing his/her exact medical condition). Deploying our algorithms to solve these problems and improving their performance remain the subjects for future research as well.

Acknowledgements. This research has been supported by the European Regional Development Fund through the Estonian Center of Excellence in Computer Science (EXCS), UaESMC project financed by the EU 7th Framework Programme under grant agreement no. 284731, and Estonian Research Council through grant IUT27-1.

References

1. BLIND SEER: Bloom index search of encrypted results,
   http://www.cs.columbia.edu/nsl/projects/blind_seer/
2. CryptDB, http://css.csail.mit.edu/cryptdb/

3. Balas, E.: An additive algorithm for solving linear programs with zero-one variables. Operations Research 13(4), 517–546 (1965)
4. Ben-David, A., Nisan, N., Pinkas, B.: FairplayMP: A system for secure multi-party computation. In: ACM CCS 2008, pp. 257–266 (2008)
5. Ben-Or, M., Goldwasser, S., Wigderson, A.: Completeness theorems for noncryptographic fault-tolerant distributed computation (extended abstract). In: STOC 1988, pp. 1–10 (1988)
6. Bogdanov, D.: Sharemind: programmable secure computations with practical applications. PhD thesis. University of Tartu (2013)
7. Bogdanov, D., Jagomägis, R., Laur, S.: A Universal Toolkit for Cryptographically Secure Privacy-Preserving Data Mining. In: Chau, M., Wang, G.A., Yue, W.T., Chen, H. (eds.) PAISI 2012. LNCS, vol. 7299, pp. 112–126. Springer, Heidelberg (2012)
8. Bogdanov, D., Laur, S., Willemson, J.: Sharemind: A Framework for Fast Privacy-Preserving Computations. In: Jajodia, S., Lopez, J. (eds.) ESORICS 2008. LNCS, vol. 5283, pp. 192–206. Springer, Heidelberg (2008)
9. Bogdanov, D., Niitsoo, M., Toft, T., Willemson, J.: High-performance secure multiparty computation for data mining applications. International Journal of Information Security 11(6), 403–418 (2012)
10. Bohli, J.-M., Li, W., Seedorf, J.: Assisting server for secure multi-party computation. In: Askoxylakis, I., Pöhls, H.C., Posegga, J. (eds.) WISTP 2012. LNCS, vol. 7322, pp. 144–159. Springer, Heidelberg (2012)
11. Burkhart, M., Strasser, M., Many, D., Dimitropoulos, X.A.: SEPIA: Privacy-preserving aggregation of multi-domain network events and statistics. In: USENIX 2010, pp. 223–240 (2010)
12. Chandran, N., Goyal, V., Ostrovsky, R., Sahai, A.: Covert multi-party computation. In: FOCS 2007, pp. 238–248 (2007)
13. Choi, S.G., Hwang, K.-W., Katz, J., Malkin, T., Rubenstein, D.: Secure multi-party computation of boolean circuits with applications to privacy in online marketplaces. In: Dunkelman, O. (ed.) CT-RSA 2012. LNCS, vol. 7178, pp. 416–432. Springer, Heidelberg (2012)
14. Elmenreich, W., Ibounig, T., Fehérvári, I.: Robustness versus performance in sorting and tournament algorithms. Acta Polytechnica Hungarica 6(5), 7–18 (2009)
15. Gentry, C.: Fully homomorphic encryption using ideal lattices. In: STOC 2009, pp. 169–178 (2009)
16. Gentry, C., Halevi, S.: Implementing Gentry's Fully-Homomorphic Encryption Scheme. In: Paterson, K.G. (ed.) EUROCRYPT 2011. LNCS, vol. 6632, pp. 129–148. Springer, Heidelberg (2011)
17. Gentry, C., Halevi, S., Smart, N.P.: Homomorphic evaluation of the AES circuit. In: Safavi-Naini, R., Canetti, R. (eds.) CRYPTO 2012. LNCS, vol. 7417, pp. 850–867. Springer, Heidelberg (2012)
18. Goldreich, O., Micali, S., Wigderson, A.: How to play any mental game or a completeness theorem for protocols with honest majority. In: STOC 1987, pp. 218–229 (1987)
19. Goyal, V., Jain, A.: On the round complexity of covert computation. In: STOC 2010, pp. 191–200 (2010)
20. Goyal, V., Mohassel, P., Smith, A.: Efficient two party and multi party computation against covert adversaries. In: Smart, N. (ed.) EUROCRYPT 2008. LNCS, vol. 4965, pp. 289–306. Springer, Heidelberg (2008)
21. Henecka, W., Kögl, S., Sadeghi, A.-R., Schneider, T., Wehrenberg, I.: TASTY: Tool for automating secure two-party computations. In: ACM CCS 2010, pp. 451–462 (2010)

22. Hirt, M., Lucas, C., Maurer, U., Raub, D.: Graceful degradation in multi-party computation (extended abstract). In: Fehr, S. (ed.) ICITS 2011. LNCS, vol. 6673, pp. 163–180. Springer, Heidelberg (2011)

23. Hirt, M., Lucas, C., Maurer, U., Raub, D.: Passive corruption in statistical multi-party computation - (extended abstract). In: Smith, A. (ed.) ICITS 2012. LNCS, vol. 7412, pp. 129–146. Springer, Heidelberg (2012)

24. Kamm, L., Bogdanov, D., Laur, S., Vilo, J.: A new way to protect privacy in large-scale genome-wide association studies. Bioinformatics 29(7), 886–893 (2013)

25. Laur, S., Willemson, J., Zhang, B.: Round-Efficient Oblivious Database Manipulation. In: Lai, X., Zhou, J., Li, H. (eds.) ISC 2011. LNCS, vol. 7001, pp. 262–277. Springer, Heidelberg (2011)

26. Lindell, Y., Pinkas, B.: Privacy preserving data mining. J. Cryptology 15(3), 177–206 (2002)

27. Malka, L.: VMCrypt: Modular software architecture for scalable secure computation. In: ACM CCS 2011, pp. 715–724 (2011)

28. Paillier, P.: Public-key cryptosystems based on composite degree residuosity classes. In: Stern, J. (ed.) EUROCRYPT 1999. LNCS, vol. 1592, pp. 223–238. Springer, Heidelberg (1999)

29. Pinkas, B., Schneider, T., Smart, N.P., Williams, S.C.: Secure two-party computation is practical. In: Matsui, M. (ed.) ASIACRYPT 2009. LNCS, vol. 5912, pp. 250–267. Springer, Heidelberg (2009)

30. Sakuma, J., Kobayashi, S.: A genetic algorithm for privacy preserving combinatorial optimization. In: GECCO 2007, pp. 1372–1379 (2007)

31. Shamir, A.: How to share a secret. Communications of the ACM 22, 612–613 (1979)

32. Takahashi, T., Emura, K., Kanaoka, A., Matsuo, S., Minowa, T.: Risk visualization and alerting system: Architecture and proof-of-concept implementation. In: SESP 2013, pp. 3–10. ACM (2013)

33. Teruya, T., Sakuma, J.: Round-efficient private stable matching from additive homomorphic encryption. In: ISC 2013 (to appear, 2014)

34. Yao, A.C.-C.: Protocols for secure computations (extended abstract). In: FOCS 1982, pp. 160–164 (1982)

35. Ye, Q., Wang, H., Pieprzyk, J., Zhang, X.-M.: Efficient disjointness tests for private datasets. In: Mu, Y., Susilo, W., Seberry, J. (eds.) ACISP 2008. LNCS, vol. 5107, pp. 155–169. Springer, Heidelberg (2008)

A   Description of the Experimental Setup

For our tests, we selected $m = 10$ threats and $n = 16$ countermeasures together with their correspondences and costs, having some typical network services in mind (e.g. social networking service, on-line banking, electronic commerce, and on-line storage service). We considered the following threats:

T1. Authentication Information Leakage from Terminal Inside

T2. Authentication Information Leakage by Shoulder Surfing

T3. Authentication Information Leakage on Data Transmission Channel (LAN)

T4. Authentication Information Leakage on Data Transmission Channel (End-to-End)

T5. Platform Information Leakage from User Terminal

T6. Privacy Information Leakage from User Terminal
T7. Privacy Information Leakage on Data Transmission Channel
T8. Classified Information Leakage from User Terminal
T9. Disable Services
T10. Financial Damage.

Against these threats we considered the following countermeasures:

C1. Authentication: Password (stored in Client Terminal)
C2. Authentication: Password (short length, not stored)
C3. Authentication: Password (long length, not stored)
C4. Authentication: Challenge and Response
C5. Authentication: Look-Up Table
C6. Authentication: Software Cryptographic Token
C7. Authentication: Hardware Cryptographic Token
C8. Anti-Virus Gateway
C9. Anti-Virus Client
C10. Channel Encryption (LAN)
C11. Channel Encryption (End-to-End)
C12. Stored Data Encryption
C13. Digital Signature
C14. Firewall
C15. Intrusion Detection System (IDS) / Intrusion Prevention System (IPS)
C16. Proxy

Based on the expert knowledge of the authors, we then selected the matrix of correspondence between the threats and countermeasures (see Table 2) and the vector of countermeasure costs (see Table 3).

Table 2. Test data for matrix of threats and countermeasures

	C1	C2	C3	C4	C5	C6	C7	C8	C9	C10	C11	C12	C13	C14	C15	C16
T1	0	1	1	1	1	1	1	0	0	0	0	1	0	0	0	0
T2	1	0	1	1	0	1	1	0	0	0	0	0	0	0	0	0
T3	0	0	0	1	1	1	1	0	0	1	0	0	0	0	0	0
T4	0	0	0	1	1	1	1	0	0	1	1	0	0	0	0	0
T5	0	0	0	0	0	0	0	0	0	0	0	1	0	0	0	0
T6	0	0	0	0	0	0	0	0	0	0	0	1	0	0	0	0
T7	0	0	0	0	0	0	0	0	0	1	1	0	0	0	0	0
T8	0	0	0	0	0	0	0	0	0	0	0	0	0	1	1	1
T9	0	0	0	1	1	0	1	0	0	0	0	0	0	0	0	0
T10	0	0	0	1	1	1	1	0	0	1	1	0	1	0	0	0

Table 3. Test data for countermeasure costs

	C1	C2	C3	C4	C5	C6	C7	C8	C9	C10	C11	C12	C13	C14	C15	C16
Cost	3	1	2	5	7	15	30	150	15	3	5	15	15	5	100	100

End-to-End Secure and Privacy Preserving Mobile Chat Application

Raja Naeem Akram and Ryan K.L. Ko

Cyber Security Lab., Department of Computer Science, University of Waikato,
Hamilton, New Zealand
{rnakram,ryan}@waikato.ac.nz

Abstract. Since the 1990s, two technologies have reshaped how we see and experience the world around us. These technologies are the Internet and mobile communication, especially smartphones. The Internet provides a cheap and convenient way to explore and communicate with distant people. A multitude of services have converged on the smartphone platform, and potentially the most notable is social networking. With increased interconnectivity and use of online services, concerns about consumers' security and privacy are growing. In this paper, we evaluate the security- and privacy-preserving features provided by existing mobile chat services. This paper also puts forwards a basic framework for an End-to-End (E2E) security and privacy-preserving mobile chat service and associated requirements. We implemented the proposal to provide proof-of-concept and evaluate the technical difficulty of satisfying the stipulated security and privacy requirements.

1 Introduction

The instant messaging services provided by applications like WhatsApp, Apple iMessage and BlackBerry Messenger are overtaking traditional SMS services [1], becoming the preferred medium of communication for millions of smartphone users[1]. However, the security and privacy-preserving features of different mobile applications have come under the spot-light [3]. There are different security and privacy features provided by different mobile chat applications, but there are not many mobile chat applications that provide an End-to-End (E2E) security and privacy-preserving service to their customers.

In this paper, we focus on such a mobile chat service. We propose a framework for building such a service and then evaluate the technical challenges involved in implementing it, to provide a proof-of-concept and understand any potential technical issues which may restrict such features from being implemented by mainstream mobile chat service providers.

---

[1] Financial Times report [1] put the number of daily instant messages at 41billion and WhatsApp has more than 200 million active monthly users [2].

D. Naccache and D. Sauveron (Eds.): WISTP 2014, LNCS 8501, pp. 124–139, 2014.

1.1   Contributions of the Paper

This paper deals with the security and privacy-related challenges faced in the design, development and maintenance of a mobile chat service. The main contributions of this study are:

1. End-to-End (E2E) security and privacy-preserving architecture for mobile chat services
2. Secure key exchange, even when communicating parties are not online (i.e. for offline messages)
3. User-to-User (U2U) authentication mechanism[2]
4. Implementation analysis of proposed architecture

1.2   Structure of the Paper

Section 2 discusses the evolution of mobile phone technology and how mobile chat is becoming a convenient method of communication. In section 3, we explore the existing commercial applications that provide different degrees of security and privacy features. In addition, we also stipulate the security and privacy requirements for an E2E secure and privacy-preserving mobile chat service. Subsequently, we describe the proposed framework along with the details of crucial operations. In section 4, practical implementation experience is presented. Section 5 provides an overall analysis of the proposed/implemented framework. Finally in section 6 we provide potential future research directions and conclude the paper.

2   Mobile Phones

In this section, we briefly visit smartphone technology in order to understand the scale of the market, which directly relates to the security and privacy concerns of mobile chat users.

2.1   Smartphones: A Paradigm Shift

The mobile phone platform has evolved a long way from the original simple medium of voice and text communication to become the hub of the digital world. Mobile phones, along with being an entertainment hub, have also developed into a social construct that has affiliations and emotional attachments for individuals. It is also becoming the predominant medium for connecting with the world through social media sites/applications [4,5].

The so-called "App Culture" promoted by Apple Inc. [6,7], has enabled users to seamlessly download any application they desire. This has opened the smartphone platform to a wide range of companies and services. One of the most

---

[2] An authentication mechanism that enables individual users to authenticate each other during a chat session without involving the respective chat servers.

prominent services provided by different applications on smartphones is mobile chat. It provides a potentially convenient and cost-effective alternative to traditional voice and SMS[3]. Mobile chat services have the potential to eclipse SMS communication and this trend is becoming more obvious on a daily basis[1]. With consumers' increasing reliance on mobile chat services, security and privacy features are becoming serious concerns [8,9].

Consumers use a mobile chat service to communicate with each other, a process that can include relaying personal information. The security and privacy of such communications should be taken seriously. However, recent episodes of vulnerability in the major chat services (i.e. WhatsApp [10]) reveal that they might not be robustly implementing security and privacy features.

In the following sections, we briefly explore the range of mobile chat applications available on Android and iOS. This discussion provides an analysis of existing work in the commercial arena. In section 2.6, we discuss existing academic work related to security and privacy-preserving chat software. The selection of commercially available chat software was made in a manner that reflects the existing approaches, and it is by no means an exhaustive list.

2.2 WhatsApp

WhatsApp is considered to be one of the biggest mobile chat services available on different platforms (e.g. iOS, and Android). The architecture of the service is proprietary and the details in this section are taken from a range of resources; notably from [11]. The main focus of the product is on messaging and privacy concerns are secondary. WhatsApp does not store any messages on the server: the chat history is stored on the client's device. The client application uses SSL [12] to connect to the server; however, a recent blog posting [10] discussed the deployment of SSL version 2. This deployment might open up WhatsApp to attacks on SSL 2.0. There is no E2E encryption to provide security in chat messages between sender and receiver. Therefore, the message server can read the messages exchanged.

2.3 BlackBerry Messenger

BlackBerry Messenger (BBM), for better or worse, is perceived to be a secure messaging service. In this section, we examine the consumer version of the BBM, not the business application. An analysis conducted by Communications Security Establishment Canada (CSEC) in 2011 found a number of issues with the BBM [13]. Messages are encrypted but the cryptographic key used is a "global key" that is common to every BlackBerry device/application. The use of a single key to encrypt all messages sent using BBM enables the message server to decrypt

---

[3] Smartphone-based mobile chat services use the Internet as the communication medium, and this might be provided by a Telecom operator. In some areas the cost for mobile data might reduce its benefits in comparison to traditional Telecom services.

the messages. In addition, there is a potential for malicious users to gain access to the "global key" and decrypt any intercepted messages sent or received via BBM.

2.4   Wickr

The most recent addition to the range of secure chat applications is Wickr. Although most of their architecture is proprietary, in this section we discuss the features they claim to offer[4]. They claim that they encrypt individual messages using a cryptographic key. However, it is difficult to determine whether these keys are generated by the message server or the clients. They only claim that users' private keys are not communicated to the server. Furthermore, it is claimed that device, location and Meta information about users and messages is protected, providing a strong privacy mechanism. Communication between the device and the message server is protected by TLS [14].

2.5   Silent Text

Similar to mobile chat applications discussed above, the complete architectural design of Silent Text is proprietary. There is fragmentary information available on their website[5]. Silent Text enables E2E key exchange and secure message communication using the Silent Circle Instant Messaging Protocol (SCIMP) [15]. Each message is encrypted with a new key that is expanded/derived from a master secret shared between the communicating entities. The message server does not handle any key material and does not store any messages. To share the master secret, the communicating entities have to exchange several messages (before they can actually communicate). It is not clear from their white paper [15] and website whether their key sharing protocol supports offline communication[6].

2.6   Related Work

Security and privacy issues in relation to smart phones have received considerable attention [16,17,18] with regard to mobile chat applications. Although there are a number of mobile chat applications that claim to provide a secure service, their complete architecture is not publicly available. To our best knowledge there are not many publications that describe such systems. Secure text messaging systems have a strong foundation in proposals like Media Path Key Agreement for Unicast Secure RTP (ZRTP) [19], Off-the-Record (OTR) [20] and A Secure Text Messaging Protocol [21]. In this paper, we aim to present a potential architecture along with security and privacy-preserving architecture to provide a complete architecture, thereby filling the gap in the existing work in the area of mobile chat applications.

---

[4] Claims were made on their website https://www.mywickr.com/en/howitworks.php

[5] Silent text website https://silentcircle.com/web/silent-text/

[6] Offline Communication: In mobile chat applications, a user can send messages to other users even when they are not online, using so-called "offline communication".

3 Secure and Privacy Preserving Mobile Chat

In this section, we first discuss the security and privacy requirements of mobile chat applications. In the remaining part of this section, we detail a proposed architecture and describe its features.

3.1 Secure and Privacy Preserving Mobile Chat Requirements

Before we present the details of the proposed architecture for mobile chat applications, this section provides a brief list of requirements that any such proposal should meet:

Req1 The sign-up process should require minimal information related to the user. The account creation process should not rely heavily on Personal Identity Information (PII)

Req2 The key exchange process should be secure, seamless and support off-line chat

Req3 Encryption/decryption of messages should not require user interaction (i.e. least interaction)

Req4 Secure offline messages can be communicated securely along with potential key share

Req5 Individual users have a mechanism to authenticate each other, assuring themselves they are communicating with the right person

Req6 Communications are not stored on the chat server. Individual chat sessions can be stored on the user's device

Req7 Local chat storage should be adequately protected

Req8 To safeguard the privacy of the users and their chat, the message-server should not be able to retrieve the messages.

3.2 Proposed Architecture

The generic architecture of a secure and privacy-preserving mobile chat application is shown in Figure 1.

After downloading a mobile chat application, the user of mobile 'A' initiates the sign-up process. The sign-up process is used either to create a new account or to sign in using an existing account (credentials). The chat server, which consists of a membership server and a message server, initiates the account creation process. The membership server manages the user's accounts, associated credentials and (optionally) the user's contact-list. The message server handles the message communication between users, whether both users are online or if the intended recipient is offline. If the recipient is offline, the message will be stored in the offline message store. These messages are temporarily stored and once they are delivered to the respective recipients they are deleted. The dotted line represents virtual communication between the users of mobiles 'A' and 'B', via the message server.

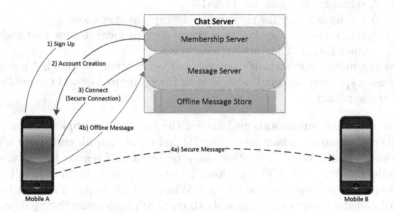

Fig. 1. Generic Architecture of a Mobile Chat Application

The communication link between the mobile application and the message server is protected using cryptography. In addition, the virtual communication link between the users of mobiles 'A' and 'B' is encrypted using the cryptographic keys generated and known only to the respective applications (of users 'A' and 'B').

The generic architecture shown in Figure 1 is essentially deployed by all of the mobile chat services discussed in section 2. However, the differentiator is the features deployed by the proposed architecture that are discussed in subsequent sections.

3.3   Signing Up

When a user completes the installation of an application and wants to create a new account or connect using existing credentials, they can initiate the sign-up process described below:

1. User selects either the new account option or an existing account.
   (a) If the user is an existing customer, then she will provide her account credentials (login/password)
   (b) If the user is a new customer, she will provide her email address[7] and provides a password (for mobile applications)
2. The server checks the provided information from the previous step, and instructs the application to generate local credentials. In addition, the server also generates a unique alphanumeric sequence that acts as the user identifier.
3. The mobile application generates a set of keys

---

[7] Email verification is carried out as part of the account creation process, in which an account only becomes active after the user clicks the account activation link sent to her (provided) email address.

(a) A signature key pair for TLS [14]
(b) A public key pair for encryption/decryption operations
(c) A symmetric storage key to encrypt/decrypt local storage that includes contact list, chat history and key store.

4. On the mobile application's request and verification by the chat server, it issues cryptographic certificates to both the signature key and the public key of the application

In subsequent communications between the mobile chat application and the chat server, a unique alphanumeric user ID and cryptographic certificate is used to authenticate the user/application and establish a TLS session (i.e. a two-way authentication-based SSL/TLS session). To add users to contact lists, their email address or unique identities can be used. When user 'A' makes a request to add user 'B' and she accepts the request, both users will then share their public keys along with associated certificates (issued by the chat server). The certificates provide the necessary guarantee that the received public key indeed belongs to the appropriate user.

3.4   Key Exchange

Keeping in mind the requirements listed in section 3.1, we have to design a key exchange process that can work even when the intended recipient(s) are offline. The requirement for an offline key exchange rules out any synchronous two-way key sharing protocols. The rationale behind having an offline key exchange is to avoid restricting a user to communicating only if a key is already shared. In addition, sharing a key only when both parties are online might not be a feasible proposition. Furthermore, in group chats all users would have to be online to share the key before they could start secure communication with each other. In this situation, if a single participant is offline then either she might not be able to read messages exchanged in the group chat or she has to be removed from the group if the chat session has to be established/continued.

Fig. 2. Key Share Message Structure

Therefore, we propose a scheme for key sharing that can accommodate such requirements. Each communicating party will generate a random key and encrypt it using the public key of the intended recipient. The encrypted message contains a number of elements shown in Figure 2. Timestamps [22] are included to avoid any potential replay attacks. Clock synchronisation between the communicating entities (users) is not required to use the timestamp, because when a mobile application connects to the chat server, it gets a time (server time) and uses it as an internal application. The timestamp included in the message is taken from this internal application time and not from the device/user time. All applications will get their internal time synchronised with the chat server whenever they connect with it, thus removing the need to synchronise device clocks between users.

The key lifetime field gives a choice to the user/mobile-application to set a limit on key usage. The key lifetime field can configured to a session-based lifetime or to any arbitrary time (e.g. seven days). The cryptographic algo field communicates the preferred symmetric key algorithm that the sender would like the receiver to use when communicating with her. The cryptographic algorithms are chosen from a list of selected algorithms which are part of the mobile chat application. The four random numbers included in the message are to generate individual message keys that are discussed in detail in section 3.6. Finally, the last block contains the master key (symmetric key) that the sender requires the receiver to use during any future communications.

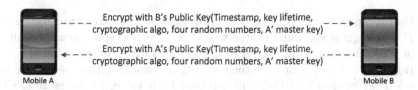

Fig. 3. Key Exchange Two Users

A point to note is that the key and cryptographic-algorithm choice shared by the sender communicates to the receiver that when decrypting any future messages from this sender, she should use them, as shown in Figure 3. Similarly, the receiver will also send the key share message shown in Figure 2 encrypted by the sender's public key. Therefore, both users will use their own generated keys to encrypt all their outgoing messages. The only difference in a group chat is that the chat organiser (group creator/administrator) will generate the master key and share it with all participants, who will then use this key to encrypt all their messages. This avoids using multiple keys (equal to the number of users in the group) to communicate with all users in the group.

3.5 Mutual User-to-User (U2U) Authentication

Mobile chat authenticates itself to the chat server, but U2U authentication is between the users themselves. This authentication process does not involve the chat server and the objective of the process is to assure communicating entities that they are talking with the right *person*. The U2U authentication process has two phases: the opt-in and the authentication phase.

In the opt-in phase, users agree on establishing a U2U authentication mechanism. To accomplish this, two users will initiate the U2U opt-in phase shown in Figure 4. The numeric items in the figure 4 relate to the process steps listed below:

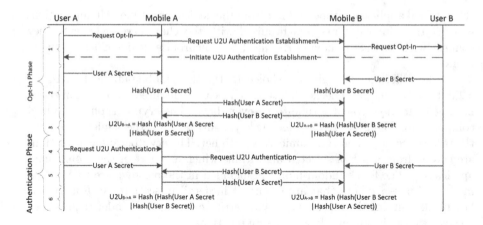

Fig. 4. Overview Of the U2U Authentication

1. User A requests establishment of a U2U authentication mechanism with user B. The request is communicated to user B: if she accepts the establishment of U2U authentication, her decision is communicated back to user A

2. Both users A and B provide their secrets (keyword) to their respective mobile chat applications that will generate hash values of the secrets. Chat applications communicate these hash values to each other.

3. In this step, the mobile applications of A and B generate U2U secrets (individually). The mobile application of A will generate its U2U secret by hashing the concatenation of the secret of A and the hash of B's secret. Similarly, the mobile application of B will generate its U2U secret by hashing the concatenation of the secret of B and the hash of A's secret. This means that both mobile chat applications have different U2U authentication values

4. Either of the users can request U2U authentication; however in figure 4, A initiates the authentication phase

5. Both A and B provide their secrets to their respective mobile chat applications

6. Individual applications will have these secrets and communicate them to each other

7. Applications will then generate the U2U secret and match with the stored value. If it matches then they can ascertain that the person with whom they are chatting is not an imposter

A point to note is that all the messages listed in Figure 4 are communicated confidentially, using the shared cryptographic keys. These messages are encrypted as if they were chat messages, which are discussed in detail in the next section. A point to note is that our mechanism is not comparable to the SafeSlinger[8] as the U2U authentication is no associated in any way with the key generation.

---

[8] Website: https://www.cylab.cmu.edu/safeslinger/

3.6   Message Communication

In this section, we discuss how individual messages are constructed and how the shared master key is used to generate message keys. The keys are then used to encrypt and decrypt the messages. Each message send by individual users is encrypted by a different key, generated using the shared master key and four random numbers (figure 2).

To generate individual message keys, we use the Pseudorandom Number Generator (PRNG) design from [23], illustrated in Figure 5. The shared (four) random numbers are taken as the seed file: for each iteration a random number (n) is encrypted using the shared master key. The output is used as the message key. The output is again encrypted using the shared master key, the output is XOR with n. The output of the XOR operation then replaces the value of n in the seed file.

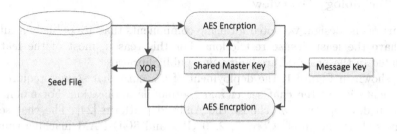

Fig. 5. Message Key Generation [23]

The message generated will then be used to encrypt the outgoing message. Similarly, each user will also have a second message key generator for messages they are receiving. For incoming and outgoing messages, each communicating entity will have two different shared master keys and seed files. Therefore, message keys for outgoing and incoming messages will be different.

3.7   Chat and Profile Storage

All data related to the application should be securely stored on the device. As chat histories are not stored on the server, users might need to have them on their devices. Therefore, chat histories, shared master keys, public key pairs, signature key pairs and contact lists should be stored on the device, protected with the user's Personal Identification Number (PIN) or password. For our proposal, we use a PIN-based mechanism with a short velocity limit (only three wrong tries permitted). If a user locks her applications, she can delete the application and then reinstall it again. If she provides her account credentials she can get her contact list back, but her application will generate new public and signature key pairs (revoking previous keys) along with establishing new master shared keys with her contacts.

In our proposal, the PIN is not the account credential that the user requires to connect with the chat server. The PIN is to authenticate the user to her mobile chat application and open her profile. The PIN is not communicated by the mobile chat application to the chat server and it is stored locally. To protect the PIN value, the application has to rely on the underlying platform and its security mechanism, which is beyond the scope of this paper.

4   Practical Implementation

Using the proposed architecture/features of the mobile chat application in the previous section, we detail the basic implementation carried out to provide a proof-of-concept for the proposed architecture. In this section, we discuss the practical implementation.

4.1   Technology Overview

As part of the design, we opted for using components that are publicly available and have the least license restrictions. For this reason, most of the features presented in the proposal are built using public libraries.

As shown in Figure 1, the deployment of a secure chat service requires the implementation of the chat server and the mobile application. For mobile application development, we choose the Android platform [24]. The chat server was hosted on the Intel[9] Core i7, 2.70 GHz and 8GB RAM machine running Ubuntu[10] 13.10.

In subsequent sections, we briefly discuss the implementation experience for both the chat server and the mobile application.

4.2   Server Side Implementation

On the chat server, we deployed two logical servers. One server ran XAMPP 1.8.3 as a membership server and Mosquitto 1.2.3 as a message server. The XAMPP server is an Apache [25] distribution containing MySQL [26], PHP [27], and Perl [28]. In addition to this, we also included Mcrypt [29] and OpenSSL [30] extensions.

Mosquitto [31] is an open source message server based on the MQ Telemetry Transport (MQTT) protocol [32]. The most recent release of Mosquitto supports the MQTT protocol version 3.1, which provides a very lightweight messaging architecture. We chose Mosquitto for its implementation of MQTT and the rationale behind the choice of MQTT is:

MQTT provided several useful features, such as "push notifications" (so that constant polling for new messages is not required by the Android-based chat application), assured message delivery and reliability, low battery usage, and

---

[9] Intel website: www.intel.com

[10] Ubuntu website: www.ubuntu.com

also "offline message delivery". Offline messages are stored on the message server until the recipient comes online, at which point these messages are sent to the recipient and removed from the server.

MQTT also provides smaller message sizes due to being a binary protocol, compared to other protocols like XMPP [33], which uses XML [34] for its messages. Using MQTT means that text messages are smaller in size than the same messages created with other message protocols such as XMPP (an example is the two character message ":)", which using MQTT generates 70 bytes, whereas the same message in XMPP is represented with 100 bytes). The low data usage for communicating the message is important from the point of view of both performance (delivery of messages) and bandwidth usage (i.e. mobile data packages).

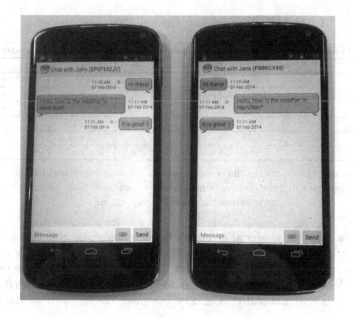

Fig. 6. Screen Shot of Mobile Chat Application Running on Two Android Devices

4.3   Mobile Side Implementation

For mobile chat, we developed an application supporting Android 4.1+. Additional APIs included GSON [35] for converting JSON, SQLCipher [36] for fully encrypted databases, Eclipse Paho [37] for MQTT messaging and Spongy Castle[11] [39] for cryptographic algorithms. The PIN is stored in the application/share preferences, and it unlocks the SQLCipher encryption/decryption key. Shared master keys, (optional) chat histories, U2U authentication secrets, and contact lists are stored in the SQLCipher database.

---

[11] Repackage of Bouncy Castle [38] for Android.

5   Overall Analysis

In section, we briefly analyse the architecture and implementation of our secure mobile chat service.

5.1   Analysis of the Proposed Architecture

In section 3.1, we list[12] seven basic requirements for a secure and privacy preserving chat service. Taking these seven requirements, we have provided a comparison between our proposal and commercially available products discussed in section 2. The comparison based on the listed requirements is shown in table 1.

Table 1. Comparison with Existing Chat Applications

Criteria	WhatsApp	BlackBerry Messenger	Wickr	Silent Text	Proposed Chat
Req1	-	*	*	*	*
Req2	-	-	(*)	(*)	*
Req3	*	*	*	*	*
Req4	-	-	-	-	*
Req5	-	-	-	-	*
Req6	*	*	*	*	*
Req7	-	*	*	*	*

Note: "*" means that it meets the requirement. "-" stands for either does not support the requirement or information is not publicly available. "(*)" means that the requirement is partially supported.

It is clear that our proposal meets all the requirements, and that one of the most widely-used mobile chat services, "WhatsApp" does not satisfy even half of the requirements. However, in support of WhatsApp we can argue that they do not market or claim to provide a secure and privacy-preserving chat service. Therefore, it is only natural that it does not meet the majority of the requirements.

5.2   Implementation Analysis

The objective of the implementation was to provide a proof-of-concept for constructing a secure and privacy-preserving mobile chat application with publicly available specifications. Therefore, this exercise was a study of the technical difficulties that a chat service provider might face in developing such a service. During our development process, we did not face any technical issues. In most cases, the important components required for such a proposed service are already present, apart from concerns about handling a large number of simultaneous connections.

---

[12] * We do not claim that this is an exhaustive list and it should be considered as a basic list of requirements.

We only tested the application for its features and whether it adequately supports the listed requirements (section 3.1). In addition, we did not test the scalability of the implementation of the chat server. However, with regard to message generation, the implementation was comparable to any commercially available mobile chat application. However, we cannot claim the same for the chat server as we did not simulate the load test to make it comparable to other mobile chat services. Such a test is beyond the scope of this work.

6   Conclusion and Future Research Directions

In this paper, we provided an open specification for a secure and privacy-preserving chat service. We described the basic requirements, architecture and implementation experience in deploying such a service. The aim of the paper is to develop mobile chat services and explore any potential complexities involved in such a service providing privacy protection to its customers. In this work, we explored the theoretical foundations and technical challenges faced if privacy protection is built into a chat service. We found that most of the theoretical and technical components are already available. With a few minor modifications, a strongly privacy-based chat service can be constructed. We have shown that a secure and privacy-preserving chat application is technically feasible. During the implementation of the framework, we did not face any serious issues concerning the technology or performance that might make this proposal infeasible. Whether it is a viable business is a different aspect of such a service, and was not considered in this paper.

In future research, we would like to experiment with the scalability and performance of the chat server: this might reveal some bottlenecks in building and maintaining a privacy-based chat server. Another potential aspect is investigation of how the text chat service proposed in this paper could be extended to a voice and video chat service. The challenges presented in providing a secure and privacy-preserving voice and/or video chat service might be more than those presented by a text-based chat service. This will give a much better insight into the development of secure and privacy-preserving services, their running costs and usability requirements, providing an opportunity to understand the underlying reasons why such services are not prevalent or widely adopted by customers.

Acknowledgements. The authors would like to thank the Faculty of Computing of Mathematical Sciences for the funds supporting this research, and acknowledge the implementation inputs of Corey Brown in this research.

References

1. Thomas, D., Bradshaw, T.: Rapid Rise of Chat Apps Slims Texting Cash Cow for Mobile Groups. Online. Financial Times (April 2013), http://www.ft.com/intl/cms/s/0/226ef82e-aed3-11e2-bdfd-00144feabdc0.html#axzz2urfG5LDi

2. Paczkowski, J.: WhatsApp: Bigger Than Twitter. Online. All Things D (April 2013), http://allthingsd.com/20130416/whatsapp-bigger-than-twitter/
3. reenwald, G.: English NSA Collecting Phone Record of Millions of Verizon Customers Daily. Online. The Guardian (June 2013), http://www.theguardian.com/world/2013/jun/06/nsa-phone-records-verizon-court-order
4. Vincent, J.: Affiliations, Emotion and the Mobile Phone. In: Esposito, A., Vích, R. (eds.) Cross-Modal Analysis. LNCS (LNAI), vol. 5641, pp. 28–41. Springer, Heidelberg (2009)
5. Ling, R.: New Tech, New Ties: How Mobile Communication Is Reshaping Social Cohesion. The MIT Press (2008)
6. Laugesen, J., Yuan, Y.: What Factors Contributed to the Success of Apple's iPhone? In: Proceedings of the 2010 Ninth International Conference on Mobile Business / 2010 Ninth Global Mobility Roundtable ICMB-GMR 2010, pp. 91–99. IEEE Computer Society, Washington, DC (2010)
7. Akram, R.N., Markantonakis, K., Mayes, K.: Building the Bridges – A Proposal for Merging different Paradigms in Mobile NFC Ecosystem. In: Xie, S. (ed.) The 8th International Conference on Computational Intelligence and Security (CIS 2012). IEEE Computer Society, Guangzhou (2012)
8. Shabtai, A., Fledel, Y., Kanonov, U., Elovici, Y., Dolev, S., Glezer, C.: Google Android: A Comprehensive Security Assessment. IEEE Security and Privacy 8(2), 35–44 (2010)
9. Becher, M., Freiling, F.C., Hoffmann, J., Holz, T., Uellenbeck, S., Wolf, C.: Mobile Security Catching Up? Revealing the Nuts and Bolts of the Security of Mobile Devices. In: 2011 IEEE Symposium on Security and Privacy (SP), pp. 96–111. IEEE (2011)
10. Goodin, D.: Crypto Weaknesses in WhatsApp "The Kind of Stuff the NSA would Love". Online. ARS Technica (February 2014), http://arstechnica.com/security/2014/02/crypto-weaknesses-in-whatsapp-the-kind-of-stuff-the-nsa-would-love/
11. The WhatsApp Architecture Facebook Bought for $19 Billion. Online. High Scalability, (February 2014) http://highscalability.com/blog/2014/2/26/the-whatsapp-architecture-facebook-bought-for-19-billion.html
12. Freier, A., Karlton, P., Kocher, P.: RFC:6101 - The Secure Sockets Layer (SSL) Protocol Version 3.0. Online. IETF (August 2011)
13. Security of BlackBerry PIN-to-PIN Messaging. Online. Communications Security Establishment Canada, http://www.cse-cst.gc.ca/its-sti/publications/itsb-bsti/itsb57b-eng.html (March 2011)
14. Dierks, T., Rescorla, E.: RFC 5246 - The Transport Layer Security (TLS) Protocol Version 1.2., Tech. Rep. (August 2008)
15. Moscaritolo, V., Belvin, G., Zimmermann, P.: Silent Circle Instant Messaging Protocol: Protocol Specification, Online, White Paper (December 2012)
16. Landman, M.: Managing Smart Phone Security Risks. In: 2010 Information Security Curriculum Development Conference, pp. 145–155. ACM (2010)
17. Felt, A.P., Egelman, S., Wagner, D.: I've Got 99 Problems, but Vibration ain't One: A Survey of Smartphone Users' Concerns. In: Proceedings of the 2nd ACM Workshop on Security and Privacy in Smartphones and Mobile Devices, pp. 33–44. ACM (2012)
18. La Polla, M., Martinelli, F., Sgandurra, D.: A Survey on Security for Mobile Devices. IEEE Communications Surveys & Tutorials, 446–471 (2013)
19. Zimmermann, P., Johnston, A., Callas, J.: ZRTP: Media Path Key Agreement for Unicast Secure RTP. IETF, RFC 6189 (April 2011)

20. Alexander, C., Goldberg, I.: Improved User Authentication in Off-the-record Messaging. In: Proceedings of the 2007 ACM Workshop on Privacy in Electronic Society, WPES 2007, pp. 41–47. ACM, New York (2007)
21. Belvin, G.: A Secure Text Messaging Protocol. Cryptology ePrint Archive, Report 2014/036 (2014), http://eprint.iacr.org/
22. Dyreson, C.E., Snodgrass, R.T.: Timestamp semantics and representation. Information Systems 18(3), 143–166 (1993)
23. Akram, R.N., Markantonakis, K., Mayes, K.: Pseudorandom Number Generation in Smart Cards: An Implementation, Performance and Randomness Analysis. In: Mana, A., Klonowski, M. (eds.) 5th International Conference on New Technologies, Mobility and Security (NTMS). IEEE Computer Society, Turkey (2012)
24. Rogers, R., Lombardo, J., Mednieks, Z., Meike, B.: Android Application Development: Programming with the Google SDK. O'Reilly, Beijing (2009)
25. Apache, Apache Tomcat (May 2007) http://tomcat.apache.org/
26. MySQL 5.6 Reference Manual, Online, Manual (March 2014), http://downloads.mysql.com/docs/refman-5.6-en.pdf
27. Wenz, C., Hauser, T.: PHP 5.1. Markt Technik, München (2006)
28. Wall, L., et al.: The Perl Language Reference Manual (for Perl version 5.12.1.). 5th edn. Perl Reference Manual (for Perl version 5.12.1), vol. 1. Network Theory Ltd, United Kingdom (2010), http://www.network-theory.co.uk/docs/perlref/
29. PHP Cryptogrpahy Extensions: Mcrypt. Online PHP (November 2013), http://nz2.php.net/mcrypt
30. The OpenSSL Project, OpenSSL: The Open Source Toolkit for SSL/TLS (April 2003), http://www.openssl.org
31. Mosquitto: An Open Source MQTT v3.1/v3.1.1 Broker, http://mosquitto.org/
32. MQ Telemetry Transport (MQTT) Protocol, http://mqtt.org/
33. Saint-Andre, P.: Extensible Messaging and Presence Protocol (XMPP): Instant Messaging and Presence. Internet RFC 3921 (October 2004)
34. Bray, T.: Extensible Markup Language - SW (XML-SW). Tech. Rep. (February 2002), http://www.textuality.com/xml/xmlSW.html
35. Singh, I., Leitch, J., Wilson, J.: GSON User Guide, User Guide, https://sites.google.com/site/gson/gson-user-guide
36. SQLCipher Documentation, http://sqlcipher.net/documentation
37. Eclipse Paho Project, http://www.eclipse.org/paho/
38. Bouncy Castle Crypto Package. Bouncy Castle, http://www.bouncycastle.org/documentation.html
39. Spongy Castle, http://rtyley.github.io/spongycastle/

S-box, SET, Match:
A Toolbox for S-box Analysis

Stjepan Picek[1,2], Lejla Batina[1], Domagoj Jakobović[2],
Barış Ege[1], and Marin Golub[2]

[1] Radboud University Nijmegen, Institute for Computing and Information Sciences
(ICIS), Postbus 9010, 6500 GL Nijmegen, The Netherlands
{s.picek,lejla,b.ege}@cs.ru.nl
[2] Faculty of Electrical Engineering and Computing, University of Zagreb
Unska 3, Zagreb, Croatia
{domagoj.jakobovic,marin.golub}@fer.hr

Abstract. Boolean functions and substitution boxes (S-boxes) represent the only nonlinear part in many algorithms and therefore play the crucial role in their security. Despite the fact that some algorithms today reuse theoretically secure and carefully constructed S-boxes, there is a clear need for a tool that can analyze security properties of S-boxes and hence the corresponding primitives. This need is especially evident in the scenarios where the goal is to create new S-boxes. Even in the cases when some common properties of S-boxes are known, we believe it is prudent to exhaustively investigate all possible sets of cryptographic properties. In this paper we present a tool for the evaluation of Boolean functions and S-boxes suitable for cryptography.

Keywords: Private-key Cryptography, Boolean functions, S-boxes, Cryptographic Properties.

1 Introduction

Boolean functions and S-boxes play important role in a number of stream and block algorithms as the only nonlinear elements. As such, if poorly chosen, Boolean functions or S-boxes can undermine the security of the whole algorithm. To be able to assess the quality of those nonlinear elements a plethora od cryptographic properties was devised over the years. Boolean functions are typically used when the output of the building blocks is one-dimensional, and S-boxes are used in the cases when the output is multi-dimensional.

There are various ways to analyze the security of a block cipher. Besides more traditional linear [1] and differential cryptanalysis [2], the most practical attacks today belong to side-channel analysis (SCA) targeting implementations of cryptography in software and hardware.

It can be concluded that nonlinear elements and their properties are of utmost importance for the security of a cryptographic algorithm as a whole. A natural question that arises is how to analyze those elements. One can question the need

D. Naccache and D. Sauveron (Eds.): WISTP 2014, LNCS 8501, pp. 140–149, 2014.

for such analysis since there are nonlinear elements in the literature with good properties. However, it is important to have a tool that can be used for the evaluation of a wider set of properties since in the time of the creation of an S-box not all properties may have been necessarily developed. Second important viewpoint is that researchers sometimes want to develop proprietary S-boxes, or S-boxes with similar functionality but of other sizes than those used before. Although it is not too difficult to check a set of main properties of S-boxes, checking several of those properties can be demanding. It is worth mentioning that many of those cryptographic properties are conflicting, so even the choice of properties that are of interest can pose a problem. In these situations we envision the need for a reliable evaluation tool as such a tool should be one of the essential parts in the evaluation process.

1.1   Related Tools

The lack of publicly available tools that can evaluate S-boxes is somewhat surprising, but this is not due to the fact that those tools would be too difficult to develop. Actually, the most demanding part of the work is to find as many relevant properties as possible. Indeed, every researcher that is interested in S-boxes uses either his own code alone or in combination with some publicly available tools. The main problem is that most of those tools are not publicly available and therefore they are not accessible to wider community. Here we mention tools that can be used to evaluate Boolean functions or S-boxes and that are publicly available.

Boolfun Package in R. R is a free software environment for statistical computing and graphics [3]. It works on various UNIX, Windows and Mac OS platforms. Although the default version of R does not have a support for the evaluation of the Boolean functions, it is possible to load a package named *boolfun* that provides functionalities related to the cryptographic analysis of Boolean functions [4, 5].

Boolean Functions in Sage. Sage is a free open-source mathematics software [6]. In Sage there is a module called *BooleanFunctions* that allows one to study cryptographic properties of Boolean functions. This tool can evaluate most of the relevant cryptographic properties (connected with linear and differential properties) of Boolean functions.

S-boxes in Sage. There is a module called *Sbox* that allows the algebraic treatment of S-boxes. This module has many options but when considering cryptographic properties it is only possible to calculate difference distribution table and linear approximation matrix.

VBF Library. For the sake of completeness we also list VBF (Vector Boolean Functions) library. Alverez-Cubero and Zufiria presented their tool for analyzing vectorial Boolean functions from cryptographic perspective that possibly could calculate various properties of S-boxes [7].[1]

---

[1] We write possibly since although this library should be publicly available, we could not find it anywhere for download.

1.2   Our Contribution

In this paper we present our software SET (S-box Evaluation Tool) that can be used to evaluate Boolean functions and S-boxes. SET can be used to analyze a wide range of properties of Boolean functions or S-boxes that are relevant for the cryptographic assessment. Naturally, this set of properties is not complete, and we plan to add new properties during the further development. Main contribution of this paper is in providing the tool for the analysis of a wide set of cryptographic properties of S-boxes or Boolean functions. In fact, as far as we know, this tool deals with the largest set of cryptographic properties that is publicly known. Furthermore, since the code is available under the GNU General Public License it is easy for other researchers to add or change the existing code.

The remainder of this paper is organized as follows: In Section 2 we give short introduction to representations and cryptographic properties of Boolean functions and S-boxes related with SET tool. In Section 3 we give the details of our tool. Finally, in Section 4 we conclude the paper.

2   Representations and Cryptographic Properties

In this section we give necessary information about the representations and cryptographic properties of Boolean functions and S-boxes. Due to the lack of space, we do not give formulas or explain the role of each property in the security of an algorithm, but rather refer to the additional literature where those information are available. When trying to classify all properties into several groups we could follow different avenues. One classification could be made on the relation to a type of cryptanalysis - properties related to differential cryptanalysis, linear cryptanalysis, algebraic/cube cryptanalysis or side-channel attacks. Another classification could be related to the properties that reflect propagations of differences induced by S-box and to properties that reflect algebraic structures of S-boxes [8]. However, we decided to classify properties on the basis of the representation we use to calculate the property.

An S-box ((n, m)-function) is any mapping F from $\mathbb{F}_2^n$ to $\mathbb{F}_2^m$. If m equals 1 then the function is called a Boolean function. Boolean functions $f_i, i \in \{1, ..., m\}$ are coordinate functions of F where every Boolean function has n variables.

2.1   Representations

A Boolean function f on $\mathbb{F}_2^n$ can be uniquely represented by a **truth table** (TT), which is a vector $(f(\mathbf{0}), ..., f(\mathbf{1}))$ that contains the function values of f, ordered lexicographically [9]. **Polarity truth table** (PTT) is a vector containing function values of $(-1)^f$ [9]. **Walsh transform** is a second unique representation of a Boolean function that measures the similarity between $f(\mathbf{x})$ and the linear function $\mathbf{a} \cdot \mathbf{x}$ [4,9]. The inner product of vectors $\mathbf{a}$ and $\mathbf{x}$ is denoted as $\mathbf{a} \cdot \mathbf{x}$ and equals $\mathbf{a} \cdot \mathbf{x} = \oplus_{i=1}^n a_i x_i$ where " $\oplus$ " is addition modulo 2.

Third unique representation of an Boolean function f on $\mathbb{F}_2^n$ is by means of a polynomial in $\mathbb{F}_2[x_0, ..., x_{n-1}]/(x_0^2 - x_0, ..., x_{n-1}^2 - x_{n-1})$. This form is called **algebraic normal form** (ANF) [9].

Autocorrelation function of a Boolean function f on $\mathbb{F}_2^n$ is real-valued function that does not uniquely determine a Boolean function [9].

Truth table of an (n, m)-function F equals the concatenation of truth tables of all coordinate functions. Walsh transform [10], algebraic normal form [10] and autocorrelation function [9] of an (n, m)-function F is the collection of all respective values of the component functions of F.

2.2 Cryptographic Properties

Next we enumerate cryptographic properties of Boolean functions and S-boxes that can be calculated with SET. With each of the properties we list the references where an interested reader can find definitions and formulas. First block of citations refers to Boolean functions and second one to S-boxes. Informally, this list can be also regarded as the dependency tree where one needs to obtain respective representation before the property listed in the group can be calculated.

Truth Table Based

– Algebraic immunity [9] [10].
– DPA Signal-to-noise ration SNR (DPA) (only for S-boxes) [11].

Walsh Transform Based

– Balancedness [9] [12].
– Nonlinearity [9] [13].
– Bias of nonlinearity (only for Boolean functions) [9].
– Correlation immunity [9] [14].
– Resilience [4] [14].

Algebraic Normal Form Based

– Algebraic degree [14] [8,9].

Autocorrelation Function Based

– Global avalanche criterion (GAC) [9,15] [14,16]. GAC property consists of absolute indicator and sum-of-square indicator.

Lookup Table Based

– Propagation characteristics [17] [9].
– Difference distribution table DDT (only for S-boxes) [9,18].
– Linear approximation table LAT (only for S-boxes) [9].
– Differential delta uniformity (only for S-boxes) [10,19].
– Robustness to differential cryptography (only for S-boxes) [2,20].
– Fixed points and opposite fixed points (only for S-boxes) [21].
– Branch number (only for S-boxes) [21,22].
– Transparency order [12,23].

These properties and corresponding functions represent only a part of available functions in SET. Full list is available in extended version of the paper published in IACR database as well as in website containing the source code of the tool (http://sidesproject.wordpress.com/).

3   SET Tool

SET (S-box Evaluation Tool) is a tool for the analysis of cryptographic properties of Boolean functions and S-boxes that is written in ANSI C code. All the properties mentioned in Section 2 can be evaluated with SET. The tool supports arbitrary input and output sizes where those sizes can differ. In the process of the development of the tool there are some challenges that had to be addressed. First and the most important one was which properties to include. We tried to add the properties that cover the most important cryptanalysis types. Therefore, we added the properties related with differential, linear, algebraic/cube cryptanalysis as well as the properties related with side-channel attacks. Some of those properties are not often used but we consider important to be able to collect as much data on S-boxes or Boolean functions as possible. Next, it was necessary to decide on the format of the tool, i.e. using a command line application, application with a GUI, or a C library. There was also an option to include it in some other tool that have support for S-boxes or Boolean functions, like Sage or R.

Currently, the program comes in two versions: first one is a stand-alone command line tool with a fixed user interface and the second version is a C library. However, since the source code is also available, users are able to customize the program for their needs. SET is available on SIDES project website: http://sidesproject.wordpress.com/.

We give description here of the stand-alone program since it encompasses all the available functionalities. In the stand-alone tool user cannot choose which properties will be calculated, but instead all the properties are calculated. It is possible to choose whether to display the results to the screen, file or both. When the program starts, a user needs to enter the basic parameters: input and output sizes and a file name. There is an option to start the program with the command line arguments (input size, output size and file name) so it can be used in a script. If the program is called with command line arguments then all results are stored to text files and are not displayed on the screen.

A file that contains a Boolean function must be defined in the truth table form and binary format. For the S-boxes case, text file must contain a lookup table of decimal or hexadecimal values with a tabular delimiter. The program can recognize between those two formats so the user does not need to provide any additional information about the format. When the program saves data to the file, the name is a concatenation of word "stats_" and input file name. Since various representations of S-box can grow large rather fast, program writes in separate file for each representation - Walsh transform, autocorrelation function, algebraic normal form and truth table, as well as for difference distribution table DDT and linear approximation table LAT. Files naming convention is "walsh_", "ac_", "anf_", "tt_", "ddt_", "lat_" + input name of the file, respectively. Program can also output S-box coordinate functions values for each property.

The code is written with the first objective being that each of the properties or representations can be calculated separately. Although one can expect that the performance is the key objective of the tool, in our opinion the option to calculate wide set of properties is of even greater importance. Performance becomes more important in the case when one needs to calculate the properties of big S-box (e.g. 16×16) or when one uses the program as a script to go through a number of S-boxes. To improve the speed of tool execution, all small functions that are often called are inlined. Furthermore, since Hamming weight is often used, instead of calling it every time we call it at the beginning and store results in lookup table for faster execution. To aid researchers in examining to code or adding new functionalities, every function is commented. Additionally, as a part of the source code package there is an extensive documentation about all functions, logic behind them and instructions on how to use them.

3.1 Time and Memory Complexity

Once the input file is loaded and transformed in the truth table form, the evaluation process starts. Most of the properties are calculated through the coefficients of the Walsh spectrum, autocorrelation spectrum and algebraic normal form. Since the formulas are the same for Boolean functions and S-boxes (only difference is that the calculation is repeated for every linear combination of the coordinate Boolean functions in the case of an S-box) we write here only complexities for Boolean function case. Computational complexity for calculating the algebraic normal form and Walsh spectrum is of order $O(n \cdot 2^n)$. We use Fast Walsh transform when calculating Walsh spectrum. Autocorrelation function has computational complexity $O(2^{2 \cdot n})$.

3.2 Program Code Examples

In this section we first show some source code of a small program and after that we show the output of that program.

```
#include <sat.h>
int main (int argc, char *argv[]){
prepare (name, argc, argv);
truth_table (tt);
linear_combinations (tt, ll);
walsh_transform (ll, wt);
is_balanced (wt);
printf ("Nonlinearity is %d\n", nonlinearity(wt));
printf ("Correlation immunity is %d\n", correlation_immunity(wt));
printf ("Transparency order is %f\n", get_transparency_order());
printf ("Delta uniformity is %d\n", get_delta_uniformity());
free_all();
}
```

When writing the program, first it is necessary to call the function *prepare* $(name, argc, argv)$ where this function sets the main variables and lookup table values for Hamming weight. After that, we simply call functions for the properties we want to calculate. At the end, function $free\_all()$ is called to free dynamically allocated arrays and matrices.

If we call this program with the AES S-box input and output sizes and the name of the file where the lookup table is, i.e.

```
SAT.exe 8 8 c:/AES.txt
```

as the output we get

```
                  SET - S-box Evaluation Toolbox
Name of the file: c:/AES.txt
Input size M is 8.
Output size N is 8.
S-box is balanced.
Nonlinearity is 112.
Correlation immunity is 0.
Transparency order is 7.860.
Delta uniformity is 4.
```

3.3 Results and Speed of Execution

In Table 1 we give a few examples for different sizes of Boolean functions and S-boxes and their execution times in milliseconds (parameter $Time$). Fields In and Out represent the number of input and output variables of S-boxes or Boolean functions and field δ represents differential uniformity. We display only a subset of available properties, but field $Time$ represents total execution time (when calculating all available properties) in miliseconds. The calculations are done on a system with Intel i5 3230M processor and 4 Gb of RAM. The tests are conducted with operating systems Debian 3.13 and Windows versions 7 and 8. It is possible to analyze larger Boolean functions or S-boxes, but the execution speed significantly goes down as expected.

Table 1. SET execution examples

Function	In	Out	Nonlinearity	Degree	δ	GAC	Time [ms]
Boolean 1	8	1	112	7	N/A	32, 133120	0.01
Boolean 2	10	1	456	9	N/A	168, 3182848	0.55
Boolean 3	12	1	1942	11	N/A	312, 48707584	450
PRESENT [24]	4	4	4	3	4	16, 1024	1
DES 3 [8]	6	4	16	5	8	48, 24064	1
AES [21]	8	8	112	7	4	32, 133120	650

It is hard to compare the execution speed of the SET tool with related tools since we offer more functionalities and therefore total time of execution for our program can be longer, depending on the number of properties that are tested. Nevertheless, in Table 2 we give execution times for some of the functions when calculated with SET and other some tools mentioned in Section 1.1. The test environment is the same as the one mentioned previously (only Debian operating system) and the times are given for the 8×1 Boolean function (as used in Raka-poshi algorithm [25]) and for 8×8 S-box (AES algorithm). We emphasize that this comparison should not be regarded as in-depth analysis of the performances ot the tools, but rather as a indication of their respective execution times. In the analysis we do not take into account specificities of each tool, e.g. precomputed values stored in memory but rather we are interested only in total time from the call of each function to the display of corresponding result. In accordance with that, presented times should serve only as a guideline.

For R, we use *rbenchmark* library and function *benchmark* [26]. For Sage, we use *timeit* function and for SET we use function *clock_gettime*. Execution times represent average times over 100 runs in microseconds. Additionally, we give necessary input arguments for functions when using SET tool.

Table 2. SET functions

| Name | Argument | R | Sage | | SET | |
			Boolean	S-box	Boolean	S-box
walsh_transform	truth table	50	0.69	N/A	1.17	2720
autocorrelation	truth table	N/A	0.8	N/A	1.3	2980
algebraic_normal	truth table	50	3160	N/A	10.02	4501
LAT	lookup table	N/A	N/A	75.6E3	N/A	1.1E5
DDT	lookup table	N/A	N/A	434E3	N/A	441
nonlinearity	walsh spectrum	70	3.31	N/A	0.66	199
correlation_immunity	walsh spectrum	40	2.5	N/A	6.6	1768
absolute_indicator	autocorrelation	N/A	27.4	N/A	0.64	192
sum_of_square_indicator	autocorrelation	N/A	2.6	N/A	0.82	259
algebraic_degree	alg. normal form	40	N/A	N/A	0.62	166
algebraic_immunity	truth table	40	2E5	N/A	12	5.2E5
propagation_characteristics	lookup table	N/A	N/A	N/A	1.58	1.58
num_fixed_points	lookup table	N/A	N/A	N/A	N/A	0.6
num_opposite_fixed_points	lookup table	N/A	N/A	N/A	N/A	0.68
snr_dpa	truth table	N/A	N/A	N/A	N/A	4019
branch_number	lookup table	N/A	N/A	N/A	N/A	277
transparency_order	lookup table	N/A	N/A	N/A	1218.7	6105

3.4   Further Work

There are several avenues that we plan to investigate in the further development of SET. First one is to add more relevant cryptographic properties (e.g. basic AI and graph AI properties of S-boxes, k-normality of Boolean functions). The following would be to make further improvements in the execution speed of the code where the goal is to be able to efficiently work with the S-boxes of sizes up to 16×16. We are also considering to make a module for Sage where we would include all the functionalities of our program.

4   Conclusion

S-boxes or Boolean functions represent important part of many algorithms. Often, some well researched and widely known S-boxes are reused (or at least the idea behind them is reused - as in the case in Rakaposhi Boolean function that uses the same irreducible polynomial as AES [25]). However, often there is a need to use new, previously not considered S-boxes or Boolean functions. Sometimes that is just due to new required sizes (as in lightweight cryptography) and sometimes it is due to the aim of having a proprietary algorithm. In any case, we consider this tool as a valuable asset to cryptographic researchers.

Acknowledgements. This work was supported in part by the Technology Foundation STW (project 12624 - SIDES), The Netherlands Organization for Scientific Research NWO (project ProFIL 628.001.007) and the ICT COST action IC1204 TRUDEVICE.

The authors would like to thank Antonio De La Piedra for his help with the speed performance tests of different tools.

References

1. Matsui, M., Yamagishi, A.: A new method for known plaintext attack of FEAL cipher. In: Rueppel, R.A. (ed.) Advances in Cryptology - EUROCRYPT 1992. LNCS, vol. 658, pp. 81–91. Springer, Heidelberg (1993)
2. Biham, E., Shamir, A.: Differential Cryptanalysis of DES-like Cryptosystems. In: Menezes, A., Vanstone, S.A. (eds.) Advances in Cryptology - CRYPTO 1990. LNCS, vol. 537, pp. 2–21. Springer, Heidelberg (1991)
3. Team, R.C.: R: A Language and Environment for Statistical Computing. R Foundation for Statistical Computing, Vienna, Austria (2013) ISBN 3-900051-07-0
4. Lafitte, F.: The boolfun Package: Cryptographic Properties of Boolean Functions (2013)
5. Lafitte, F., Heule, D.V., Hamme, J.V.: Cryptographic Boolean Functions with R. The R Journal 3(1), 44–47 (2011)
6. Stein, W.A., et al.: Sage Mathematics Software (Version 5.10). The Sage Development Team (2013), http://www.sagemath.org
7. Alvarez-Cubero, J., Zufiria, P.: A c++ class for analysing vector boolean functions from a cryptographic perspective. In: Proceedings of the 2010 International Conference on Security and Cryptography (SECRYPT), pp. 1–9 (July 2010)
8. Knudsen, L.R., Robshaw, M.: The Block Cipher Companion. Information Security and Cryptography. Springer (2011)
9. Braeken, A.: Cryptographic Properties of Boolean Functions and S-Boxes. PhD thesis. Katholieke Universiteit Leuven (2006)
10. Crama, Y., Hammer, P.L.: Boolean Models and Methods in Mathematics, Computer Science, and Engineering, 1st edn. Cambridge University Press, New York (2010)
11. Guilley, S., Pacalet, R.: Differential Power Analysis Model and Some Results. In: Proceedings of CARDIS 2004, pp. 127–142. Kluwer Academic Publishers (2004)
12. Prouff, E.: DPA Attacks and S-Boxes. In: Gilbert, H., Handschuh, H. (eds.) FSE 2005. LNCS, vol. 3557, pp. 424–441. Springer, Heidelberg (2005)

13. Carlet, C.: On highly nonlinear S-boxes and their inability to thwart DPA attacks. In: Maitra, S., Veni Madhavan, C.E., Venkatesan, R. (eds.) INDOCRYPT 2005. LNCS, vol. 3797, pp. 49–62. Springer, Heidelberg (2005)
14. Burnett, L.D.: Heuristic Optimization of Boolean Functions and Substitution Boxes for Cryptography. PhD thesis. Queensland University of Technology (2005)
15. Zhang, X., Zheng, Y.: GAC-the criterion of global avalanche characteristics of cryptographic functions. Journal of Universal Computer Science 1(5), 316–333 (1995)
16. Clark, J.A., Jacob, J.L., Stepney, S.: The design of S-boxes by simulated annealing. New Generation Computing 23(3), 219–231 (2005)
17. Preneel, B., Van Leekwijck, W., Van Linden, L., Govaerts, R., Vandewalle, J.: Propagation characteristics of Boolean functions. In: Damgård, I.B. (ed.) Advances in Cryptology - EUROCRYPT1990. LNCS, vol. 473, pp. 161–173. Springer, Heidelberg (1991)
18. Heys, H.M.: A Tutorial on Linear and Differential Cryptanalysis. Technical report (2001)
19. Nyberg, K.: Perfect Nonlinear S-Boxes. In: Davies, D.W. (ed.) Advances in Cryptology - EUROCRYPT 1991. LNCS, vol. 547, pp. 378–386. Springer, Heidelberg (1991)
20. Seberry, J., Zhang, X.M., Zheng, Y.: Systematic Generation of Cryptographically Robust S-boxes (Extended Abstract). In: Proceedings of the First ACM Conference on Computer and Communications Security, pp. 172–182 (1993)
21. Daemen, J., Rijmen, V.: The Design of Rijndael. Springer-Verlag New York, Inc., Secaucus (2002)
22. Saarinen, M.-J.O.: Cryptographic Analysis of All 4 x 4-Bit S-Boxes. In: Miri, A., Vaudenay, S. (eds.) SAC 2011. LNCS, vol. 7118, pp. 118–133. Springer, Heidelberg (2012)
23. Fan, L., Zhou, Y., Feng, D.: A Fast Implementation of Computing the Transparency Order of S-Boxes. In: The 9th International Conference for Young Computer Scientists, ICYCS 2008, pp. 206–211 (2008)
24. Bogdanov, A., Knudsen, L.R., Leander, G., Paar, C., Poschmann, A., Robshaw, M.J., Seurin, Y., Vikkelsoe, C.: PRESENT: An Ultra-Lightweight Block Cipher. In: Paillier, P., Verbauwhede, I. (eds.) CHES 2007. LNCS, vol. 4727, pp. 450–466. Springer, Heidelberg (2007)
25. Cid, C., Kiyomoto, S., Kurihara, J.: The RAKAPOSHI Stream Cipher. In: Qing, S., Mitchell, C.J., Wang, G. (eds.) ICICS 2009. LNCS, vol. 5927, pp. 32–46. Springer, Heidelberg (2009)
26. Kusnierczyk, W.: Rbenchmark: Benchmarking routine for R (2012)

Policy-Based Access Control
for Body Sensor Networks

Charalampos Manifavas[1], Konstantinos Fysarakis[2], Konstantinos Rantos[3],
Konstantinos Kagiambakis[1], and Ioannis Papaefstathiou[2]

[1] Dept. of Informatics Engineering,
Technological Educational Institute of Crete, Heraklion, Crete, Greece
harryman@ie.teicrete.gr, kostiskag@gmail.com
[2] Dept. of Electronic & Computer Engineering,
Technical University of Crete, Chania, Crete, Greece
kfysarakis@isc.tuc.gr, ypg@mhl.tuc.gr
[3] Dept. of Computer and Informatics Engineering,
Eastern Macedonia and Thrace Institute of Technology, Kavala, Greece
krantos@teikav.edu.gr

Abstract. Sensor nodes and actuators are becoming ubiquitous and
research efforts focus on addressing the various issues stemming from
resources constraints and other intrinsic characteristics typically associated with such devices and their applications. In the case of wearable
nodes, and especially in the context of e-Health applications, the security issues are exacerbated by the direct interaction with the human
body and the associated safety and privacy concerns. This work presents
a policy-based, unified, cross-platform and flexible access control framework. It adopts a web services-compliant approach to enable secure and
authorized fine-grained access control to body sensor network resources
and services. The proposed scheme specifically considers the very limited
resources of so-called nano nodes that are anticipated to be used in such
an environment. A proof-of-concept implementation is developed and a
preliminary performance evaluation is presented.

Keywords: body sensor networks, policy-based access control, XACML,
DPWS, web services, security.

1 Introduction

Sensor nodes and wireless sensor networks constitute a well-established technology with many applications, ranging from home and industrial automation,
to smart cities, agriculture and power metering, logistics, e-Health and assisted
living monitoring. A leading solution adopted by many schemes for enabling
interaction with and providing sensitive information to remote parties is Service Oriented Architecture (SOA). It constitutes an attractive design approach
for many types of networks, including those that consist of nodes with limited
capabilities. Such a network is a body sensor network (BSN) [29] which comprises a number of low-power implanted, wearable (on-body) or in close distance

D. Naccache and D. Sauveron (Eds.): WISTP 2014, LNCS 8501, pp. 150–159, 2014.

wireless sensors and actuators. The environmental and physiological sensors of a BSN provide vital information to medical staff, who can remotely monitor and possibly control users medical treatment. For such an application there are many security concerns [8], including secure transmission of sensitive information to (remote) medical staff, unaltered instructions that reach patients actuators, robust entity authentication and access control mechanisms.

Among the access control schemes that have gained popularity are those where decisions are made based on policy restrictions, such as the standardized by the OASIS, eXtensible Access Control Markup Language (XACML), an XML-based general purpose policy decision language. Besides being used for representing authorization and entitlement policies for managing access to resources, XACML provides a processing model for evaluating requests and making decisions based on a well-defined set of policies. The architecture presented in this paper is an implementation of the XACML solution outlined in [19], adapted to the environment of a BSN. Access to BSN nodes resources is controlled by the use of XACML, facilitating the separate and scalable deployment of nodes on heterogeneous networks and platforms, based on patients' needs.

This paper is organized as follows: Section 2 analyzes the basic characteristics of a BSN network architecture and presents related work, section 3 details the proposed scheme and presents a proof-of-concept implementation and, finally, section 4 features the closing remarks.

2 The Body Sensor Network Case

In a typical BSN used for e-Health purposes, environmental and physiological sensors are deployed to gather and send medical staff important information, such as blood pressure and body and room temperature. Actuators controlled by authorized medical staff can also be deployed for remote treatment, such as an automatic insulin injection device. These sensitive actions need strict access control decisions before being authorized so that users privacy andor safety are not threatened. Security requirements related to BSNs are well documented in the literature [8,22] and include data confidentiality, message authentication and availability.

The types of nodes, in terms of computing capabilities, found in a BSN include *power nodes*, i.e. nodes with medium to high performance computing power and no particular resources restrictions (e.g. a mobile phone, a laptop or a dedicated sink node) and *micro/nano nodes*, i.e. small devices with limited capabilities and resources, such as computational power, memory, storage space and energy. The latter are typically the on-body or implanted nodes found in a BSN and their resource constraints have been considered in the design of the proposed solution.

2.1 Related Work

Many access control schemes have been proposed for wireless sensor networks, yet most of them focus on authentication and authorization schemes and on enhancing basic access control models to address privacy matters. Such schemes can be found in [13,12,30,16].

Some of the proposed mechanisms are based on the use of public-key cryptography, a choice that is very expensive for nano nodes found in a BSN. More importantly, little work has been carried out on policy-based access control (PBAC). The EU-project Internet-of-Things Architecture (IoT-A) worked on the adoption of XACML in the Internet of Things [25] and proposed a generic model whose functional modules are mapped to a set of well-defined components that comprise the IoT-A. The authors use a logistics scenario for demonstration purposes, which has different requirements than a BSN considered in this paper.

In [11] the authors also utilize XACML but focus on the privacy of e-Health data within the mobile environment. In contrast to the work presented here, a complete framework is not included and, moreover, the authors choose computationally intensive security mechanisms such as XML encryption digital signatures. In [31], the authors propose a lightweight policy system for body sensors but they do so by presenting a custom API and policy definitions, thus sacrificing interoperability with existing standards and infrastructures.

3   Proposed Framework

The framework presented in this paper is based on the standardised XACML architecture to provide a cross-platform solution that can typically be deployed in various types of embedded systems while satisfying interoperability, an important requirement for next-generation pervasive computing devices.

An XACML architecture typically consists of the following main components:

- *Policy Enforcement Point (PEP):* Performs access control, by making decision requests and enforcing authorization decisions [18,27].
- *Policy Decision Point (PDP):* Evaluates requests against applicable policies and renders an authorization decision [18].
- *Policy Administration Point (PAP):* Creates and manages policies or policy sets [18].
- *Policy Information Point (PIP):* Acts as a source of attribute values [18].

In the proposed architecture the sensor nodes and actuators, which have direct access to resources, expose their functional elements to the PEP. These nodes are micro/nano nodes and are not expected to have the capacity to accommodate additional functionality. All the above XACML components can run on a single system or, in a more distributed approach, on different systems based on their distinctive capabilities. The latter is the model that fits the environment of a BSN comprising a number of nodes.

3.1   Implementation Approach

There is a variety of tools and APIs available to implement the presented access control framework, each with its own merits and peculiarities, although application development on micro and nano nodes is a challenging task due to inherent resource constraints. For the entities deployed on power nodes, i.e. the PIP, PDP and PAP, the XACML handling and decision-making engine can be adopted from any open source implementation, including Suns XACML implementation [4], PicketBox XACML [2] and the Enterprise Java XACML project [1]. Considering the available options, Suns XACML is a solid choice, as it remains popular among developers and is actually the basis of various current open source and commercial offerings.

Regarding the use of web services to expose the various node features and services to the rest of the entities and users, the authors propose the adoption of the Devices Profile for Web Services (DPWS) specification [7]. A multifunctional sensor embedded on a patient's body will have a single hosting service but may feature various hosted services (e.g. a temperature service, a heart-rate service etc.). Discovery services are included [17], thus the device can advertise its presence on the network and search for other devices. Publish and subscribe eventing mechanisms allow clients to subscribe to services provided by devices.

In terms of opensource resources aimed at developing DPWS-compliant applications for resource-constrained devices, Service-Oriented Architecture for Devices (SOA4D, [3]) provides development toolkits in C and Java. Alternatively, Web Services for Devices (WS4D, [5]) is another open source initiative which provides a number of toolkits for various platforms.

For the proposed scheme to be operational each devices functional elements must be represented by an appropriate DPWS entity and its corresponding operations. Assuming a simple temperature sensor, for instance, a node is programmed as a DPWS device which hosts a temperature service featuring various operations:

- A *GetTemperature* operation which, when invoked, will return the patients current temperature.
- A more complex *TemperatureEvent* operation which, by exploiting the WS-Eventing [9] mechanism, allows a client device (e.g. doctors device) to subscribe to the service and get temperature updates at set intervals as well as event notification messages when the temperature exceeds a certain threshold.
- An additional *SetTemperatureThreshold* operation which, when invoked, allows setting/updating the abovementioned warning threshold.

Similarly, the XACML-related elements of each node must be represented as DPWS devices, clients or peers. The approach adopted by the authors involves a DPWS client on the temperature sensor node described above. DPWS is then used to discover and use the PDP service implemented on a control/gateway node. The process followed when a user tries to access a sensors functional elements (e.g. the temperature reading) is depicted in Fig. 1.

In more detail, assuming a doctor tries to access the temperature sensors features (Step 1), the request is automatically forwarded to the devices PEP (Step 2). The PEP can then invoke the *AccessRequest* operation on the control nodes PDP service (Step3), sending a properly formulated access request to the PDP. When the PDP is done evaluating (Step 4) the request based on subjects

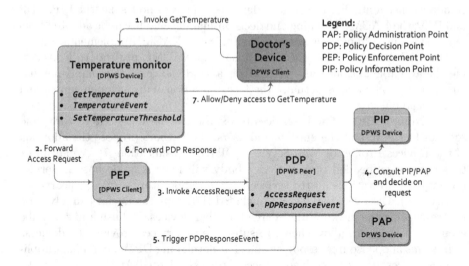

Fig. 1. PBAC implementation using DPWS

attributes and policy rules, it can, in turn, trigger its *PDPResponseEvent* (to which the sensors PEP client subscribes during initialization), returning the authorization decision. This decision is then conveyed to the functional operation of the device, thus granting or denying access to the *GetTemperature* operation the doctor tried to invoke. The PDP to PAP and PIP entities functionality are, equivalently, developed as DPWS devices and clients, exploiting the integrated discovery and subscription mechanisms, thus bypassing the need to use other protocols (e.g. LDAP).

Protection of PBAC Messaging. Unprotected policy messages would expose the systems security, revealing private information to attackers who might also try to identify policy restrictions and do a mapping of the security measures taken for the specific environments. One could also masquerade as a legitimate entity or modify policy related messages, in an attempt to downgrade adopted measures and bypass access controls.

Security measures can be deployed on various layers of the network stack, with the most prominent being those that protect messages at the application or network layer and can provide end-to-end message protection. Well-known security mechanisms for these layers are the TLS (Transport Layer Security) [10] protocol and the variant proposed for securing UDP messages, namely DTLS [24], as well as IPsec and its variants that utilize header compression [21,20,23], for the network layer. An alternative approach would be to utilize a subset of the mechanisms detailed in the WS-Security [15] specification, but the X509-based public key schemes included in said specification can impose a significant performance overhead [14].

Communications between the context handler and the PIP can typically utilize any protection mechanism as it is anticipated they will operate on a power node, hence without significant restrictions.

3.2   Proof-of-Concept Implementation

A proof of concept implementation of the PBAC scheme presented in this work was developed using Suns XACML as a basis for the policy and access control mechanisms. The WS4D-JMEDS API [6] was used for the creation of the necessary DPWS devices. The implementation consists of the following modules:

- An application that runs on the sensors and which implements the access to the functional elements of the sensor (e.g. temperature reading) as well as the communication with the sink node. A security mechanism was also developed, based on the AES algorithm in CBC mode and pre-shared secret keys, to guarantee that only the legitimate sink node/bridge can access the sensors. When connected to the bridge, sensors ignore all other connection requests. Moreover the security mechanism protects the messages from eavesdropping on the sensors-sink node communications.
- A sink node application that bridges the BSN, which in this case operates over 802.15.4, to the standard network infrastructure. This application has to be deployed on a device equipped with dual 802.15.4 & Ethernet/wireless Ethernet functionality.
- The DPWS Provider module which discovers available sensors (via the sink node), probes said sensors to discover their functionality and then maps this functionality to a corresponding DPWS device. The DPWS device created for each of the discovered sensors includes the necessary operations to realize the PEP functionality, as well as the conversion of all low level messages transmitted to and from the sensors to a DPWS compatible form. The communication of the PEP(s) to the PDP must also be protected, as malicious tampering of the policy messages exchanged by the PBAC entities can compromise the access control efforts. To this end, a security mechanism based on the AES/CCM [28] authenticated encryption algorithm was implemented. Deployment of this mechanism guarantees that the PBAC-related messages exchanged between PEP and PDP (when the former seeks the authorization status of a specific clients request), are fully protected in terms of confidentiality, integrity and authenticity.

Performance Evaluation. The performance of the proof of concept implementation was evaluated on a test-bed featuring a SunSPOT mote [26] running the sensing application. Another Sun-SPOT mote was connected to a personal computer acting as a sink node. The DPWS Provider application was deployed on the same computer system. In a real-world application the bridge/DPWS Provider functionality could be deployed on any smart device with dual 802.15.4 & Ethernet/wireless Ethernet connectivity, even a small embedded or wearable

device, as depicted in Fig. 2. The PDP/PIP/PAP application was running on
a separate computer system which also stored the policy files. This system also
featured a client application developed to query the sensors for benchmarking
purposes. SunSPOTs communicate via the 802.15.4 radio, while the personal
computers communicated via wired Ethernet.

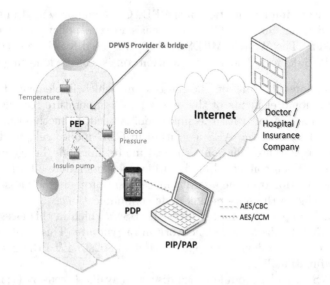

Fig. 2. Proposed deployment of the proof-of-concept PBAC application

A total of 50 consecutive requests were issued from the client application to
the sensor. In order to evaluate the delay imposed by the proposed scheme, the
sensor featured both a PEP-protected operation (*GetTemperature*) that the test
client was allowed to invoke by the current policy set and an unprotected operation (*GetTemperatureUnprotected*) which could be invoked immediately (without
going through the policy enforcement point for authorization). Aiming to also
weigh the impact of the security mechanisms, the assessment included scenarios
with and without encryption on both the SunSPOT-Provider link (plaintext vs.
AES-CBC) and the PEP-to-PDP link (plaintext vs. AES/CCM). The response
time, averaged over 50 requests, including the overhead when considering a totally unprotected (access control- and security-wise) operation as baseline, can
be seen in Fig. 3.

The bulk of the delay can be attributed to the communication between the
SunSPOT and the Provider, as was evident from timing tests run concurrently
on the client side and the Provider side. E.g. the results of such a test, run
with AES-CBC protection on the SunSPOT messages and no protection on the
PEP-PDP communication, indicated that out of the 527,3ms client-side delay
(on average, for 50 requests) when invoking an unprotected (i.e. no PBAC involved) operation, 449,45ms was the average time that the Provider had to wait
until it got a reply from the SunSPOT. Therefore the overhead of the DPWS

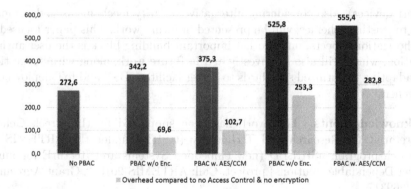

Fig. 3. Response time (in ms) for a single request, averaged over 50 data points. Columns in dark gray depict the scenario where there is no security between the sensor and the Provider, while black columns correspond to the scenarios where AES-CBC encryption was used to protect said link.

communication between client and the Provider (i.e. the DPWS device that mirrors the sensors functionality) was 77,85ms. Another important aspect is that when changing the policy so that the invocation of the protected operation by our test client is denied, the response time is negligible, as the request is rejected by the PEP and is never forwarded to the sensor. In a test run of 50 such unauthorized requests, the average response time of the DPWS device was just 8,39ms. It should be noted that, regarding policy look-ups, the authors chose to implement the system so that the PEP checks with the PDP for every single request, considering scenarios where policies change dynamically (even in an automated fashion when certain conditions are triggered), and where it is desirable to have the access control system enforce said changes in real-time. In deployments where policy changes are expected to be infrequent or less dynamic in nature, access tokens with a predetermined validity period (e.g. 30 minutes) could be introduced to reduce the load on the PDP.

4   Conclusions

In this paper we proposed a framework for controlling access in BSNs comprising of nodes with limited resources based on systems policy. Instead of proposing a proprietary solution typically applicable only to a network comprising of homogeneous nodes, the proposed framework is based on existing Internet and access control standards, facilitating the deployment of interoperable solutions. The aforementioned technologies and their applicability to various heterogeneous types of nodes have been investigated and relevant solutions have been identified. The results of these efforts include a proof-of-concept implementation, which is presented in this work along with an initial performance assessment. Further evaluation, including deployment on alternative platforms, both in terms of the sensors (to include devices less capable than the SunSPOTs) as well as the bridge/Provider and access control entities (to include embedded systems and smart devices), also considering alternative security mechanisms and comparison to existing schemes, will be presented in future work. This paper focused on authorization aspects, but another important building block is the user authentication, which will also be investigated in future work, along with suggestions on adapting the utilized standards to better facilitate BSN and IoT deployments in general.

Acknowledgments. This work has been supported by the Greek General Secretariat for Research and Technology (GSRT), under the ARTEMIS JU research program nSHIELD (new embedded Systems arcHItecturE for multi-Layer Dependable solutions) project. Call: ARTEMIS-2010-1, Grant Agreement No.:269317.

References

1. Enterprise Java XACML, http://code.google.com/p/enterprise-java-xacml/
2. PicketBox XACML,
   https://community.jboss.org/wiki/PicketBoxXACMLJBossXACML
3. Service-Oriented Architecture for Devices (SOA4D), http://cms.soa4d.org/
4. Sun Microsystems Laboratories, XACML, http://sunxacml.sourceforge.net
5. Web Services for Devices (WS4D), http://ws4d.e-technik.uni-rostock.de
6. WS4D-JMEDS DPWS Stack, http://sourceforge.net/projects/ws4d-javame/
7. Devices profile for web services, version 1.1 (2009),
   http://docs.oasis-open.org/ws-dd/dpws/1.1/os/
8. Alhaqbani, B., Fidge, C.: Access control requirements for processing electronic health records. In: ter Hofstede, A., Benatallah, B., Paik, H.-Y. (eds.) BPM Workshops 2007. LNCS, vol. 4928, pp. 371–382. Springer, Heidelberg (2008)
9. Box, D., Cabrera, L.F., Critchley, C., Curbera, F., Ferguson, D., Graham, S., Hull, D., Kakivaya, G., Lewis, A., Lovering, B., Niblett, P., Orchard, D., Samdarshi, S., Schlimmer, J., Sedukhin, I., Shewchuk, J., Weerawarana, S., Wortendyke, D.: Web Services Eventing, WS-Eventing (2006),
   http://www.w3.org/Submission/WS-Eventing/
10. Dierks, T.: Rescorla, E.: RFC 5246 - The Transport Layer Security (TLS) Protocol Version 1.2 (2008), http://tools.ietf.org/rfc/rfc5246.txt
11. El-Aziz, A.A.A., Kannan, A.: Access control for healthcare data using extended XACML-SRBAC model. In: 2012 International Conference on Computer Communication and Informatics. Dept. of Information & Science Technology, Anna University, pp. 1–4. IEEE (January 2012)
12. Faye, Y., Niang, I., Noel, T.: A survey of access control schemes in wireless sensor networks. In: Proc. World Acad. Sci. Eng. Tech (Laboratory LID), pp. 814–823 (2011)
13. He, D., Bu, J., Zhu, S., Chan, S., Chen, C.: Distributed Access Control with Privacy Support in Wireless Sensor Networks. IEEE Transactions on Wireless Communications 10(10), 3472–3481 (2011)
14. Lascelles, F., Flint, A.: WS-Security Performance (2006),
    http://websphere.sys-con.com/node/204424
15. Lawrence, K., Kaler, C., Nadalin, A., Monzilo, R., Hallam-Baker, P.: Web Services Security: SOAP Message Security 1.1 (2006),
    http://docs.oasis-open.org/wss/v1.1/

16. Maerien, J., Michiels, S., Huygens, C., Hughes, D., Joosen, W.: Access Control in Multi-party Wireless Sensor Networks. In: Demeester, P., Moerman, I., Terzis, A. (eds.) EWSN 2013. LNCS, vol. 7772, pp. 34–49. Springer, Heidelberg (2013)
17. Nixon, T., Regnier, A., Jeyaraman, R.: SOAP-over-UDP Version 1.1 (2009), http://docs.oasis-open.org/ws-dd/soapoverudp/1.1/
18. Parducci, B., Lockhart, H., Rissanen, E.: eXtensible Access Control Markup Language (XACML) Version 3.0 (2003), http://docs.oasis-open.org/xacml/3.0/
19. Rantos, K., Papanikolaou, A., Fysarakis, K., Manifavas, C.: Secure policy-based management solutions in heterogeneous embedded systems networks. In: 2012 International Conference on Telecommunications and Multimedia (TEMU), pp. 227–232. IEEE (July 2012)
20. Rantos, K., Papanikolaou, A., Manifavas, C., Papaefstathiou, I.: Ipv6 security for low power and lossy networks. In: Wireless Days (WD). IFIP, pp. 1–8 (November 2013)
21. Rantos, K., Papanikolaou, A., Manifavas, C.: Ipsec over ieee 802.15.4 for low power and lossy networks. In: Proceedings of the 11th ACM International Symposium on Mobility Management and Wireless Access, MobiWac 2013, pp. 59–64. ACM, New York (2013)
22. Ray, P., Wimalasiri, J.: The need for technical solutions for maintaining the privacy of EHR. In: Proceedings of the International Conference of IEEE Engineering in Medicine and Biology Society, vol. 1, pp. 4686–4689. IEEE (2006)
23. Raza, S., Duquennoy, S., Chung, T., Yazar, D., Voigt, T., Roedig, U.: Securing Communication in 6LoWPAN with Compressed IPsec. In: Proceedings of the 7th IEEE International Conference on Distributed Computing in Sensor Systems (IEEE DCOSS 2011), Barcelona, Spain (June 2011)
24. Rescorla, E., Modadugu, N.: Datagram Transport Layer Security (2012), http://tools.ietf.org/rfc/rfc6347.txt
25. Serbanati, A., Segura, A.S., Oliverau, A., Saied, Y.B., Gruschka, N., Gessner, D., Gomez-Marmol, F.: Internet of Things Architecture, Concept and Solutions for Privacy and Security in the Resolution Infrastructure. EU project IoT-A, Project report D4.2 (2012), http://www.iot-a.eu/
26. Smith, R.: SPOTWorld and the Sun SPOT. 2007 6th International Symposium on Information Processing in Sensor Networks (2007)
27. Westerinen, A., Schnizlein, J., Strassner, J., Scherling, M., Quinn, B., Herzog, S., Huynh, A., Carlson, M., Perry, J., Waldbusser, S.: Terminology for Policy-Based Management (2001), http://www.ietf.org/rfc/rfc3198.txt
28. Whiting, D., Housley, R., Ferguson, N.: Counter with CBC-MAC (CCM) (2003), http://tools.ietf.org/rfc/rfc3610.txt
29. Yang, G., Yacoub, M.: Body sensor networks. 6. Springer, London (2006)
30. Yu, S., Ren, K., Lou, W.: FDAC: Toward Fine-Grained Distributed Data Access Control in Wireless Sensor Networks. IEEE Transactions on Parallel and Distributed Systems 22(4), 352–362 (2011)
31. Zhu, Y., Keoh, S., Sloman, M., Lupu, E.: A lightweight policy system for body sensor networks. IEEE Transactions on Network and Service Management 6(3), 137–148 (2009)

Personal Identification
in the Web Using Electronic Identity Cards
and a Personal Identity Provider

André Zúquete[1], Hélder Gomes[2], and Cláudio Teixeira[1]

[1] DETI, IEETA, University of Aveiro, Portugal
[2] ESTGA, IEETA, University of Aveiro, Portugal

Abstract. This paper presents a new paradigm for implementing the authentication of individuals within Web sessions. Nowadays many countries have deployed electronic identity cards (eID tokens) for their citizens' personal identification, but these are not yet well integrated with the authentication of people in Web sessions. We used the concept of Personal Identity Provider (PIdP) to replace (or complement) the role ordinarily given to institutional Identity Providers (IdPs), which are trusted third parties to which service providers delegate the identification and the authentication of their clients. By running locally on a citizen's computer, the PIdP paradigm is well suited to assist his/her eID-based authentication. In this paper we describe an eID-based authentication protocol handled by a PIdP, its implementation and its integration in a production scenario (a campus-wide, Shibboleth IdP-based authentication infrastructure used in University of Aveiro).

1 Introduction

Within a Web context, user authentication is critical, especially when accessing personalized services/information. When the Web first appeared, people had to setup accounts on each and every service requiring client authentication. Then the Web evolved towards a more centralized and less annoying client authentication paradigm, using Identity Providers (IdPs). An IdP can centralize the authentication of a set of persons and provide identity attributes of authenticated individuals to authorised services. Authentication paradigms such as SAML 2.0 Web browser based SSO profile [1] explore this IdP-based authentication and identification services.

In this paper we build upon this IdP paradigm but we introduce a novelty: the authentication is performed by personal cryptographic tokens (smartcard-based identity cards, or eIDs) and the IdP is deployed and managed by the persons being authenticated, instead of some trusted third party. The benefits are the following: (i) people don't have to use more than their own eID to get authenticated, (ii) neither people nor services need to trust on third-party IdP services, other than the eID providers, and (iii) we can achieve a higher control over the authentication with an eID when comparing with the one performed by Web "transport" layers (e.g. by HTTPS [2]).

D. Naccache and D. Sauveron (Eds.): WISTP 2014, LNCS 8501, pp. 160–169, 2014.

1.1 Motivation

According to [3], there are three types of eID solutions: password-based systems, Public Key Infrastructures (PKI) and attribute-based credentials. Our work is targeted to the PKI type, which is actually available in 26 European countries.

In eID solutions based on PKI, part of the citizens' identity attributes (name, civil identity number, birthday, sex, etc.) are sealed inside public key certificates, which also contain the public key corresponding to the private one with which signatures can be made. Signatures with personal private keys can only be made with the help of the eID. For this purpose, the eID is frequently a tamperproof smartcard with cryptographic capabilities and simultaneously a digital container for personal attributes. Private keys are maintained secret inside the eID smartcard, and their use in signature operations needs to be authorized with a personal 4-digit PIN. The physical protection provided by the smartcard, together with the PIN knowledge, provides a multi-factor authentication of the eID owner.

Most Public Administration Services, as well as many other public or private services (utility services, banks, insurance companies, etc.), usually require citizens to provide face-to-face their real identity to become clients. An eID simplifies the access of a citizen to all these services, since a citizen can use it to create an account through the Internet without having to show up somewhere for a face-to-face identification, and can use the same eID for accessing afterwards that account. Moreover, the exact same eID can be used to access many of such services services.

The trustworthy identity attributes that an eID can provide to online services depends on each eID. For eID solutions based on a PKI, these attributes must be part of a public key certificate associated with the eID (more precisely, associated to a private key stored in the eID).

Public key certificates (PKC) corresponding to eID private keys are signed documents that can be checked by anyone using certificate hierarchies provided by national PKIs. Any service should be able to check the validity and correctness of a personal PKC with the help of PKI validation services (e.g., CRL [4] distribution points). Thus, a person can get identified and authenticated by signing some challenge provided by the target service (the authenticator) with one of the person's private keys and presenting, together with the signed data, his/her corresponding PKC. The PKC enables the service to both (i) authenticate the person and (ii) get his/her identity attributes present in the PKC.

1.2 Problem

Currently, most browsers are able to explore cryptographic tokens (namely, eIDs) to authenticate the client side of an HTTPS session with an asymmetric key pair. However, server-side Web applications are designed in a way that make them independent from the so-called *transport layer*, which can be either HTTP or HTTPS. In other words, the exploitation of HTTPS instead of ordinary HTTP is a concern of the HTTP server, and not a concern of the applicational logic. Consequently, applicational sessions are completely independent from HTTPS sessions, thus although the former are able to receive information about the authentication and identification of clients, they cannot completely rely on it, simply because they are unable to control it.

Since application-layer sessions cannot use the client authentication provided by the transport layer, they need to manage their own authentication policies and mechanisms. Thus, the application session control manager should directly interact with clients to authenticate them, possibly with an eID. But how can this be done without changing client applications, namely the Web browsers?

1.3   Contribution

For solving this problem, we propose to adopt the current IdP-based paradigms for authenticating people, namely SAML 2.0 Web browser based SSO profile [1], which is based on HTTP redirections, but using a personal IdP (**PIdP**) for making the proper interface with eIDs. The PIdP does not need to be a component trusted by the authenticating service; that will solely trust on the security robustness of eIDs and on the correctness of the eIDs PKI. From the service's perspective, the PIdP will act as a functional extension of a browser (it may inclusively be implemented as a plugin).

We designed a new authentication protocol involving a service provider (authenticating part), a PIdP and an eID, namely the Portuguese one. This protocol is robust against the theft of identity proofs, and protects also the identity of the authenticated person from networks eavesdroppers. A prototype of the PIdP was implemented in Java, as well as a set of Servlets for handling the authentication on the server side, and both components were integrated and temporarily deployed for demonstration purposes with the campus-wide, centralized and IdP-based authentication system used in the University of Aveiro.

2   Related Work

One methodology currently in use for exploring the authentication with eID cards in Web iterations is based on the download and execution, just in time, of Java applets that interact with the eID. This approach is being explored by the majority of the Portuguese sites that allow Portuguese citizens to use their eID to authenticate themselves. However, this is not a good solution for several reasons. First, because browsers usually present a danger warning regarding the execution of such applets, because they can interact extensively with the user machine. Second, because users need to trust code that can be malicious (the service requesting eID authentication can be managed by attackers).

This approach is also the one followed by the e-Contract company[1] for the Belgian eID and by the eID Identity Provider project[2]. In this project they developed an IdP that interacts closely with an eID Applet that interacts with the eID. Our goal was different, we do not want to provide a completely new,

---

[1] http://www.e-contract.be
[2] http://code.google.com/p/eid-idp

fully-fledged IdP capable of interacting with eIDs. Instead, we provide a basic identification and authentication protocol, involving installed PIdPs for dealing with eIDs (see Section 4), which can then be used by existing IdP's.

A different approach [5], also put forward for the Belgian eID, consists in using a different HTTP protocol anchor (auth). In a browser, this anchor could be associated to a client authentication application, which could use the URI host and path following the anchor to contact an authentication server, or some IdP. The authentication protocol, which may, or may not, involve an eID, includes some HTTP client-server state information (e.g. an SSL session identifier) to establish the link between the authentication proofs and the relationship with existing (SSL) sessions. This approach involves changing all browsers to tackle this new anchor, and entangles the authentication proof with transport information (the SSL session identifier), which is not advised to keep application-level session management separated from secure transport management.

3   Architectural Overview

In Web interactions, the most frequent way to separate the authentication and identification of people (service clients) from the actual service provisioning is based on the SAML 2.0 Web browser based SSO profile, presented in Figure 1 (top-left). When a browser first accesses a Service Provider (SP), the SP redirects the client to an IdP (for this reason, the service is also called Relying Party). The IdP authenticates the browser user, using some Web interface, and redirects the browser to an identity management module of the Relying Party. In this redirection, the IdP sends an assertion containing a set of identity attributes associated with the authenticated user. Upon validating the IdP assertion, the identity management module will select an existing profile matching the provided attributes and will thereafter use it in the subsequent interaction with the client (using a cookie returned after a profile match). Different services using the same IdP can get different sets of identity attributes for the same person.

Our simplest eID-based identification architecture consists in replacing the IdP by a PIdP located in the client host (top-right diagram of Figure 1). The PIdP conducts the eID-based user authentication and provides a user identification assertion, in the form of a datum signed by the eID, to the Relying Party's identity module. The user identity attributes are the identity attributes contained in the PKC that goes along with the signature. Upon validating the user signature, the identity management module will select an existing profile matching the user's PKC identity attributes.

A more complex but richer approach can be achieved by combining both concepts (bottom diagram of Figure 1). In fact, a Relying Party can use an IdP for hiding all user authentication details, and the IdP can interact with the PIdP for authenticating the user with his/her eID and get his/her PKC identity attributes.

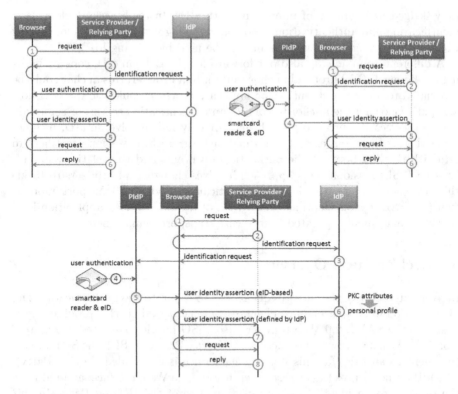

Fig. 1. Common IdP-based client identification architecture in Web interactions (top-left), alternative architecture using a PIdP and an eID (top-right) and a combined architecture using an IdP service and a PIdP (bottom)

4   PIdP-Based Identification and Authentication

Our new identification architecture uses eID cards and a PIdP local to the person that wants to get identified (see Fig. 2). In terms of interface, the PIdP is a Web server. Along this text we will use the term *user* to refer the person that will be identified and authenticated by a service using his/her eID.

Whenever a service handling a client request requires the identification of the requesting user (1), it requires it to the client's PIdP (2), which must run on the client's host (thus, in the IP address 127.x.x.x). The identification request is made with a redirection of the client browser to its local PIdP, together with some authentication parameters. The PIdP interacts with the user in order to conduct his/her authentication with an eID (3), upon which it uses a parameter of message 2 to redirect the client browser to the service's identification module (IM) (4), which will validate the authentication proof and collect the user PKC, both provided by the PIdP. Upon success, the IM stores the user PKC in the proper session context, and redirects the client to its original target service (5), which will then provide the service to an already identified client (6).

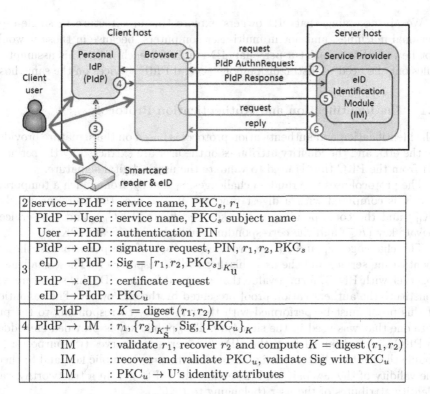

Fig. 2. Proposed user identification architecture (top), using a PIdP (Personal IdP) to handle the authentication and identification of a client user with his/her eID, and the protocol details (below), using the same interaction numbering. $\lceil x \rceil_y$ stands for the "'the value x signed with private key y".

The PIdP is the only component that interacts with the eID and it does not need to be integrated with the client browser. It has its own graphical interface for interacting with the local user in order to customize the exploitation of the eID. The benefits of this approach are twofold: (1) the client cannot be fooled by a phony browser interface requiring credentials to use the user's eID; and (2) this approach works with all browsers (or other HTTP user agents) capable of supporting server replies containing HTTP redirections. This decision holds little impact over the security mechanism of the user eID, as it is basically an exploitation facilitation decision. The PIdP may very well use the native local interface of the eID middleware (for example, for getting an authorization PIN).

The PIdP is a local service of the user, therefore it doesn't need to be available to other machines in the Internet. Consequently, it can use a localhost IP address (e.g. 127.0.0.1). However, both this address and the TCP port used to receive HTTP requests have to be standard (in order to be known by the authentication requester). Alternatively, these elements can be conveyed by the browser as HTTP header fields.

We are assuming that eID owners explore this architecture in single-user, personal machines, and not in multi-user computers, because in those it would not be trivial to connect a personal eID reader for each user. This assumption rules out the need to distinguish among several PIdP services on the same host.

4.1   The Identification and Authentication Protocol

The identification and authentication protocol is based on the signature provided by the eID, and the identity attributes of the user are extracted by the service's IM from the PKC that is used to validate the user's digital signature.

The protocol uses two random challenges, r_1 and r_2, from which a temporary key K is computed with a digest function. It also uses the users' private key (K_u^-) and the corresponding public key certificate (PKC$_u$), and the service's private key (K_s^-) and the corresponding public key certificate (PKC$_s$).

The challenges r_1 and r_2 are provided by each of the participants: the authenticating service and the user (his/her PIdP), respectively. These challenges, together with PKC$_s$, form a value that is signed by the eID; this signature will constitute the authentication proof presented by the eID owner. The validation of this proof must be performed with the public key corresponding to the private one that was used in the signature. This public key is provided embedded in PKC$_u$, also obtained from the eID. This certificate serves two purposes: (1) enable the IM to validate the signature with the proper public key, and to check the validity of the key pair, and (2) enable the IM to get, in a trustworthy way, identity attributes of the user (belonging to PKC$_u$).

The value of r_1 may optionally include a subcomponent with a service timestamp. This timestamp can help the IM to discard authentication requests happening after a threshold timeout defined solely by the service.

The purpose of the random value r_2 is to prevent a malicious service to collect specific r_1 values signed with users' private keys. The protection principle here is that the eID never signs a value that is solely provided by a third party; it must always include a random component generated locally by the PIdP.

4.2   Identification of Services and Protection of User's Privacy

The user identity elements, contained in his/her PKC$_u$, should not be delivered to services in clear text for preserving the users' privacy from eavesdroppers. Furthermore, attackers running rogue services should not be able to impersonate legitimate services just to know the identity of clients.

To protect against these issues, all critical elements provided to the IM are protected with the service's public key, K_s^+, contained in PKC$_s$. Namely, the challenge r_2 is encrypted with K_s^+, thus can only be recovered by the owner of K_s^-, and the user's identity attributes, conveyed in his/her PKC$_u$, are encrypted with K, a temporary key derived from both r_1 and r_2. Therefore, a malicious service using a stolen PKC$_s$ can not recover r_2 nor K, thus cannot observe PKC$_u$.

The services' certificates are not validated by the PIdP using certification chains or validity dates. Furthermore, they can be different from the certificates used by the services' underlying HTTPS servers. The PIdP should use a strategy similar to SSH [6] to handle relationships between services names and their certificates: if yet unknown, the user is asked whether or not it should be maintained; if already known, the PIdP checks if it has changed and, upon a change, asks the user if it authorizes the update of the existing information.

Note that the whole system is prepared to validate services' certificates according with X.509 rules at any time, but in our opinion it is excessive. As we will see, the main drawback of this approach is the possibility to provide a PKC_u to an attacker. This topic will be further addressed in the next section.

5   Security Analysis

In this section we will evaluate the security of our authentication protocol regarding two kinds of attacks against authentication protocols: (i) identity stealing and (ii) identity surveillance.

A user may be fooled by a rogue service provider presenting a misleading identity (name and certificate). Two situations can occur: (i) the server presents a stolen certificate, for which it has no corresponding private key; or (i) the server presents its own certificate, for which it has a private key.

In the first case, the server would not be able to interpret the PIdP response, namely to get PKC_u, because it doesn't know K_s^-. For the exact same reason, a network eavesdropper would not also be able to interpret the user response, and therefore would not be able to get any information about the user identity.

In the second case, the server is able to interpret correctly the PIdP response, with his/her identity attributes. This allows the server to become aware of the user identity, but not to impersonate him/her, because the response cannot be reused (either as it is or after some manipulation). In fact, the values r_1 are different on each authentication run and the certificates PKC_s are different for each server. Therefore, a signature made by an eID once for an authentication process cannot be used in another authentication process (because either r_1 or PKC_s are different). We are assuming, of course, that given a signed piece of data it is impossible to find another one, different from the former, where the same signature fits. Therefore, the response provided by the PIdP when interacting with a particular authentication service cannot be stolen and reused with another server. This is true as well for a network eavesdropper, which has even less control over the PIdP response than a server being able to interpret the response.

Consequently, the protocol is secure against identity theft attempts based on stolen PIdP responses, either when the attacker does not know K_s^- (network eavesdroppers or rogue services using stolen certificates) or when the attacker knows K_s^- (rogue service using its own certificate). In the worst case, a rogue service may be able to learn the user identity after being able to convince the user to participate in a eID-based authentication. However, with password-based systems this risk is incomparably higher, since in that case the rogue service can, in fact, steal the user's authentication credentials.

Finally, certificate validation would not help most users to protect themselves against false certificates presented by rogue services. In fact, the vast majority of users doesn't know anything about certificates and certification chains, thus they are not likely to react appropriately to error messages provided upon errors detected in the validation of certificates. Therefore, they can always be misled by rogue certificates when asked to proceed or not upon validation errors.

6 Implementation and Experimentation

We have implemented a prototype of the authentication protocol using the PIdP and HTML mechanisms. The prototype was tested with the IdP-based identification infrastructure of University of Aveiro, which was adapted to perform the identification and authentication of the client using his/her PIdP and the Portuguese eID. The prototype was designed to work with all browsers, therefore we only used standard HTML mechanisms. Furthermore, we restrained ourselves from using facilities such as Java Script, because users and/or domain-wide policies may block them for security reasons.

The PIdP is a stand-alone, graphical application programmed in Java. It is based on the HttpServer class and uses Swing for managing the graphical interface. Upon a first authentication contact by a local client (browser), the PIdP launches a thread that conducts the interaction with the user and with his/her eID. In the meanwhile, the PIdP main thread keeps a dialog with the browser for showing a minimum of information regarding the current interaction with the eID. Once this interaction finishes, the PIdP redirects the browser to the validation service provided in the initial redirection URL.

The interaction with the eID uses native PKCS #11 C libraries. Regarding other crypto, r_1 and r_2 have 16 bytes each and K is computed with SHA-1 (first 16 bytes of the output). The symmetric encryption of PKC_u with K is with AES-128 (with ECB and PKCS5 padding). The encryption of r_2 with K_S^+ is with RSA (ECB mode and OAEP with SHA-1 and MGF1 padding).

The authentication request to the IdP is an HTTP GET request to URL http://127.0.0.1:[port]/authenticate with 4 parameters: the 3 presented in the protocol description (see Fig. 2) plus the URL where the response should be returned; port will be discussed below. The authentication response is also an HTTP GET request, to the URL provided in the request, with the 4 parameters presented in the protocol description. All byte array parameters are transmitted encoded as hexadecimal strings.

The PIdP is addressed using a standard and uniform IP address for the client host (127.0.0.1) and a TCP port. The IP address does not pose any addressing issues, as it is interpreted by the client browser. On the contrary, dealing with the PIdP TCP port is more complex. According to standards [7], a port in a URI is expressed solely with digits; names are not allowed, therefore we could not rely on some existing port name resolver.

For our first experiments we chose and used a fixed port number (666) for the PIdP. As this is not an elegant solution, we are actually working on a name server using a well-known port number, which could appropriately redirect requests to local services (such as a PIdP). But for the sake of the experimental tests, the result is exactly the same.

7 Conclusions

In this paper we have presented a new approach for dealing with the Web authentication with eID tokens. This approach is based on a local application, called PIdP (Personal Identity Provider) that does not need to be trusted by the authenticator. On the other hand, the PIdP should be trusted by the eID owner, and in that sense our approach is more is more likely to fulfill this requisite than Java Applets or other form of dynamic code downloaded just-in-time by browsers. Finally, users are free to choose, or even develop, their own PIdP. This means that they have the power to define which application interacts with their eID, which is an advantage for managing personalization features (e.g. PIN recording for particular services) and for preventing abusive interactions with eIDs (e.g. multiple signature requests instead of a single one).

The PIdP-based authentication architecture is completely independent from browsers and can be used directly by service providers or by identity providers. Our prototype, based on a Java PIdP and on Java Servlets, was tested in both scenarios. Currently it works only with the Portuguese eID, but it can be easily extended to deal with eIDs of other countries or even companies. Furthermore, we can use other alternative physical locations of the user credentials (files, USB dongles, etc.) other than an eID, because it is up to the PIdP to look for them.

References

1. Hughes, J., Cantor, S., Hodges, J., Hirsch, F., Mishra, P., Philpott, R., Maler, E.: Profiles for the OASIS Security Assertion Markup Language (SAML) 2.0. OASIS. (March 2005) http://docs.oasis-open.org/security/saml/v2.0/saml-profiles-2.0-os.pdf.
2. Rescorla, E.: HTTP Over TLS. RFC 2818 (Informational) (May 2000)
3. Bour, I.: Electronic Identities in Europe: overview of E-ID solutions connecting citizens to public authorities. UL Transaction Security Whitepaper (April 2013)
4. Cooper, D., Santesson, S., Farrell, S., Boeyen, S., Housley, R., Polk, W.: Internet X.509 Public Key Infrastructure Certificate and Certificate Revocation List (CRL) Profile. RFC 5280 (May 2008)
5. Verhaeghe, P., Lapon, J., De Decker, B., Naessens, V., Verslype, K.: Security and Privacy Improvements for the Belgian eID Technology. In: Gritzalis, D., Lopez, J. (eds.) SEC 2009. IFIP AICT, vol. 297, pp. 237–247. Springer, Heidelberg (2009)
6. Ylonen, T., Lonvick, C.: The Secure Shell (SSH) Protocol Architecture. RFC 4251 (January 2006)
7. Berners-Lee, T., Fielding, R., Masinter, L.: Uniform Resource Identifier (URI): Generic Syntax. RFC 3986 (January 2005)

CAN Bus Risk Analysis Revisit

Hafizah Mansor, Konstantinos Markantonakis, and Keith Mayes

Information Security Group, Smart Card Centre,
Royal Holloway, University of London, United Kingdom
Hafizah.Mansor.2011@live.rhul.ac.uk,
{K.Markantonakis,Keith.Mayes}@rhul.ac.uk

Abstract. In automotive design process, safety has always been the main concern. However, in modern days, security is also seen as an important aspect in vehicle communication especially where connectivity is very widely available. In this paper, we are going to discuss the threats and vulnerabilities of a CAN bus network. After we have considered a number of risk analysis methods, we decided to use FMEA. The analysis process allowed us to derive the security requirements of a CAN bus. Experimental setup of CAN bus communication network were implemented and analysed.

Keywords: Risk analysis, ECU, FMEA, CAN bus network.

1   Introduction

Safety is always the first priority in automotive application. With the advanced technologies and introduction of multiple intelligent applications for automotive, security is now a very crucial criteria to ensure the safety and reliability of a car.

In modern vehicles, the operations are controlled by embedded microcontrollers called ECUs (Electronic Control Units). These ECUs are interconnected through multiple network buses, such as Controller Area Network (CAN) [9], Media Oriented Systems Transport (MOST) [13], Local Interconnect Network (LIN) [14] and FlexRay [12].

This paper will discuss the risk analysis of a CAN bus network using Failure Mode and Effect Analysis (FMEA). The objective of this paper is twofold. While analysing the security requirements on CAN bus network, we also want to highlight the method we used for risk analysis.

The next section will discuss background and related works on vulnerabilities and threats on vehicular networks, their method for risk analysis and their proposals for secure solutions. Our CAN bus risk analysis using FMEA is decribed in the following section. From the analysis, we discuss the security requirements of a CAN bus network. The last section describes the experimental CAN bus implementation that we conducted with basic communication and incorporating crypto operations to introduce security to the CAN bus communications.

D. Naccache and D. Sauveron (Eds.): WISTP 2014, LNCS 8501, pp. 170–179, 2014.

1.1 Background

Since in-car network connectivity is becoming very widely used and available, people are interested on how this may improve the operations of a vehicle. Thus, some parties have higher motivation, whether to gain financial profit or recognition by attacking the system. This is even easier by the availability of many interfaces (On board diagnostic (OBD), Bluetooth, wireless) and the weaknesses proven [10][5][8] in the current system.

1.2 Related Work

In this section, we are going to discuss a number of industrial projects and their security requirements analysis methods.

The focus of EVITA project [2] was security for onboard networks. In their security requirement analysis, they identified use cases and threat scenarios to obtain the security requirements. Hence, they designed a secure onboard architecture and secure onboard communications protocols.

In the SeVecom project [1], they introduced cluster analysis for security requirement analysis process [11]. The objective of SeVecom project was to find a future-proof solution to the problem of vehicle to vehicle (V2V) and and vehicle to infrastructure (V2I). Focusing on communication specific to road traffic, it proposed a security architecture and security mechanisms by proposing cryptographic algorithms and secure device for vehicular networks.

The PRESERVE project [4] combines the results of several projects such as SeVecom, PRECIOSA (Privacy Enabled Capability in Co-operative Systems and Safety Applications) [3], EVITA and OVERSEE. The objective of this project is to create an integrated vehicle to X (V2X) security architecture. In this project, they use the method introduced by [11] to obtain their security requirements and countermeasures [15].

In European Telecommunication Standard Institute (ETSI), a standard for Intelligent Transport Systems (ITS) was made to ensure efficient and reliable communication in transport system. In [6], the ETSI (ITS) document lists seven steps to identify risks using threat, vulnerability and risk analysis (TVRA). In the TVRA method, the security requirements are listed first, then only the threats to the requirements are analysed.

2 Risk Analysis

There are different methods and tools available to conduct a risk analysis of a system. In this paper, we conduct our risk analysis based on FMEA. In FMEA, risk is the product of the probability that an event (potential failure mode) may occur in a specified system and the impact on the system if the event occurs and to what extent the event can be detected in the existing environment.

2.1   CAN Bus Risk Analysis Using FMEA

In this security risk analysis, we take the approach of viewing the risks of a CAN bus from four different views, i.e car lifecycle, CAN bus operations, entities involved and ECUs. While the lists are not exhaustive, our analysis mainly focuses on common use cases without V2V and V2I communications. From the different views of risks, we can highlight the risk levels and thus propose proper mitigation actions to overcome the threats and vulnerabilities accordingly.

Table 1. Probability Rating

Probability of failure	Failure	Rating
Very High	>=1 in 2	10
	1 in 3	9
High	1 in 8	8
	1 in 20	7
Moderate	1 in 80	6
	1 in 40	5
	1 in 2,000	4
Low	1 in 15,000	3
	1 in 150,000	2
Remote	1 in 1,500,000	1

Table 2. Severity Rating

Effect	Severity of effect			Rating
	Safety	Reliability	Financial	
Catastrophic	Multiple deaths	Overall system failure	Total loss	10
Extreme	At least one death	System failure	Extremely high loss	9
Very High	Major injury	Partial system failure	Very high loss	8
High	Bad injury	Very bad distraction	High loss	7
Moderate	Moderate injury	Distraction	Moderate loss	6
Low	Small injury	Loss of comfort	Small loss	5
Very low	Very small injury	Uncomfortable	Very low loss	4
Minor	Minor injury	Minor loss of comfort	Minor loss	3
Very Minor	Very minor injury	Very minor loss of comfort	Very minor loss	2
None	No effect	No effect	No effect	1

In FMEA, the ratings for probability, severity, detection and risk depend on the process or product being analysed. In this analysis, the ratings scale is an initial starting point that could be refined following discussion with industry. Tables 1, 2, 3 are ratings related to probability, severity and detection respectively. Table 4 assigns the risk priority number (RPN) values, which is the product of probability, severity and detection, to the different risk levels.

Table 3. Detection rating

Detection	Likelihood of detection	Rating
Absolute uncertainty	Control cannot detect	10
Very remote	Very remote chance the control will detect	9
Remote	Remote chance the control will detect	8
Very low	Very low chance the control will detect	7
Low	Low chance the control will detect	6
Moderate	Moderate chance the control will detect	5
Moderately high	Moderately high chance the control will detect	4
High	High chance the control will detect	3
Very high	Very high chance the control will detect	2
Almost certain	Control will detect	1

Table 4. Risk level

Risk level	RPN	Label
Unacceptable	301<=RPN<=1000	U
High	201<=RPN<=300	H
Moderate	101<=RPN<=200	M
Low	1<=RPN<=100	L

Car Life Cycle. Car life cycle starts from the manufacturing state, followed by selling, use by owner, reselling and forensics. In each state of the life cycle, there are many different potential failure modes. Table 5 shows the FMEA for car life cycle. From the analysis, we conclude that the highest risk is during the usage of the car by the user or the owner. During this state of life cycle, the CAN bus network is most vulnerable whether to attacks or to any failure modes that might occur deliberately or not.

Entities. There are a number of different entities involved in a car lifecycle. They are the car manufacturer, car parts supplier, firmware developer, technician and mechanic at workshop, car agent and dealer, insurance agent, owner, user and interested parties in car hacking (car manufacturing competitor, hobbyist, researcher, technical enthusiast, thief and terrorist). From the analysis, the car manufacturer and the insurance agent are seen as low risk entities, while car parts supplier is considered at moderate risk. Other entities are found to be at unacceptable risk level.

CAN Bus Operations. The risks are also analysed from the weaknesses of CAN bus operations that might be used by the attacker to cause failure modes. For example, for message reception, an attacker can cause failure by making improper filtering. Other general weaknesses that can be threats to the CAN bus are the broadcast nature of the network, priority bus based arbitration and unlimited number of nodes. These manipulations can cause severe effects if they involve critical ECUs. The detection level for failure mode is very remote.

Table 5. FMEA of car life cycle

Life cycle	Failure mode	Entity	Mechanism	Why	Effect	Probability	Severity	Detection	RPN	Risk level	Mitigation
Car manufacturing	Wrong parts	Manufacturer		Financial/ negligence	safety/ comfort	4	7	2	56	L	Parts authentication
	Counterfeit parts				safety/ comfort	4	8	2	64	L	Parts authentication
	Incompatible firmware				safety/ comfort	8	6	4	192	M	Firmware version control
	Bad parts				safety	4	8	2	64	L	Parts authentication
Car selling	Change of firmware	Car agent/ Technician		Financial	safety/ comfort	1	8	7	56	L	Firmware version control
	Broken wire				safety/ comfort	1	8	7	56	L	ECUs authentication
	Change of data in ECU				safety/ comfort	1	8	7	56	L	Authentication, data integrity
Service	Change of firmware	Owner/ Technician		Financial	safety/ comfort	7	9	5	315	U	Firmware version control
	Change of data in ECU				safety/ comfort	5	7	5	175	M	Authentication, data integrity
	Counterfeit parts				safety/ comfort	7	7	9	441	U	Parts authentication
	Used parts				safety/ comfort	7	7	8	392	U	Parts authentication
	Bad parts	Technician		Financial/ Negligence	safety	4	9	1	36	L	Parts authentication
Repair	Counterfeit parts	Owner/ Technician		Financial	safety/ comfort	7	7	9	441	U	Parts authentication
	Used parts				safety/ comfort	7	7	8	392	U	Parts authentication
	Bad parts	Technician		Financial/ Negligence	safety	4	9	1	36	L	Parts authentication
On the road (OTR)	Bad handling of car	User (faulty parts)		Negligence	safety/ comfort	7	9	4	252	H	Data logging on ECU states
	Sudden breakdown			-	safety/ comfort	4	9	9	324	U	Data logging on ECU states
	Sudden breakdown	Attacker		Financial/ Crime/ Interest	safety	3	9	10	270	H	Authentication
Insurance	Undeclared upgrades	Owner		Financial	safety/ comfort	8	7	10	560	U	Data logging on ECU states
	Undeclared accidents				safety/ comfort	8	9	5	360	U	Firmware version control
Reselling	Change of firmware	Car agent/ Technician		Financial	safety/ comfort	8	8	5	320	U	Firmware version control
	Broken wire				safety/ comfort	8	8	2	128	M	ECUs authentication
	Change of data in ECU				safety/ comfort	8	8	5	320	U	Authentication, data integrity
Forensics	Data not available	Technician/ Insurance agent		-	reliability	8	10	10	800	U	Backup of latest state
	Unretrieved data				reliability	8	10	10	800	U	Backup of latest state
	Broken ECU				reliability	8	10	10	800	U	Backup of latest state

ECUs and Car Operations. Each ECU has different functionalities. Using FMEA, we can conclude which ECUs are more critical in terms of safety and therefore require extra protection. The ECUs related to comfort are considered as lower risk ECUs as the severity of failure is less compared to ECUs related to safety. There is minimal control to detect any failure mode that might occur to these ECUs, and thereby causing the risk to be higher.

FMEA as a Risk Analysis and Security Design Tool. With the increasing reliance on car technology and security, FMEA should be given greater attention in the future. From Table 5, it shows that risk analysis has better coverage by not only considering threats, vulnerabilities and attacks, but also considering the potential failure modes in the overall life cycle of a car and the entities involved. Attacks are conducted intentionally on vulnerabilities of the system, but unintentional actions may also lead to failure modes of the system. Therefore, it is important to consider all possible failure modes in our risk analysis. The detection attribute in the FMEA helps to address the effectiveness of countermeasures being introduced.

2.2 Security Requirements

After the preliminary analysis, the security requirements for a CAN bus are concluded in Table 6. We divided the security requirements of a CAN bus into two parts. They are the security of the nodes (ECUs) and the security of the communication protocols.

Table 6. Security requirements of a CAN bus

Security requirements	Node	Communication protocol
Authentication	✓	✓
Integrity	✓	✓
Availability	✓	✓
Non-repudiation		✓
Freshness		✓
Confidentiality	✓	
Access control	✓	✓
Tamper resistance	✓	

3 Experimental Work

From the analysis it appears that the CAN bus will be a weak link in our system unless the traffic can be better secured. However security may come at a performance cost and so to investigate this, an experimental system was created.

3.1 Method

Components. In this experiment, we tried to emulate the communications between the wheel rotation and the odometer on the instrument panel cluster

(IPC). We chose MCP25050 and PIC18F4580 (with built in CAN driver) as the CAN processors and MCP2551 as the CAN transceivers. MCP25050 is a configurable chip which makes the CAN bus setup much easier without the need of a microcontroller. The setup is as shown in Figure 1 and 2. The nodes were connected using MCP25050 development board with an oscillator clock of 16MHz. The communications at 125kbps were observed using CAN bus analyser. The CAN bus analyser application monitored the messages sent across the CAN bus.

Setup. Firstly, we used MCP25050 for Node 1 and Node 2. Node 2 was an exact copy of Node 1 in terms of its firmware. It would transmit the same message as Node 1 (including ID and data) once it received a wheel rotation signal from the sensor. In our experiment, the signal from wheel rotation was emulated using a switch pulse. For the IPC node, we used PIC18F4580. The IPC was programmed so that it would receive the messages (with specific ID) sent to the CAN bus and increment its counter once the message was successfully received. The counter was shown using LEDs at the output port.

Security Implementation. To incorporate security into the network, we included encryption and MAC using AES on the data field. Table 7 shows the different configurations of setups. For these setups, we used PIC18F4580 for IPC and Node 1, because MCP25050 is just a configurable IC and is not able to perform security computation as required. In this simple security experiment, we append the MAC as part of the data field in the message to be sent. For MAC computation, we used AES128 and concatenated the result to 2 bytes, then appended the MAC as part of the data field. For a standard frame format, the total number of bits per message is 108 bits (1 bit of start of frame, 11 bits of ID, 1 bit of remote transmission request, 1 bit of ID extension bit, 1 bit of reserved bit, 4 bits of DLC (data length code), up to 8 bytes of data field, 15 bits of CRC, 1 bit of CRC delimiter, 1 bit of ACK slot, 1 bit of ACK delimiter and 7 bits of end-of-frame). Therefore, we decided to put the MAC in the data field and truncate the MAC to 2 bytes only. The firmware codes for CAN communications (transmit and receive functions) and AES computation used for these experiments were taken from Microchip website given as part of PIC18 library [7]. The total code size for AES computation was about 4700 bytes and CAN communication was about 2500 bytes. No optimisation in terms of code size or performance was implemented.

3.2   Result

The latency caused by implementation of security features are as shown in Table 8. These operations executed at external clock of 16MHz using the development board's oscillator. For a 125kbps communication, this would result in a total messages of 1157 for a standard ID (108 bits) in a second. By adding security, it took up 0.737% of total capacity of bus for send and receive operations.

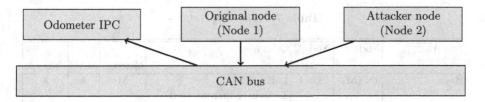

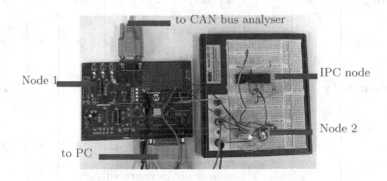

Fig. 1. CAN bus experimental setup

Fig. 2. Actual CAN bus experimental setup

3.3   Discussion

In the basic setup, it was clear that CAN bus network is very vulnerable to attacks such as sniffing, denial of service, message manipulation and many others. In our experiment, we were able to demonstrate masquarading attack on CAN bus. The attacker node sent the same message as the original node and accepted by the IPC node. From this experiment, we can conclude the requirements of a CAN bus as discussed earlier and summarised in Table 6.

In the setup with MAC, only valid nodes (nodes that have the key to generate the MAC) were able to send messages across the bus. The MAC introduced authenticity and integrity to the network. However attacker can still participate in the bus communication by listening to the network (sniffing).

Finally, in the setup with encrypt and MAC, valid nodes can transmit messages across the bus. If any node attempted to sniff the messages sent across the CAN bus, the messages were encrypted. This setup introduced confidentiality to the network while the MAC gave authenticity and integrity. However, the attacker can still send the same message by replaying the message. Therefore, freshness is further required in the communication. Freshness can be introduced by using counter or timestamp.

The key management needs to be handled properly to ensure successful security implementation, especially considering the car lifetime. It is expected for parts replacements, which include ECUs, and hence the cryptographic keys need proper handling. The synchronisation of counter or timestamp is also crucial.

Table 7. Steps of operations

Setup	Node 1	Node 2	Odometer	Message	MAC	Encrypt
Basic	Tx (M)		1. Rx (M)	M	✗	✗
			2. counter incremented			
		Tx (M)	1. Rx (M)	M	✗	✗
			2. counter incremented			
With MAC	Tx (M1)		1. Rx (M1)	M1	✓	✗
			2. verify MAC			
			3. counter incremented			
		Tx (M)	1. Rx (M)	M	✗	✗
			2. verify MAC			
			3. counter not incremented			
Encrypt+MAC	Tx (M2)		1. Rx (M2)	M2	✓	✓
			2. verify MAC			
			3. decrypt data			
			4. counter incremented			
		Tx (M)	1. Rx (M)	M	✗	✗
			2. verify MAC			
			3. counter not incremented			

Table 8. Additional computation time for security implementation

Process	Operation	Time (ms)
Generate MAC	AES encryption	1.59
Verify MAC	AES encryption	1.59
Encrypt data	AES encryption	1.59
Decrypt data	AES decryption	2.58

While security is important, cryptographic implementation alone does not guarantee a successful system. We also have to consider the limitations and constraints of the system. The latency caused by including the security features can be further optimised to ensure availability of messages in time. Appending MAC as part of the message in the data field may cause potential unavailability since some messages may require to send 8 bytes of data in one message transmission. Furthermore, MAC is not able to provide non-repudiation. A message has to be signed in order to provide non-repudiation. Therefore, this requires further work in order to provide overall security to the CAN bus which include security to the nodes as well as the communication protocol. This includes attestation during start up of operation. The constraints of automotive applications will have to be considered in proposing a secure solution. This will be included in our future work.

4   Conclusion

This paper discusses the security risk analysis of CAN bus network using FMEA and it shows that security is a process required in the automotive applications. Our experimental CAN bus communications showed that the processing appears to be quite efficient and so adding a security protocol may well be feasible. With the increase use of networks connectivity to improve and assist performance of vehicles, this justifies the need of security to ensure privacy, safety and reliability.

References

1. SeVeCom project, http://www.sevecom.org/
2. EVITA project, http://www.evita-project.org/
3. PRECIOSA, http://www.preciosa-project.org/
4. PRESERVE project, http://www.preserve-project.eu/
5. Checkoway, S., McCoy, D., Kantor, B., Anderson, D., Shacham, H., Savage, S., Koscher, K., Czeskis, A., Roesner, F., Kohno, T.: Comprehensive experimental analyses of automotive attack surfaces. In: USENIX Security Symposium (2011)
6. ETSI. ITS: Security: Threat, Vulnerability and Risk Analysis (TVRA). Technical report, ETSI (2010)
7. Flowers, D.: AN953: Data Encryption Routines for the PIC18 (2005)
8. Miller, R., Rouf, I., Mustafa, H., Oh, S., Taylor, T., Xu, W., Gruteser, M., Trappe, W., Seskar, I.: Security and privacy vulnerabilities of in-car wireless networks: A tire pressure monitoring system case study. In: 19th USENIX Security Symposium, Washington DC, pp. 11–13 (2010)
9. Road vehicles – Controller Area Network (CAN) – part 1: Data link layer and physical signalling. Standard, International Organization for Standardization (February 2003)
10. Koscher, K., Czeskis, A., Roesner, F., Patel, S., Kohno, T., Checkoway, S., McCoy, D., Kantor, B., Anderson, D., Shacham, H., et al.: Experimental security analysis of a modern automobile. In: 2010 IEEE Symposium on Security and Privacy (SP), pp. 447–462. IEEE (2010)
11. Kung, A.: Security architecture and mechanisms for V2V/V2I. Technical report, SeVeCom (2008)
12. Makowitz, R., Temple, C.: Flexray- A communication network for automotive control systems. In: 2006 IEEE International Workshop on Factory Communication Systems, pp. 207–212 (2006)
13. Media Oriented Systems Transport Specifications (2006)
14. Ruff, M.: Evolution of Local Interconnect Network (LIN) solutions. In: 2003 IEEE 58th Vehicular Technology Conference, VTC 2003-Fall, vol. 5, pp. 3382–3389. IEEE (2003)
15. Stotz, J.P., Bißmeyer, N., Kargl, F., Dietzel, S., Papadimitratos, P., Schleiffer, C.: Security requirements of vehicle security architecture. Technical report, PRESERVE (2011)

AU2EU: Privacy-Preserving Matching of DNA Sequences*

Tanya Ignatenko[1] and Milan Petković[2,3]

[1] Electrical Engineering Department,
Eindhoven University of Technology, The Netherlands
t.ignatenko@tue.nl
[2] Mathematics and Computer Science Department,
Eindhoven University of Technology, The Netherlands
[3] Philips Research Eindhoven, The Netherlands
milan.petkovic@philips.com

Abstract. Advances in DNA sequencing create new opportunities for
the use of DNA data in healthcare for diagnostic and treatment purposes, but also in many other health and well-being services. This brings
new challenges with regard to the protection and use of this sensitive
data. Thus, special technical means of protection should safeguard critical DNA data and create trust for patients and consumers of lifestyle
services. In particular an interesting research challenge is to design secure
operations on DNA sequences in the encrypted domain that allow a person to engage into a DNA-based service and obtain required (medical)
answers without revealing his/her DNA. We focus in this paper on this
topic and present a solution to a particular problem of privacy-preserving
matching of DNA sequences which can be used in clinical trials or other
DNA services.

1 Introduction

To be competitive and efficient, multiple independent organizations often have
to form virtual collaborations to work together on critical applications or to
share sensitive data. In order to facilitate such collaborations, a widely deployed
network infrastructure can be used to allow access to either cloud-based environments or directly grant access through the involved parties to each other's
systems and resources. Given the fact that such applications have to deal with
sensitive data, organizations feel reluctant to move their resources to the cloud
or safely rely on the (authentication) claims coming from the members of the
collaboration. As a result trust becomes an important component of such collaborations. Cross-organizational and jurisdictional nature of these collaborations
makes it hard to relate different attributes and policies of different collaborating
parties and thus build mutual trust.

* This work has been partially funded by the EC via grant agreement no. 611659 for
the AU2EU project.

D. Naccache and D. Sauveron (Eds.): WISTP 2014, LNCS 8501, pp. 180–189, 2014.

The problem of establishing trust lies in the lack of authentication and authorization infrastructures supporting high level of assurance, privacy as well as cross-domain and jurisdictional collaborations. Thus, there is a clear need for an adequate infrastructure for authentication and authorization in establishing trust. To address this need and general requirements of distributed eAuthentication and eAuthorization infrastructures for trusted secure information sharing, the EU FP7 project called AUthentication and AUthorization for Entrusted Unions (AU2EU) was initiated. The project is a joint collaboration between seven EU partners and five research institutes and universities in Australia. The main objectives of this project are to: (a) deploy a composable architecture that builds on the best existing practices and novel emerging techniques to design the eAuthentication and eAuthorization infrastructure for cross-organizational and jurisdictional collaborations; (b) extend the joint eAuthentication and eAuthorization framework with four novel functionalities: (i) assurance of claims to increase trust by introducing the ability to assess reliability of claims; (ii) trust indicators to assess trustworthiness of the involved devices, platforms and services; (iii) cryptographic policy enforcement to ensure data confidentiality in cloud-based and offline scenarios inherent to distributed systems; and (iv) mechanism to perform operations under encryption to enable processing data in a privacy-preserving way; (c) implement the resulting joint eAuthentication and eAuthorization framework and deploy it in two real-life pilots in Australia and Europe; and (d) evaluate its security, maturity, scalability, and usability.

The project is driven by four use cases, namely bio-security, eHealth, and two healthcare use cases related to picture archiving and communication systems (PACS) and DNA data management. The joint eAuthentication and eAuthorization infrastructure is designed by combining the XACML-based authorization framework [3], ABC4Trust [2] authentication architecture and TDL [1] authentication framework. In our framework we deploy novel mechanisms for semantic mapping to translate policies and attributes to the required authentication claims that can be verified in our authentication framework. To guarantee strong authentication and privacy at the same time, idemix technology [4] for attribute-based authentication is used as a building block of our authentication architecture. To support privacy as well as ease of use for collaborating parties, the idemix is integrated as a cloud-based service in the AU2EU architecture. The platform will be deployed and evaluated in the bio-security and eHealth pilots.

In the rest of this paper, we focus on the DNA use case that fall under one of the AU2EU research directions, which is operations under encryption. When sensitive data, e.g. patient DNA or bio-security incident data, need to be accessed and processed by various parties in the distributed collaborative systems, restricting access to only partial data is a difficult task, since processing and extracting partial information from the data often requires access to the whole dataset. Policy enforcement mechanisms alone cannot guarantee this fine-grained level of access control. It would be ideal if we could perform operations on the encrypted data that are equivalent to the operations one need to perform on the corresponding non-encrypted data, without the need to decrypt them. Processing in the encrypted domain that builds on homomorphic encryption techniques [5], secure multi-party computation [6], and code-based security [7] suggest possible solutions. It would allow a party to engage into applications dealing with sensitive data (e.g. medical trial or disease risk profiling that use DNA data) and obtain required answers without revealing particular data or without 'seeing' user's data in plain text.

In this paper we concentrate on the problem of privacy-preserving similarity search in DNA databases for clinical trials and medical research. Clinical trials and genome-wide association studies are typical tools to evaluate effectiveness of certain treatments and drugs, and to determine dependencies between DNA patterns and diseases. In clinical trials, the eligibility criteria for inclusion in a trial might include patients with DNA sequences that have similar phenotype (e.g. race) and functionality (e.g. a gene is on or off). In genome-wide association studies, to conduct tests, one need to select DNA sequences that can be formed into cases (e.g. sequences that contain a mutation) and controls (sequences that do not contain a mutation). Therefore, to find eligible patients for a clinical trial or data for research purposes, various parties like pharmacies that conduct a trial, and clinical researchers have to be able to look up patient's primary medical records and research repositories containing DNA information and check DNA sequences against inclusion criteria. However, accessing DNA information in such databases poses privacy and security concerns. Remarkably, DNA sequences are self-identifying sensitive data. They are a unique identifier of human beings; moreover these sequences contain information used for disease risk profiling, ancestry determination and, potentially, other more personal physiological aspects. It is important to realize that since DNA data are identifiers by themselves, DNA sequences, unlike other medical information, cannot be anonymized. Thus realization of clinical trials and research experiments that use genetic information as a subject selection criterion requires a proper DNA management infrastructure in place. In the next section we present our solution to a particular problem of privacy-preserving indexing of DNA sequences to support similarity search.

2   Privacy-Preserving DNA Indices

Consider the problem when a third party (e.g. a pharmacy) has to query a (distributed) DNA database in order to find patients (e.g. volunteers for a clinical trial) whose DNA sequences are similar to a query (example) DNA sequence. To guarantee privacy of DNA information stored in the database, we only store privacy-preserving DNA indices that can be used for similarity measurements. We propose to use DNA sequences processed into context trees as index-information that can be used to facilitate privacy-preserving matching and similarity search in DNA databases. The context trees are built by estimating the underlying model of (a set of similar, in a certain sense) DNA sequence(s) using the universal compression technique called context-tree weighting (CTW) [8]. As a retrieval criterion the mutual information, that characterizes the inherent dependence of two variables, see e.g. [19], between a query DNA sequence and database sequences is used. We compute this mutual information as a difference between the codeword length of a query DNA sequence computed using CTW and the codeword length of this DNA sequence computed given the stored DNA-indices. Privacy of DNA information is achieved by only storing the context trees that represent the DNA source generating the sequences, as the context trees along are insufficient to reconstruct the underlying DNA sequences.

2.1 DNA Preliminaries

Genome is entire organism hereditary information containing the complete set of instructions for constructing an organism. The human genome consists of tightly coiled threads of deoxyribonucleic acid (DNA) which basic building blocks are four nucleobases or bases that are adenine (A), thymine (T), cytosine (C), and guanine (G). The particular order of the nucleobases is called the DNA sequence which is measured in base pairs (bp). The human genome contains roughly 3 billion bp. DNA sequences contain instructions for manufacturing all proteins, in this way to form proteins triplets of DNA bases (codons) are interpreted as amino acids, and amino acids in their turn are added to a growing chain that forms protein. Thus DNA sequences are not random and have logical sequential organization.

Individual genomes vary in about 1 in 1000 bp. Remarkably these small variations account for significant phenotype differences including disease susceptibility, medication response etc. Typically variations are accumulated over time from mutations, structural polymorphisms, chromosome recombination. On a structural level, these variations include single-nucleotide polymorphisms (SNP), that is substitutions variation in a DNA at a single nucleotide position; structural polymorphism, that is a large scale structural changes characterized by indels - insertion or deletion of short nucleotide sequences.

2.2 Context-Tree Weighting (CTW) Method

The context-tree weighting (CTW) method [8] is a universal source coding method that finds a good coding distribution for an observed (DNA) source sequence in a sequential way. This coding distribution corresponds to all tree-models whose depth does not exceed D. The distribution can be used to compress an observed sequence using arithmetic coding techniques. The CTW method also approaches entropy for ergodic stationary sources. The CTW method can also be used as a two-pass method [18]: in the first step it is used to determine the statistical model matching an observed (DNA) sequence, and in the second step this model is encoded and the observed (DNA) sequence is encoded (compressed) given the model.

The CTW method uses a concept of context trees. A context tree, see Fig.1, consists of nodes that correspond to contexts s up to a certain depth D. Each node s in the context tree is associated with the subsequence of source symbols that occurred in the observed sequence after context s. Moreover, to each node s

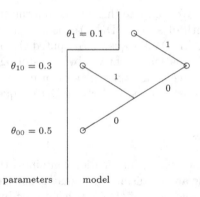

$\theta_1 = 0.1$

$\theta_{10} = 0.3$

$\theta_{00} = 0.5$

parameters   model

Fig. 1. An example of a binary context-tree of depth 2 with parameters, from [8]

there corresponds a parameter θ_s that give s the probability of the next symbol being one (in the binary case) in the sequences when context s was observed.

The DNA sequence structure is such that it codes for amino acids and subsequently for proteins in a sequential way. This makes the CTW particularly suitable for this type of data. For example, it was shown in [9] that CTW performs well for DNA compression. Let x^T denote an observed DNA sequence. Then CTW can be used to estimate $P(x^T)$, where x^T corresponds to a DNA vector with values from alphabet $A = \{1, 2, 3, 4\}^1$. Denote with x_t a symbol at position t in the observed sequence x^T. A statistical model for the DNA sequence is estimated by building the context tree and estimating the distribution $P(x^T)$ using the CTW algorithm as $P(x_t | \{x_{t-b}, b \in B\})$, where B is a set of well-chosen integers. The "context" $\{x_{t-b}, b \in B\}$ consists of a set of values from alphabet A obtained from $|B|$ different locations of x^T. Typically, B is defined as a set of values preceding x_t. All possible contexts (that actually occurred in the observed DNA sequence) together with probability distribution $P(x_t | \{x_{t-b}, b \in B\})$ constitute the context-tree (model) and the parameters, respectively. Thus, for a DNA sequence the context-tree model constitutes an ensemble of short subsequences that occurred there.

2.3   Similarity Measure

Consider an observed DNA sequence x^T. Suppose $\{S, \Theta_S\}$ are a model (contexts) and parameter set (conditional probabilities) describing some tree source of depth not larger than D. Then if we use $\{S, \Theta_S\}$ to compress this sequence, the length of the compressed sequence will be given by

$$L(x^T | x^1_{-D}, \{S, \Theta_S\}) = -\sum_{t=1}^{T} \log_2 P(x_t | x^{t-1}_{-D}, \{S, \Theta_S\}) = -\sum_{t=1}^{T} \log_2 \theta^{x_t}_{\sigma_{\{x^{t-1}_{-D}\}}},$$

(1)

---

[1] Since DNA alphabet is $\{A, T, G, C\}$, we can replace it with $\{1, 2, 3, 4\}$ without loss of generality.

where $\sigma_{\{x_{-D}^{t-1}\}}$ is a mapping of x_{-D}^{t-1} to a context from S and

$$P(x_t|x_{-D}^{t-1}, \{S, \Theta_S\}) = \theta_{\sigma_{\{x_{-D}^{t-1}\}}}^{x_t} \in \Theta$$

is the probability of symbol x_t to occur after subsequence $\sigma_{\{x_{-D}^{t-1}\}}$ was observed in x^T. When $\{S, \Theta_S\}$ describes the actual source that produced x^T then $L(x^T|x_{-D}^1, \{S, \Theta_S\})$ corresponds to the ideal codeword length. However, if $\{S, \Theta_S\}$ describes some other source then $L(x^T|x_{-D}^1, \{S, \Theta_S\})$ will be larger than the ideal codeword length as the used model does not help to describe the observed sequence, this also relates to MDL principle see e.g. [15]. Note that when CTW is used to estimate model and parameters of an observed (DNA) sequence, then the resulting codeword length will have the smallest distance (redundancy) from the ideal codeword length.

Now suppose y^N and x^T are two observed DNA sequence not necessarily of the same length. Let $\{S_x, \Theta_{S_x}\}$ be the model and parameter set for x^T, estimated using the CTW method and $L_{ctw}(y^N)$ be the codeword length for y^N estimated using the CTW method. Then if we consider the difference

$$\frac{1}{N}L_{ctw}(y^N) - \frac{1}{N}L(y^N|\{S_x, \Theta_{S_x}\})$$

$$= -\frac{1}{N}\sum_{t=1}^{N}\log_2 P_{ctw}(y_t|y_{-D}^{t-1}) + \frac{1}{N}\sum_{t=1}^{N}\log_2 P(y_t|y_{-D}^{t-1}, \{S_x, \Theta_{S_x}\})$$

$$= -\frac{1}{N}\sum_{t=1}^{N}\log_2 \frac{P_{ctw}(y_t|y_{-D}^{t-1})}{P(y_t|y_{-D}^{t-1}, \{S_x, \Theta_{S_x}\})} = -\frac{1}{N}\sum_{t=1}^{N}\log_2 \frac{P_{ctw}(y_t|y_{-D}^{t-1})}{\theta_{S_x, \sigma_{\{y_{-D}^{t-1}\}}^{y_t}}}, \quad (2)$$

we see that this difference tells how much we can gain if we use the distribution of x^T instead of y^N in order to describe (compress) y^N. If the gain is high then $\{S_x, \Theta_{S_x}\}$ corresponds to the source that fits well y^N, and it is more likely that both y^N and x^T are generated by the same source, thus they belong to the same sequence class. If the gain is low, then codeword length for y^N estimated using $\{S_x, \Theta_{S_x}\}$ has very high redundancy and thus $\{S_x, \Theta_{S_x}\}$ does not help to describe y^N, which means that it corresponds to some other source generating other types of (DNA) sequences. Hence we can say that y^N and x^T are generated by different sources and they are not similar. In general, the higher the gain the better the model and parameter set describe sequence y^N. Thus it is the more likely, that the source with $\{S_x, \Theta_{S_x}\}$ generated y^N.

The codeword length per source symbol estimated using the CTW method gives (a good) estimate of the entropy of the (DNA) source sequence. Hence the similarity measure given above can be seen as an estimate of the mutual information between a DNA sequence Y^N and a DNA source that produced some DNA sequence X^T. Note that mutual information is non-negative, while our estimate can take up negative values. This underestimate partially comes from the fact that query sequence can have deletions, insertions and substitutions that are not part of the source model used for the codeword length estimates.

Now consider the mutual information between a database DNA sequence X^N and the query DNA sequence Y^N

$$
\begin{aligned}
I(Y^N; X^T) &= I(Y^N; X^T, \{S_x, \Theta_{S_x}\}) \\
&= I(Y^N; \{S_x, \Theta_{S_x}\}) + I(Y^N; X^T | \{S_x, \Theta_{S_x}\}),
\end{aligned}
\tag{3}
$$

where in the first step we use the fact that $\{S_x, \Theta_{S_x}\}$ is a function of X^T and the data-processing inequality, see e.g. [19]. Note that when $\{S_x, \Theta_{S_x}\}$ matches the source that generated Y^N, the second term in the last step becomes negligible, on the other hand if Y^N and X^N are produced by different sources this term is also small. We see that mutual information between X^N and Y^N sequences is equivalent to the mutual information $I(Y^N; \{S_x, \Theta_{S_x}\})$. Thus in order to find the closest sequence we may concentrate on finding the estimated model and parameters that maximize $I(Y^N; \{S_x, \Theta_{S_x}\})$.

2.4   Proposed System

Set-up
Create a database of privacy-preserving DNA-indices for a (sets of) DNA sequence(s) $x_i^{T_i}, i = 1, 2, \ldots, n$. In order to do it, estimate the models and parameters for each (sets of) DNA sequences $x_i^{T_i}, i = 1, 2, \ldots, n$ applying the CTW method. Store $\{S_{x_i}, \Theta_{S_{x_i}}\}$ in the database together with some other relevant information.

Retrieval
Given the query (example) DNA sequence y^N, perform the following steps:
1. Apply CTW and estimate the codeword length per source symbol

$$
\frac{1}{N} L_{ctw}(y^N), \text{ for } y^N;
\tag{4}
$$

2. For each DNA record $i, i = 1, 2, \ldots, n$ in the database, compute the estimate of the codeword length for y^N given $\{S_{x_i}, \Theta_{S_{x_i}}\}$, by mapping subsequences in y^N to the contexts from S_{x_i} and using the corresponding parameters as

$$
\frac{1}{N} L(y^N | \{S_{x_i}, \Theta_{S_{x_i}}\}) = -\sum_{t=1}^{N} \log_2 \theta_{S_{x_i}, \sigma_{y_{-D}^{t-1}}^{y_t}},
\tag{5}
$$

note that if there is no context in S_{x_i} for some subsequence from y^N, then the corresponding parameter equals $1/2$. Observe that this parameter $1/2$ will also contribute to dissimilarity of the close DNA sequences when deletion or insertion occurred.
3. Find the record i that maximizes

$$
\frac{1}{N} L_{ctw}(y^N) - \frac{1}{N} L(y^N | \{S_{x_i}, \Theta_{S_{x_i}}\})
\tag{6}
$$

and return the relevant information to the querying party.

2.5 Security Discussion

Observe that in the DNA database in order to perform privacy-preserving similarity search one only need to store the model and the parameter set $\{S_{x_i}, \Theta_{S_{x_i}}\}$ corresponding to a (set of) DNA sequence(s). Note that the model consists of short subsequences that occurred in the DNA sequences, but contains no information on temporal arrangement of the subsequences. Moreover, due to DNA variable length, also probabilistic information contained in the parameters is insufficient to characterize the number of the subsequences. Note also that an average typical length of DNA sequence is around 3.2×10^9bp. Thus our model and parameter set can be seen as a hash of DNA sequences that allows for prohibitively large number of sequences being produced based on it.

2.6 Toy Example

Here we consider a toy example where we use 14 DNA sequences from GenBank. Suppose we need to arrange the database per chromosome. Then we create the corresponding privacy-preserving indices using CTW with depth 9 (this corresponds to three codons) by estimating the models and parameter sets for each chromosome, i.e. for chromosome 1, 2, 3, 5, 8, 9, 10, 14 in our example. These models and parameter sets are stored in the database.

Next a researcher presents a piece of a DNA sequence and he would like to find from which chromosome it comes from. Using the system described above he can calculate the estimates of the mutual information between the available

Query chromosome	Mutual Information estimates per chromosome							
	1	2	3	5	8	9	10	14
1	-0.16883	-0.17662	-0.19062	-0.19116	-0.17525	-0.17702	-0.18031	-0.18617
1	-0.0237	-0.02721	-0.03196	-0.03766	-0.03254	-0.02697	-0.03561	-0.03784
1	-0.20133	-0.21518	-0.22017	-0.2222	-0.21824	-0.21132	-0.21977	-0.22331
2	-0.00613	0.085012	-0.00542	-0.00982	-0.00741	-0.00223	-0.00618	-0.00994
3	-0.02269	-0.01402	0.041464	-0.01267	-0.01713	-0.00675	-0.0218	-0.01881
5	-0.07684	-0.06272	-0.06162	-0.00854	-0.06846	-0.05452	-0.07161	-0.07257
5	-0.0971	-0.0648	-0.07114	-0.06463	-0.07918	-0.05804	-0.08502	-0.08603
8	-0.01266	-0.01229	-0.01528	-0.01913	0.05676	-0.0103	-0.01446	-0.01544
8	-0.02475	-0.02566	-0.04455	-0.03514	-0.02306	-0.02315	-0.02324	-0.03107
9	-0.02467	-0.01264	-0.01365	-0.01563	-0.01858	0.073098	-0.02074	-0.02068
10	-0.04395	-0.02693	-0.03615	-0.03762	-0.03394	-0.02079	-0.00575	-0.04144
10	-0.04919	-0.03164	-0.03858	-0.04385	-0.0395	-0.02606	-0.00923	-0.04534
10	-0.04458	-0.02924	-0.0371	-0.04147	-0.03617	-0.02454	-0.0071	-0.0417
14	-0.05247	-0.05541	-0.05562	-0.05696	-0.05506	-0.05147	-0.05438	0.04525

Fig. 2. Estimates for mutual information from the toy example. A shaded cell corresponds to the maximum mutual information.

piece of the DNA sequence and the models and parameters corresponding to different chromosomes, and then find the chromosome that maximizes the mutual information. Fig.2 shows the results of such estimates for a number of query sequences. From this table we observe that the proposed method can correctly detect which chromosome the query piece of DNA comes from.

3 Related Work

Work in the direction on privacy-preserving operations on DNA data focuses on privacy-preserving calculation of edit (Levenshtein) and set distances. E.g. in [10] oblivious automata for privacy-preserving approximate DNA matching and searching is proposed. This approach is using Levenshtein distance as a similarity metric for DNA sequences. In [11] edit distance between two DNA sequences is derived using homomorphic encryption. In [12] and [17] homomorphic encryption and secure two-party computations ares used to match short tandem repeats that are used for human identification and for parental tests. Finally, in [13] Privacy-Enhanced Invertible Bloom Filter (PEIBF) is proposed for set distance computations based on compressed DNA sequences, where DNA sequence compression is defined as sets of differences from the DNA reference string.

The approaches in [10] and [13] are effective for human authentication and identification, a well as verification if a certain pattern is a part of a given DNA. Methods based on homomorphic encryption like [11] are prohibitively expensive to be used in large databases and can be effectively used for authentication. The approach presented in [12] is applicable to human authentication and identification, forensic investigations and parental tests. However, the approaches mentioned above are not sufficient if one has to determine whether DNA sequences have a similar functionality, since e.g. it was shown that chimpanzee and human genomes are 96% similar [16], while the corresponding edit distance between two genomes is very large. Therefore, to compare DNA sequences more complex similarity metrics than edit or set distance, like divergence [16] and mutual information [14] are needed, as these metrics also takes into account temporal structure of DNA sequences. Note that work in [16] and [14] does not focus on privacy, while our approach aims at privacy-preserving similarity search based on mutual information. To the best of our knowledge this is the first work in this direction.

4 Conclusions

In this paper we have presented a particular solution for privacy-preserving search and matching in DNA databases. Our approach is based on the universal source coding technique, CTW [8]. Further investigations of the proposed solution, as well as design of a wide range of operations on DNA sequences still remain as the future work in the AU2EU project.

References

1. Bjones, R.: Architecture serving complex Identity Infrastructures. Trust in Digital Life, p.21 (2012)
2. Camenisch, J., Krontiris, I., Lehmann, A., Neven, G., Paquin, C., Rannenberg, K., Zwingelberg, H.: Architecture for Attribute-based Credential Technologies, ABC4Trust,
   `https://abc4trust.eu/index.php/pub/results/107-d21architecturev1`
3. Rissanen, E.: eXtensible Access Control Markup Language (XACML) Version 3.0., OASIS standard (2010),
   `http://docs.oasis-open.org/xacml/3.0/xacml-3.0-core-spec-cs-01-en.pdf`
4. IBM Research Zurich, Specification of the Identity Mixer Cryptographic Library Version 2.3.1 (2010)
5. Fontaine, C., Galand, F.: A Survey of Homomorphic Encryption for Nonspecialists. EURASIP Journal on Information Security (2007)
6. Damgård, I., Pastro, V., Smart, N., Zakarias, S.: Multiparty Computation from Somewhat Homomorphic Encryption. In: Safavi-Naini, R., Canetti, R. (eds.) CRYPTO 2012. LNCS, vol. 7417, pp. 643–662. Springer, Heidelberg (2012)
7. Finiasz, M., Sendrier, N.: Security Bounds for the Design of Code-Based Cryptosystems. In: Matsui, M. (ed.) ASIACRYPT 2009. LNCS, vol. 5912, pp. 88–105. Springer, Heidelberg (2009)
8. Willems, F.M.J., Shtarkov, Y.M., Tjalkens, T.J.: The Context-Tree Weighting Method: Basic Properties. IEEE Trans. on Information Theory 41(3), 653–664 (1995)
9. Matsumoto, T., Sadakane, K., Imai, H.: Biological Sequence Compression Algorithms. Genome Informatics Workshop 11, 43–52 (2000)
10. Troncoso-Pastoriza, J.R., Katzenbeisser, S., Celik, M.: Privacy Preserving Error Resilient DNA Searching Through Oblivious Automata. In: Proceedings of the 14th ACM Conference on Computer and Communications Security (CCS 2007), pp. 519–528. ACM, New York (2007)
11. Jha, S., Kruger, L., Shmatikov, V.: Towards Practical Privacy for Genomic Computation. In: The 2008 IEEE Symposium on Security and Privacy, May 18-21, pp. 216–230 (2008)
12. Bruekers, F., Katzenbeisser, S., Kursawe, K., Tuyls, P.: Privacy-Preserving Matching of DNA Profiles, IACR Cryptology ePrint Archive (2008)
13. Eppstein, D., Goodrich, M.T., Baldi, P.: Privacy-Enhanced Methods for Comparing Compressed DNA Sequences, CoRR abs/1107.3593 (2011)
14. Adami, C.: Information Theory in Molecular Biology. Physics of Life Reviews 1(1), 3–22 (2004)
15. Cilibrasi, R., Vitanyi, P.: Clustering by Compression. IEEE Trans. on Information Theory 51(4), 1523–1545 (2005)
16. Chimpanzee Sequencing and Analysis Consortium, "Initial Sequence of The Chimpanzee Genome and Comparison with the Human Genome". Nature 437(7055), pp.69–87
17. De Cristofaro, E., Faber, S., Gasti, P., Tsudik, G.: Genodroid: Are Privacy-Preserving Genomic Tests Ready For Prime Time? In: WPES 2012, pp. 97–108 (2012)
18. Willems, F.M.J., Nowbahkt-Irani, A., Volf, P.A.J.: Maximum a-Posteriori Tree Models. In: ITG 2002, Berlin, Germany (February 2002)
19. Cover, T.M., Thomas, J.A.: Elements of Information Theory. 2nd edn. John Wiley and Sons Inc., New York (2006)

Early DDoS Detection
Based on Data Mining Techniques

Konstantinos Xylogiannopoulos[1], Panagiotis Karampelas[2], and Reda Alhajj[1]

[1] University of Calgary, Calgary AB T2N 1N4, Canada
[2] Hellenic Air Force Academy, Dekelia Air Force Base, Attica, Greece

Abstract. In the past few years, internet has experienced a rapid growth in users and services. This led to an increase of different type of cyber-crimes. One of the most important is the Distributed Denial of Service (DDoS) attack, which someone can unleash through many different isolated hosts and make a system to shut down due to resources exhaustion. The importance of the problem can be easily identified due to the huge number of references found in literature trying to detect and prevent such attacks. In the current paper, a novel method based on a data mining technique is introduced in order to early warn the network administrator of a potential DDoS attack. The method uses the advanced All Repeated Patterns Detection (ARPaD) Algorithm, which allows the detection of all repeated patterns in a sequence. The proposed method can give very fast results regarding all IP prefixes in a sequence of hits and, therefore, warn the network administrator if a potential DDoS attack is under development. Based on several experiments conducted, it has been proven experimentally the importance of the method for the detection of a DDoS attack since it can detect a potential DDoS attack at the beginning and before it affects the system.

1 Introduction

The proliferation of the internet enabled smart mobile devices all over the world along with the available networked corporate or home personal computers has created an enormous battlefield for cyberwar and cyber games. New devices have become the target of malevolent hackers who desire to take advantage of the security weaknesses of the newly available applications together with the illiteracy of the new users of this technology. By taking control of the innumerous devices, cyber criminals can materialize their plans easily e.g., to invade users privacy, to steal users identity, to start different types of attacks such as Distributed Denial of Service (DDoS) attacks, scan attacks or Trojan attacks [1]. According to recent reports [2], more than 4,800 DDOS attacks per day take place, more than 80 GBPs bandwidth is utilized for these attacks and more than 900 active botnets are ready to flood the Internet and disrupt the legitimate services. Monitoring and detecting such types of attacks has become increasingly demanding since the DDoS attacks correspondingly have become sophisticated and the Internet traffic due to the increasing number of the new devices has become enormous

D. Naccache and D. Sauveron (Eds.): WISTP 2014, LNCS 8501, pp. 190–199, 2014.
© IFIP International Federation for Information Processing 2014

[3] and thus difficult to monitor. DDoS attacks as the abovementioned statistics reveal are launched by very big botnets or computers infected with software that allows their remote control by the attacker. All the infected hosts, which typically are some thousands, then attack one or different legitimate services by sending thousands or millions of requests in a few seconds. The attacked host is flooded with different types of packets such as SYN, FIN or other types of packets and as a result stops responding and offering the legitimate service. Several known internet sites such as Yahoo, Dell, eBay, Amazon, ZDNet, British Telecom and countries such as Georgia, Estonia [4] and more recently Syria and Ukraine have been targeted by DDoS attacks that caused either financial losses or serious problems in the operation of public services correspondingly.

The protection of critical infrastructure and services against DDoS attacks has occupied researchers working in the fields of networking and cybercrime a lot. Several different techniques have been proposed either to prevent or to detect DDoS attack. A task that is not easy due to the existence of diverse characteristics of the attack. More specifically, J. Mikrovic [6] in her PhD thesis identified the characteristics of DDoS attacks that make DDoS defense very complicated. The characteristics mentioned are the diverse methods the attackers use, e.g., the different stream of packets they sent, the coordination of the distribution of the attack makes very complicated the detection of the attack e.g., geo-dispersed botnets are used, the sophisticated coverage of the traces of the attacker e.g., through IP address spoofing, the availability of several tools that can launch DDoS attacks, e.g., Trinoo, Stacheldraht, etc. and the illiteracy of the Internet users e.g., users who do not update their operating systems in order to address potential security holes. These characteristics of DDoS attacks have obliged researchers to propose different approaches in order to either prevent the infrastructure from DDoS attacks or early detect the DDoS attack and safeguard the infrastructure. A classification of DDoS Mechanisms [5] suggests two generic categories, the preventive and reactive methods. Preventive methods can be further distinguished to Attack prevention methods that increase the security of the hardware or software resources of an organization e.g., by deploying automatic updating schemes, by continually monitoring the access rights, by deploying security related infrastructure such as firewalls or intrusion detection systems. Another type of preventive methods attempt to prevent specifically DDoS attacks. These methods either balance the load of an attack intelligently or utilize a very large number of resources that can endure DDoS attacks. The reactive methods on the other hand focus on the early detection of a DDoS attack and the elimination of its impact to the infrastructure. Reactive methods are further distinguished in pattern detection methods or anomaly detection methods. The pattern detection methods usually monitor the system under protection by identifying and comparing possible patterns against stored signature of known attacks. The anomaly detection methods on the other hand attempt to identify anomalies in the normal or standard operation of the network under protection. All these different types of preventive or reactive methods cannot provide 100% protection of a system against DDoS attacks and that is why the research in the field of defense against those types of attacks is on-going and new methods are constantly introduced. The contribution of this paper is the proposal of an innovative DDoS detection method that combines anomaly with pattern detection. A data mining technique developed by the authors which can identify all the repeated patterns of a sequence is applied to the data received in the network. When several IP addresses from the same domain are detected by this technique a potential DDoS attack may occur. Based on the experiments, the time needed to identify the launch of the DDoS attack ranges from 1-4 seconds depending on the initial parameters provided to the algorithm.

The rest of the paper is organized as follows: Section 2 presents a review of pattern and anomaly detection methods. Section 3 presents the approach proposed using the pattern detection method that is developed by the authors. Section 4 presents the experimental results by the application of the proposed methodology to an existing publicly available dataset with DDoS attack data and discusses the experimental results. Finally, the conclusions and future work is presented.

2   Related Work

Several researchers have focused on the detection of patterns or signatures of DDoS attacks using various methods such as statistical methods, artificial neural networks, data mining techniques, hybrid techniques, etc. Statistical-based methods [7] monitor and model normal traffic patterns by using advanced statistical analysis techniques and are able to detect anomalies based on a predefined threshold. An example of this method is described in [7]. This type of technique may provide relatively accurate results depending on the statistical analysis technique used. However, the selection of threshold is very important since either real DDoS attacks may not be detected or legitimate requests may be tagged as DDoS attacks. If the threshold selected is rigid it may increase the false positive detections while it will decrease the false negative detections [10]. Especially in cases where there is an increase of traffic as for example when an event such as a music concert occurs the corresponding website of the event may be visited by several people who wish to learn information about the event, the accessibility of the venue, etc. and thus the traffic will increase as the event approaches. The increasing traffic may be identified as DDoS attack because it does not follow the normal traffic patterns processed by the statistical based detection method and thus a false alarm may be issued.

Neural network based methods aggregate already identified patterns related to DDoS attacks and by applying machine learning techniques, develop a neural network that can analyze the traffic in a network and decide whether a DDoS attack is in progress or not. Such a technique is presented in [9]. The algorithm described operates in two stages. In the first stage it monitors various features of the traffic and estimates the likelihood ratios for a DDoS attack. In the second stage the algorithm combines the result of each feature identified and the results are forwarded to the neural network that provides the final decision whether a

DDoS attack has been detected or not. The result of such techniques are heavily dependent on the selection of features. If the features selected do not correspond to the type of DDoS attack carried then the detection will not be possible.

Data mining based techniques have also been introduced in the detection of DDoS attacks. Data mining algorithms can be employed in the automatic feature selection for monitoring and the classification of the traffic patterns as in [8] in which the decision tree algorithm is used to select the traffic attributes that need to be analyzed. Then using a classification algorithm it is possible to decide whether there is a DDoS attack or not. Other data mining algorithms such as C4.5 algorithm association rule mining have been applied to detect attack patterns in [11]. The C4.5 algorithm is first applied to develop a learning model for known attack types and then association rule mining is used for in-depth semantic interpretation of the attack type. This approach combines different data mining techniques for the detection and analysis of the monitored traffic and notifies the network managers regarding possible DDoS attacks.

Hybrid methods finally combine elements of the above mentioned techniques in order to improve the positive detection rates of DDoS attacks. Such a system is proposed in [12] that combines anomaly detection with weighted association rules in order to produce signatures of attacks. These signatures are used in order to identify similar new and unknown future attacks. The combination of these techniques according to the results reported in [12] outperforms the corresponding individual methods used. In another work statistical based methods and data mining techniques are used to propose a multistage detection of DDoS attacks [13]. The method is based on various statistical analysis model e.g., Markov based prediction at the first stage and wavelet based singularity detection for sending DDoS attack alerts.

Most of the methods presented in this section are addressing three stages of the DDoS defense process: the detection phase, the classification phase whether it is a DDoS attack or not and finally the response [14]. The proposed method in this paper focuses on the first phase of the defense process by detecting an anomaly in the network traffic using a novel pattern recognition algorithm which discovers all the repeated patterns in a given sequence. In other words the proposed method acts as an early warning system and reports abnormal activity in network traffic.

3   Our Approach

The method proposed in this paper is based on the Suffix Array data structure that is used to detect all repeated patterns in a sequence. More specifically, the ARPaD Algorithm [19] is used as it has been derived by COV Algorithm [15], [16], [17]. A Suffix Array is a data structure that contains an array of all suffixes of a string [20] and it is mainly used for pattern detection. However, with the use of the actual suffix strings we can construct a similar to a suffix array data structure for fixed width substring such as the IP strings of length 12 by adding leading zeros in octets that do not have length three. By doing this, ARPaD Algorithm can analyze the strings of the IPs and detect all repeated patterns, which in this case are domains, subnets or actual hosts when the string is a full IP address of length 12.

The first step to apply the ARPaD algorithm in the log files of traffic is to convert the IP addresses found to actual strings that will be used in order to detect all repeated patterns. For this reason, each one of the triplets of the IPs that are not full (i.e. have less than three digits) is converted to a full triplet by adding in front of each number the necessary number of zeros. This transformation will allow ARPaD Algorithm to search into IP addresses as they were simple strings.

The second step that is required is to sort all the IP addresses alphabetically since now all have been converted to strings. This is needed for the ARPaD Algorithm in order to perform the analysis as the strings have directly come from a Suffix Array data structure. This is the most time consuming part since it has complexity $O(nlogn)$, while ARPaD Algorithm has been proven experimentally to have on average complexity $O(n)$ [16], [18], [19]. Therefore, the total complexity of the method is on average $O(nlogn)$ which allows a very fast analysis of the IP addresses data.

The last step in the proposed methodology is to execute ARPaD Algorithm on the sorted array of IP address strings and retrieve as results all the repeated substrings (IP prefixes of the domains or subnets) or strings (full IP addresses). Having the results a Network Administrator can set a threshold in the occurrences of the substrings (IP prefixes) that are detected in order to characterize the traffic from a specific domain, or subnet or host as possible abnormality and, therefore, a potential DDoS attack. The specific threshold has to be set depending on the type of analysis, hits number or time. Based on the defined threshold and the detected traffic, the proposed method can send a warning of a potential DDoS attack to the administrator. Furthermore, the Network Administrator can use the proposed method to continue monitoring the traffic and can opt to perform further analysis based on specific time interval or a specific number of hits on the router. This is something that a specialist can decide, yet, the proposed methodology allows both implementations to be applied interchangeable. Depending on the traffic and the potential DDoS attack warning, these intervals (time or numbers) can change dynamically to accelerate the analysis and prevent an attack at the beginning. For example, in a normal traffic situation you can analyze the hits per minute but when a warning is issued instead of time interval, a specific number of hits e.g., 100,000 can be analyzed. In a DDoS attack situation this is expected to be reached in a few seconds depending on the magnitude of the attack.

4   Experimental Results

For the experiments a laptop with Intel i5 quad core processor and 8Gb RAM has been used. The code of ARPaD algorithm has been written in C# and a 64bit operating system has been used. The data come from the Computer Science Department of University of California Los Angeles (UCLA) website that holds information about packet traces. We have used Trace Set 2 for the UDP packets that includes 16 files. Each one of the first 15 files has 100,000 hits generated from a DDoS attack. The last file holds less information and we haven't used it in order to have a uniform distribution of the hits per file and thus to be comparable. There have been contacted in total three major experiments. In each experiment different number of hits (100,000 IPs, 500,000 IPs and 1,500,000 IPs) has been used. For the first experiment, the ARPaD algorithm run 15 times to analyze all the 15 files. In the second experiment the algorithm run three times and in the third one the algorithm run once. For each experiment, two different versions of the algorithm run in order to just detect all repeated patterns (IPs prefixes) or all repeated patterns including the positions of each one in timeline. The latter is more time consuming that the first yet can provide more detail information for further analysis.

Table 1. IP Detection Time per File (100,000 rows per file)

From	To	Detect IPs	Detect IPs & Positions	DDoS Attack
1	100	0.992	3.22	9.57
100,001	200	0.988	3.26	8.93
200,001	300	0.991	3.22	8.86
300,001	400	0.994	3.23	9.77
400,001	500	0.988	3.17	11.15
500,001	600	0.989	3.13	9.81
600,001	700	1.006	3.23	11.00
700,001	800	0.992	3.22	10.65
800,001	900	1.013	3.17	10.56
900,001	1,000,000	0.975	3.23	10.68
1,000,001	1,100,000	0.993	3.20	10.77
1,100,001	1,200,000	0.988	3.22	9.75
1,200,001	1,300,000	1.021	3.24	10.73
1,300,001	1,400,000	0.995	3.19	10.79
1,400,001	1,500,000	0.991	3.17	13.10

In Table 1 we can see the time analysis per single file. The table includes the time ARPaD Algorithm needs to simply detect all repeated patterns and the time the Algorithm needs to detect the patterns and their position in the timeline. The position of each pattern can be further used to detect density or increase in hits or other attributes per pattern (IP prefix) that might be useful to detect DDoS attack. Moreover, the table includes the time the attack last for each one of the 100,000 hits based on the data provided in the files from UCLA. As we can see from Table 1 the time ARPaD Algorithm needs to detect all repeated patterns is approximately 1 second on average, including the sorting process time when we do not record the actual positions of the hits in timeline. If the time factor needs to be calculated then the Algorithm needs approximately 3.2 seconds on average for each file. However, what is very important to be mentioned here is that the attack needs approximately 10 seconds while the analysis can be performed in 1 or 3.2 seconds depending on which variation of the algorithm is used. Therefore, the analysis can be performed faster than the attack as in case there is a DDoS attack with 100,000 hits per second, the algorithm can provide the results of the analysis the next second. As a result, we can run a pattern detection analysis every few seconds and have an early warning when something abnormal is happening and before the next sequence of IPs will need to be analyzed. The time interval to analyze the data can change automatically depending on the results found in the previous run of the algorithm.

Table 2. IP Detection Time per 5 Files (500,000 rows)

From	To	Detect IPs	Detect IPs & Positions	DDoS Attack
1	500	4.32	14.30	48.29
500,001	1,000,000	4.31	14.53	52.69
1,000,001	1,500,000	4.33	14.21	55.15

Table 3. IP Detection Time for the Whole Data Set (1,500,000 rows)

From	To	Detect IPs	Detect IPs & Positions	DDoS Attack
1	1,500,000	11.67	43.20	156.12

In Table 2 the results of the second experiment (the hits per 500,000 IPs) are presented. Again we have the same information as in Table I regarding times and we can observe that the detection of all repeated patterns is approximately 4.3 seconds on average while when all repeated patterns and their position in timeline is detected the ARPaD Algorithm needs approximately 14.3 seconds. In this experiment, the total attack time per 500,000 hits is approximately 52 seconds, time considerably longer than the time ARPaD Algorithm needs to detect all repeated patterns. ARPaD Algorithm it has been proved to be linear on average [15], [16], [19] and that is why it preserves the ratio of 1/10 for the simple pattern detection and approximately 1/4 for the full pattern detection (including positions). Finally, we run one more experiment for the whole data set for the 1.5 million IPs (Table 3). The time for the single detection is 12 seconds, for the full detection is 43 seconds while the whole DDoS attack lasted 156 seconds approximately according to the files provided by UCLA.

The fact that our method can perform a very fast analysis in real time can have several benefits and can also allow variation of implementations of the method. One way is to have a fixed width analysis per time or number of hits as we have already described with the experiments and the results in Table 1 through Table 3. However, we can apply a dynamic execution of the method and allow the Network Administrator to fully parameterize it and decide how the pattern detection will be executed. The process can be the following: In a normal environment we run checks based on a fixed, wide, interval which can be based on either on time or number of

IPs. If the system detects an abnormality then it can manually or automatically decrease the width of the intervals in order to prevent a DDoS attack. For example, we can have a fixed width of 500,000 hits. The analysis of these needs approximately 4.3 seconds while the time needed for the hits is 52 seconds. So, in time t we execute an analysis for the 500,000 hits and the system detects an abnormality in time t+4.3. Now the system can change the time interval and perform an analysis per 100,000 hits. This will happen at t+10 or 5.7 seconds after the first analysis has been conducted by the ARPaD Algorithm. Therefore, the network administrator can specify intervals that can easily be executed without overlapping or without lags in order to have a flexible, dynamic early warning DDoS attack detection system. When the traffic will return to normal level then the system can again increase its intervals.

We can see in Table 4 the full list of results for the domains and subnets in the whole 1.5 million hits that the 15 files have. The first and third column contains all repeated patterns detected and the second and fourth column contains the number of occurrences of each pattern (IP prefixes) correspondingly. The table is sorted based on the IP prefixes. The domain 1.1.139.x has been detected 1,500,00 times during the DdoS attack. For each subnet of the previous domain we have 588,537 for the 1.1.139.0x, 583,884 for the 1.1.139.1x and 327,579 for the 1.1.139.2x. The subnet with the most occurrences 59,941 has IP Prefix 1.1.139.17x and the subnet with the least occurrences 29,826 has IP Prefix 1.1.139.25x. The single IP addresses have not been included because the list is very large and almost all the possible IP addresses from the specific domain have been used in the DDoS attack in this data set. The IP with the most occurrences (hits) is the IP with address 1.1.139.149 with 6,140 hits and the IP with the least hits is the 1.1.139.181 with 5,752 hits. From the results presented in Table 4 we can detect the hits from a specific domain and further how this can be analyzed per subnet or even per host. For example, we can observe in Table 4 the hits per subnet are almost uniformly distributed which it cannot be a real life situation. Therefore using this analysis, it is possible to determine if a system is under DDoS attack or not.

Table 4. Full IPs List Ordered By Occurrences

IP Prefix	Occurrences	IP Prefix	Occurrences	IP Prefix	Occurrences
1001139	1,500,000	100113906	59,909	100113916	53,74
10011390	588,537	100113907	59,675	100113917	59,941
10011391	583,884	100113908	59,796	100113918	59,291
10011392	327,579	100113909	59,539	100113919	53,886
100113900	53,548	100113910	59,352	100113920	59,616
100113901	59,151	100113911	59,396	100113921	59,22
100113902	59,088	100113912	59,654	100113922	59,213
100113903	59,444	100113913	59,679	100113923	59,913
100113904	59,173	100113914	59,777	100113924	59,791
100113905	59,214	100113915	59,168	100113925	29,826

5 Conclusions

We have proposed in the current paper a novel methodology that can allow a network administrator to prevent a DDoS attack manually or automatically. Our method, based on an advanced data mining technique, takes advantage of the very fast ARPaD Algorithm that can detect all repeated patterns in a sequence. Using this algorithm, abnormal number of hits from specific domains or subnets can be detected and characterized as a potential DDoS attack. Such analysis allows to use our method as an early warning system of DDoS attack that can help to stop the attack at the beginning. The method has been applied in a 1,500,000 hits data set from the Computer Science Department of UCLA and the results showed that the method can analyze and detect the potential DDoS attack in 1/10 of the total time of the attack.

In future work, we can also use more characteristics of the ARPaD Algorithm and more specifically the detection of each IP hit in the timeline. This can help detecting any further attributes of the hits such as density and increase of the hits over time. For example, we may have periodic attacks from different hosts. The proposed method can detect the periodic pattern and correctly alert the network administrator for further action. Additionally, after the early warning of potential DDoS attack the system can also continue further investigation in order to determine if abnormal traffic from specific domain or IPs can be defined as a positive DDoS attack. This can be accomplished by analyzing further attributes included in the traffic, e.g., packets, time, etc. Finally, analyzing the IPs it is possible to very fast identify whether the traffic from a specific host is legitimate or spoofed and as a result has a very good indication if the traffic is in the context of a DDoS attack or not.

References

1. Hoque, N., Monowar, H., Bhuyan, R.C., Baishya, D.K., Bhattacharyya, J.K.: Kalita, Network attacks: Taxonomy, tools and systems. J. Netw. Comput. Appl. 40, 307–324 (2014)
2. ARBOR Networks, DDOS and Security Reports Live Feed, http://www.arbornetworks.com/asert/2014/03/ pravail-security-analytics-packetloop/ (retrieved March 20, 2014)
3. Wang, D., Yufu, Z., Jie, J.: A multi-core based DDoS detection method. In: 2010 3rd IEEE International Conference on Computer Science and Information Technology (ICCSIT), July 9-11, vol. 4, pp. 115–118 (2010)
4. Loukas, G., Oke, G.: Protection against denial of service attacks: A survey. Computer J. British Computer Society. 53, 1020–1037 (2010)
5. Mirkovic, J., Reiher, P.: A taxonomy of DDoS attack and DDoS defense mechanisms. SIGCOMM Computer Communication Review 34(2), 39–53 (2004)
6. Mirkovic, J.: D-WARD: DDoS network attack recognition and defense, PhD disseration prospectus. UCLA (January 23, 2002)
7. Thapngam, T., Yu, S., Zhou, W., Makki, S.K.: Distributed Denial of Service (DDoS) detection by traffic pattern analysis. Peer-to-Peer Networking and Applications, 1–13 (2012)

8. Kim, M., Na, H., Chae, K.-J., Bang, H., Na, J.-C.: A combined data mining approach for DDoS attack detection. In: Kahng, H.-K., Goto, S. (eds.) ICOIN 2004. LNCS, vol. 3090, pp. 943–950. Springer, Heidelberg (2004)
9. Oke, G., Loukas, G.: A Denial of Service Detector based on Maximum Likeli-hood Detection and the Random Neural Network. The Computer Journal 50(6), 717–727 (2007)
10. Rahmani, H., Sahli, N., Kamoun, F.: DDoS flooding attack detection scheme based on F-divergence. Computer Communications 35, 1380–1391 (2012)
11. Yu, J., Kang, H., Park, D., Bang, H.-C., Kang, D.W.: An in-depth analysis on traffic flooding attacks detection and system using data mining techniques. Journal of Systems Architecture 59(10-B),1005–1012 (2013)
12. Hwang, K., Cai, M., Chen, Y., Qin, M.: Hybrid Intrusion Detection with Weighted Signature Generation over Anomalous Internet Episodes. IEEE Transactions on Dependable and Secure Computing 4(1), 41–55 (2007)
13. Wang, F., Wang, H., Wang, X., Su, J.: A new multistage approach to detect subtle DDoS attacks. Mathematical and Computer Modelling 55(1), 198–213 (2012)
14. Oke, G., Loukas, G., Gelenbe, E.: Detecting denial of service attacks with bayesian classifiers and the random neural network. In: IEEE International Fuzzy Systems Conference, FUZZ-IEEE 2007, pp. 1–6. IEEE (2007)
15. Xylogiannopoulos, K., Karampelas, P., Alhajj, R.: Periodicity Data Mining in Time Series Using Suffix Arrays. In: Proc. IEEE Intelligent Systems IS12 (2012)
16. Xylogiannopoulos, K., Karampelas, P., Alhajj, R.: Exhaustive Patterns Detectio. In: Time Series Using Suffix Arrays (2012) (manuscript in submission)
17. Xylogiannopoulos, K., Karampelas, P., Alhajj, R.: Minimization of Suffix Arrays Storage Capacity for Periodicity Detection in Time Series. In: Proc. IEEE International Conference in Tools with Artificial Intelligence (2012)
18. Xylogiannopoulos, K., Karampelas, P., Alhajj, R.: Experimental Analysis on the Normality of pi, e, phi and square root of 2 Using Advanced Data Mining Techniques. Experimental Mathematics (2014) (in press)
19. Xylogiannopoulos, K., Karampelas, P., Alhajj, R.: Analyzing Very Large Time Series Using Suffix Arrays. Applied Intelligence (2014) (submitted for publication)
20. Manber, U., Myers, G.: Suffix Arrays: A New Method for On-Line String Searches. In: Proceedings of the first Annual ACM-SIAM Symposium on Discrete Algorithms, pp. 319–327 (1990)

Author Index